# APERTURE

A FEW MONTHS BEFORE HIS DEATH in 1976, Paul Strand wrote: "I think of myself fundamentally as an explorer who has spent his life on a long voyage of discovery."

This issue of *Aperture* embraces the last twenty-five years of Paul Strand's discoveries—from 1950, when he expatriated to France from the McCarthyism of the United States, until his death in 1976. Geographically, his explorations ranged farther than any he had previously undertaken: Paul and his wife Hazel Kingsbury traveled throughout France and to other places including Italy, Romania, the Hebrides, Morocco, Ghana, and Egypt during this period. Photographically, one begins to discover an almost unearthly wisdom in his work that grasps at mysteries of human experience.

In Strand's portraits, both the photographer and his subject are free of self-consciousness, and qualities are revealed that are pure, detached—existing beyond the moment. *Young Boy, Gondeville, France,* 1951, has provoked every conceivable interpretation. After forty years as one of the world's best-known portraits, that boy's scowl remains as unfathomable as the *Mona Lisa*'s smile. In other portraits, both individual and group, association of place, history, and the triumphs and pitfalls of life transcend superficial identity.

The iconographic nature of the portraits carries over into studies of landscapes, villages, even machinery. These resonate with a passion for what Paul called "dynamic realism," and embody his and humanity's ancient faith in change for the better and the growth of human freedom. These images offer no conclusion; instead there is a sense of the ineffable and a rare sense of grace that can be universally experienced.

Paul Strand's images, for all their lucidity, beckon us with enigmas, which is why the intent of this issue of *Aperture* is more inquiring than elegiac. Strand was one of the great explorers in twentieth-century art. That does not mean he was a helpful guide. He believed the viewer must find his own way within the image, an experience that would be unique to each individual, and would evolve over time—given sufficient patience and perseverance.

Our individual voyages of perception provoked by Paul Strand's photography are enhanced here by the sensitive reminiscence by Catherine Duncan—a friend and trusted colleague of the Strands almost from the moment they arrived in France. And our journey is further facilitated by the accompanying exhibition of "Paul Strand: The World on My Doorstep," co-curated by Anthony Montoya, director of the Paul Strand Archive, and Michael E. Hoffman, Executive Director of the Aperture Foundation. The show will travel throughout Europe beginning in April 1994 at the Folkwang Museum in Essen, Germany, under the direction of Ute Eskildsen.

In Strand's last photographs, there is a prevailing sense of time and mortality. *Fall in Movement, The Garden, Orgeval,* 1973, the frontispiece of this issue, is a mysterious icon filled with decay, death, and implied renewal. The poetic correlative can be found in a writer who inspired Strand throughout his life. The closing poem in Edgar Lee Master's *Spoon River Anthology,* "Webster Ford," is in fact a hymn to Apollo at the hour of death:

> *When I seemed to be turning to a tree with trunk*
>     *and branches*
> *Growing indurate, turning to stone, yet burgeoning*
> *In Laurel leaves, in hosts of lambent laurel,*
> *Quivering, fluttering, shrinking, fighting the numbness*
> *Creeping into their veins from the dying trunk and  branches!*

"Continually our eyes are opened wider, the depth of our vision is increased," wrote the astronomer Harlow Shapley. It was a remark that deeply moved the photographer in later life, as his "voyage of discovery" turned inward. The details, nuances, and experiences of his immediate surroundings, or, as he put it, "the world on my doorstep," inspired Strand's compelling photographic explorations at the end of his life. In these final images of his Orgeval garden, three of which open this issue, Paul Strand was able to fulfill—in what appear to be the simplest and most concise forms—the challenge he faced in all his work: to evoke the everlasting.

—THE EDITORS

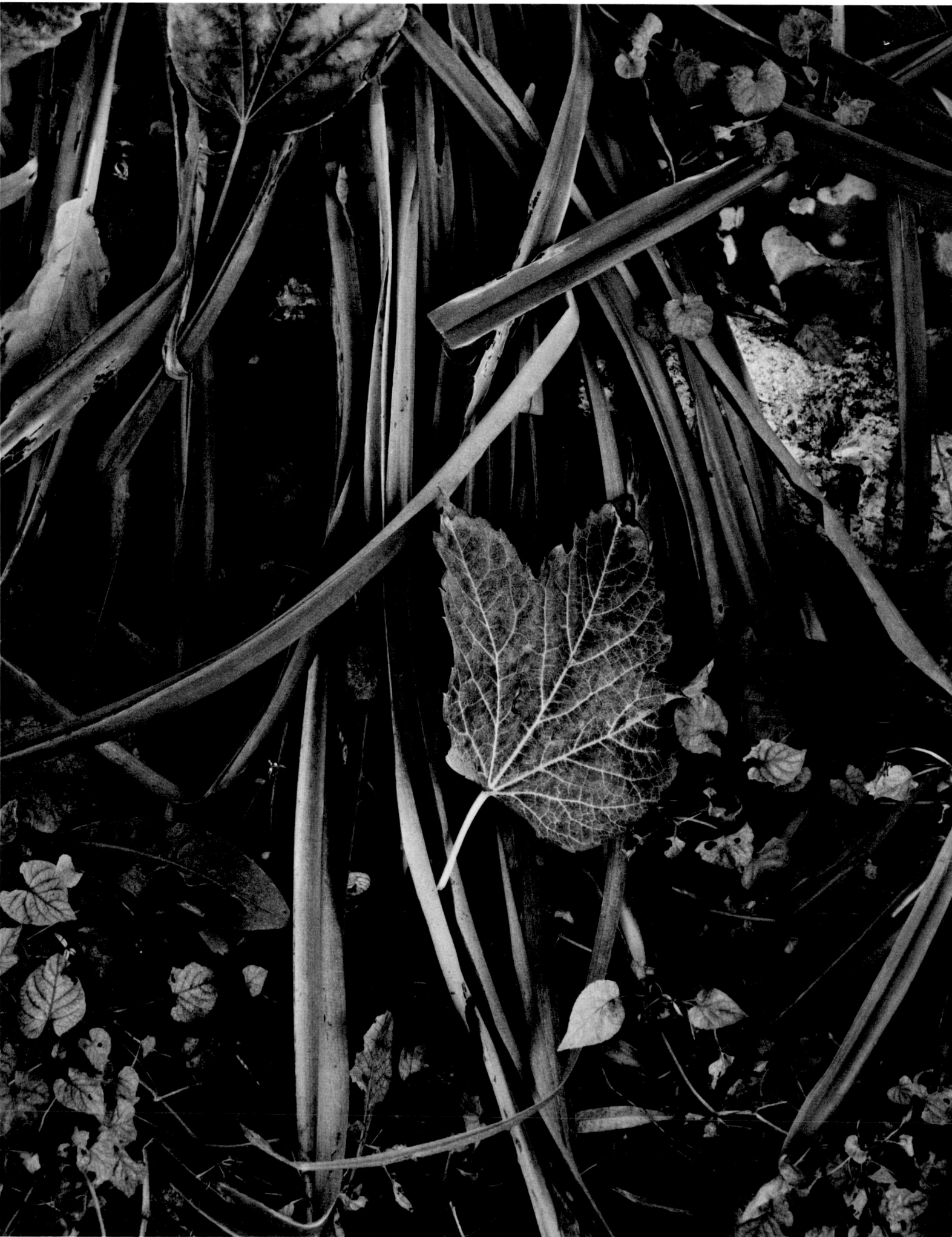

# THE WORLD ON PAUL STRAND MY DOORSTEP

An Intimate Portrait
Catherine Duncan

APERTURE

**W H E R E V E R** I happened to be, in the Southwest, in Mexico, in an Italian village, in Ghana or Egypt, in Morocco or on the islands of the Outer Hebrides, I sought the signs of a long partnership that give each place its special quality and create the profiles of its people....

So finally, it can be seen that what I have explored all my life is the world on my doorstep. And if the things that come close to me today are those literally only a few feet away in our garden at Orgeval, this too is another phase of the voyage.

When it is no longer possible to get about with the same energy and freedom, a man usually tries to find a way around the difficulty so that he can continue to do the things he wants to do. The question he asks is: What can the obstacle lead to that is new, positive and useful? In my case, the answer has been an intensified awareness of what has always been there to see in my immediate surroundings.

The material of the artist lies not within himself nor in the fabrications of his imagination, but in the world around him. The element which gives life to the great Picassos and Cézannes, to the paintings of van Gogh, is the relationship of the artist to content, to the truth of the real world. It is the way he sees this world and translates it into art that determines whether the work of art becomes a new and active force within reality, to widen and transform man's experience.

The artist's world is limitless. It can be found anywhere far from where he lives or a few feet away. It is always on his doorstep.

Paul Strand, from the Introduction
to the "On My Doorstep" portfolio,
Orgeval, December 1975.

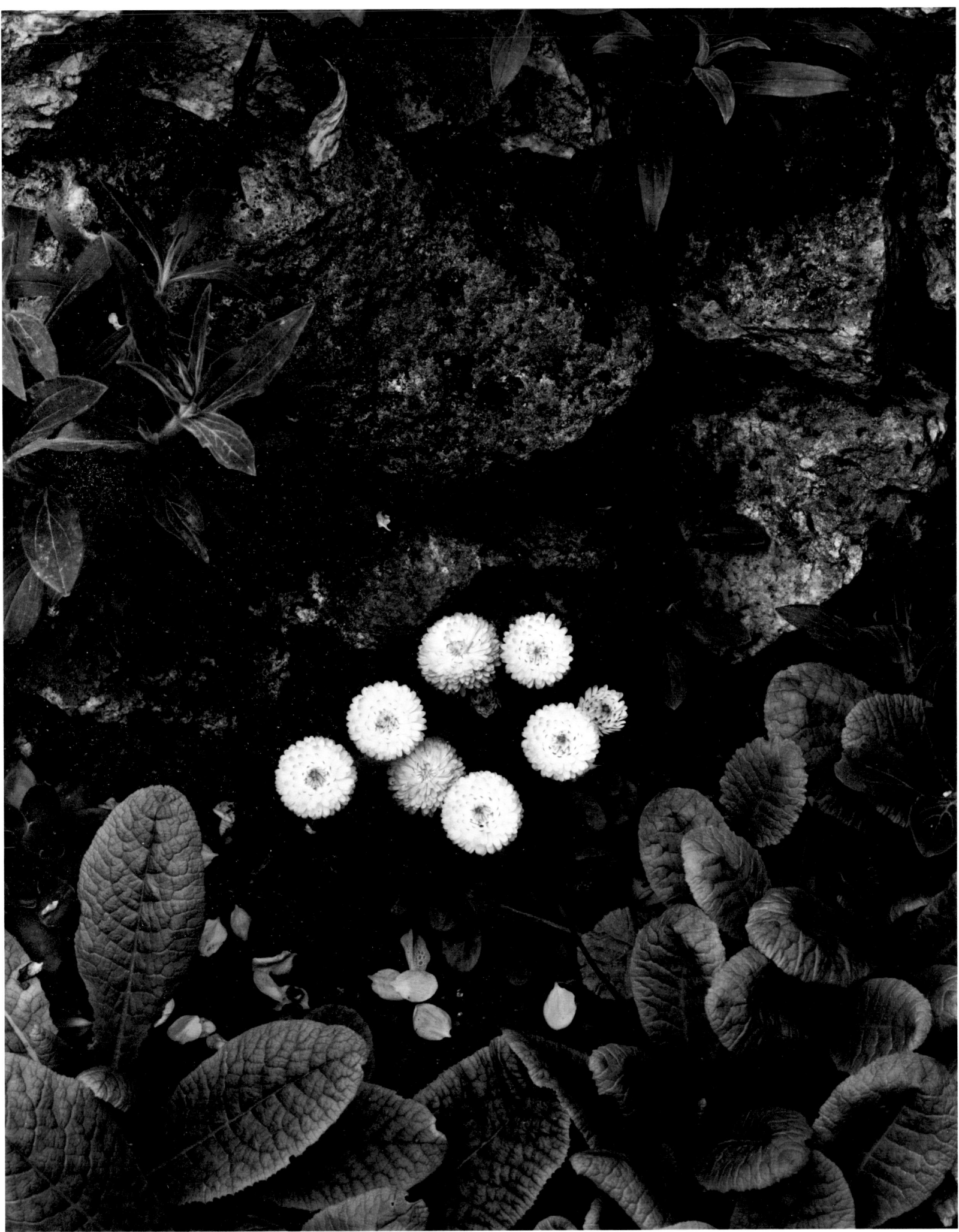

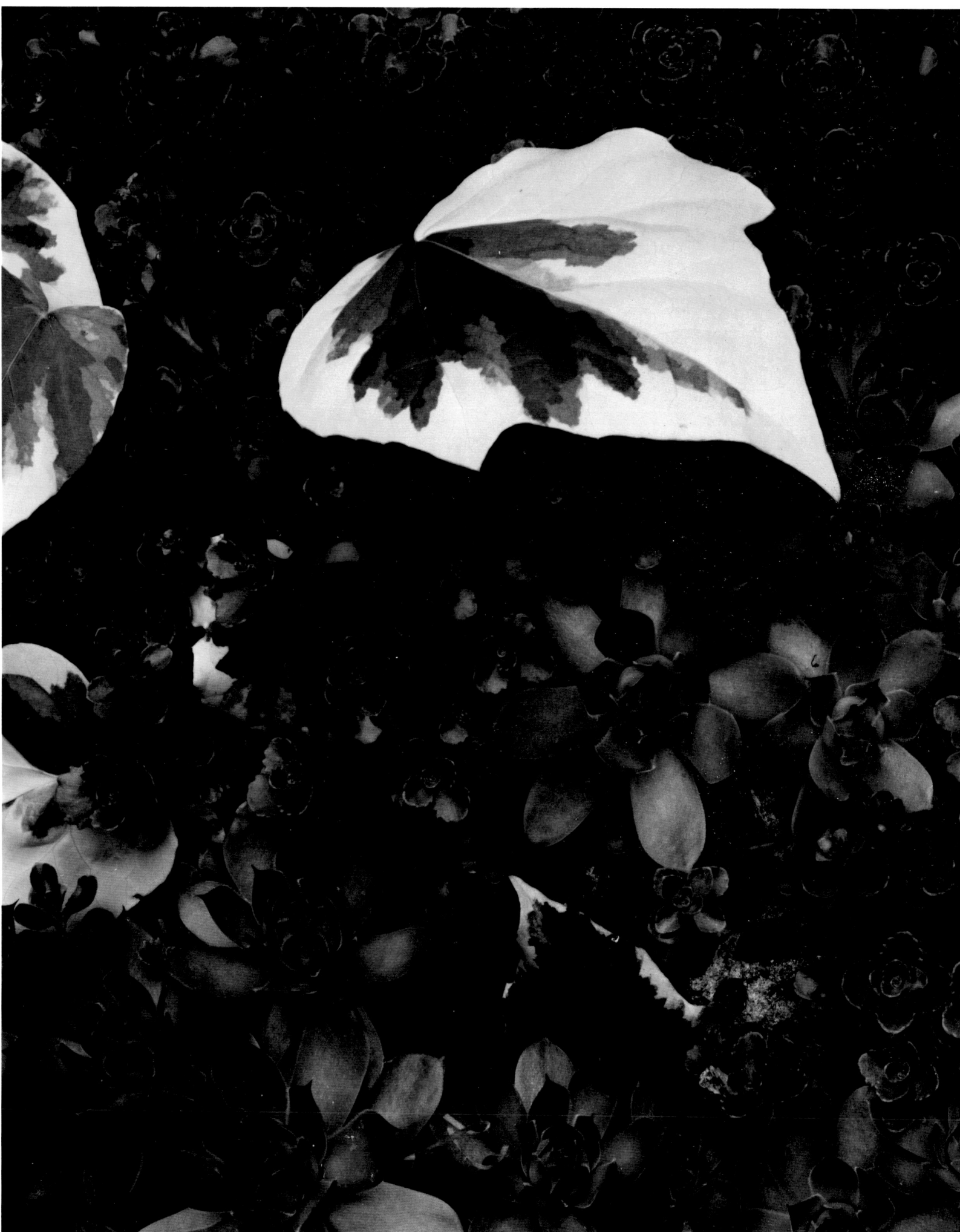

# A N   I N T I M A T E

# P O R T R A I T

PAUL AND HAZEL STRAND stood in the garden beside the old willow tree gazing back at the house, and as they looked it seemed to become transparent. The khaki-colored walls would have to be repainted white, the ugly fireplace rebuilt. Then the eye would travel comfortably from the front garden, through the big living room to include the weeping birch in the back courtyard. On the upper floor, the gallery could be filled in to make a studio for Paul, his darkroom behind it.... The main bedroom, like the living room, ran the width of the house with windows on both gardens, front and back, an inside/outside relationship Paul had often photographed in New England houses. But this was France, and the house stood in a village called Orgeval in the Yvelines, thirty-six kilometers from Paris.

*What do you think, Hazie?*

Having made over the house in imagination, Hazel turned her attention to the garden and its rows of espaliered pear trees, the drive up from the front gate straddling a bed of primroses. Old trees, simple flowers, a cloud of mauve wisteria clinging to the latticed walls of the house. And suddenly she had an urgent desire to get her hands into the earth and make it flourish. Instead of the earth she had known as a Red Cross photographer during the war, churned up by tanks and jeeps, bombed, toxic, a place for the dead, she would have a garden. The garden she had never owned, where she could grow corn and Mother Hubbard squash, cucumbers for dill pickles, and the pears for ginger-pear jam.

The little room upstairs would become *her* workroom, housing a loom on which to weave the traditional patterns of early America, with still enough space to assemble pieces for a patchwork quilt. Her hands, practical hands, could do all these things as once they had worked helping Louise Dahl-Wolf make fashion photographs for *Harper's Bazaar*. But that was before the war, in New York. This was France, and one photographer was quite enough in the family, particularly if he were Paul Strand, whose name already figured among the great pioneer photographers of America.

Remembering Paul's question, she said: *I think we could work here.*

Meanwhile, Paul's eye had been traveling beyond the garden to the old farm opposite on the other side of the road, then sloping down the hill, across the cultivated valley, moving left, climbing again, this time to the woods, and from there, returning full circle to the house.

*It's not far from Paris*, he thought aloud. *We could get in easily and friends could come out.* To which he added another thought: *And we could travel.*

*To find that village you're always looking for?* Hazel

teased him. *You'd have one right here on the spot with Orgeval.* But she knew it was useless suggesting what or where Paul should photograph.

"MONSIEUR ET MADAME STRAND," the new owners of the property in Orgeval, were newlyweds, married recently by the mayor of Orgeval, who was profoundly relieved when Hazel Kingsbury became Madame Strand, a name he could pronounce without stuttering. The gossips of the village confirmed that Madame Strand was his third wife and a good deal younger than her husband. At least she spoke a little French. All he seemed to manage was *bonjour* and *au revoir. Americans,* stated the oldest inhabitant. *They won't last long. The house will be up for sale again in no time.*

*En France,* Hélène Letutour remarked crisply, *ce n'est que le temporaire que dure.* An old saying used ironically when referring to the longevity of the temporary.

Nobody in the village was better informed about the new owners than Hélène and her husband, Raymond Letutour, who had been engaged as housekeeper and gardener by the Strands. The gossips would have liked to ask on what grounds Hélène based her remark suggesting that the Strands had come to stay, but Hélène and Raymond were notoriously tight-lipped about their employers.

Perhaps, in those early days, Hélène herself would have found it difficult to explain why she felt the coming of the Strands was more than temporary. Even Paul and Hazel were unaware, the day they decided to buy the house in Orgeval, that they were laying the ground plan of their life together for the next twenty years.

MORE THAN A DECADE LATER, Susan Barron, a young American photographer, came to France repeating *Orgeval, Orgeval* like a talisman. Driving to Normandy, the name jumped out of the road map

she was following. Taking an impulsive turn left, Susan began asking where Paul Strand lived.

*I had to go where the pictures were taken, though the only pictures I knew then were in the book* La France de Profil. *Finally, a cyclist pointed to the gate and something compelled me to go in. The garden was like fairyland. Walking up the drive with forget-me-nots and tiny pansies, the first thing you noticed were steps up to the lawn, rock gardens, and a willow to make you weep. It was early spring, you saw your breath and the buds just starting to come out. The house seemed very open. I peered in. You could see right through to the little backyard, holding the sun like a cloister. I knocked on the door and heard a noise upstairs as if I was being watched.*

*What do you want?* The voice was forbidding, a woman's voice.

*Is this where Paul Strand lives?*

*Yes. Who sent you?*

*Nobody sent me.*

*What do you want?*

*I'm not sure. I just saw some photographs Mr. Strand made.*

There was a pause. The wall between Paul and the public seemed to be deciding whether or not it would let her through. Finally the voice said: *If you wait a little he'll see you.*

So Susan sat in the garden waiting, while the birds fossicked between freshly weeded vegetables and the strawberry patch, or landed on the sanded *boules* court under the plum tree. After fifteen minutes of what Hazel called the editing process, the voice called out: *You'd better come in. It's chilly out there.*

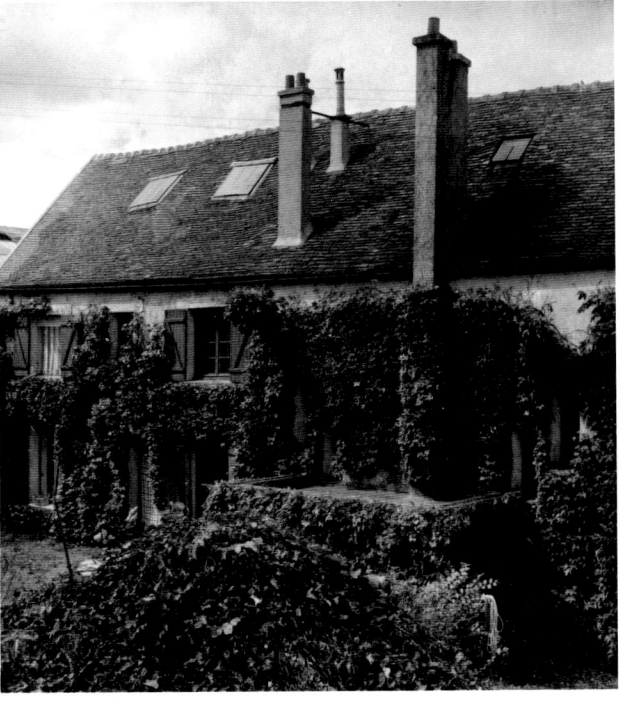

The House at Orgeval.
Photograph by Hazel Strand

*The room was cold but thoughtful*, Susan remembers. *Craft materials, a flagged floor, and on the wall, original prints. Not even the wonderful reproductions of the book could do them justice. Then Paul came into the room. Backlit, he was much bigger than I expected. His center of gravity seemed higher. He had on a tweedy sport coat and sweater. Gray hair. Eyes light blue, with a strange look I discovered afterwards was cataract. Not athletic, but handsome, very welcoming and sweet. "You waited quite a long time, didn't you?" I was looking at a picture,*

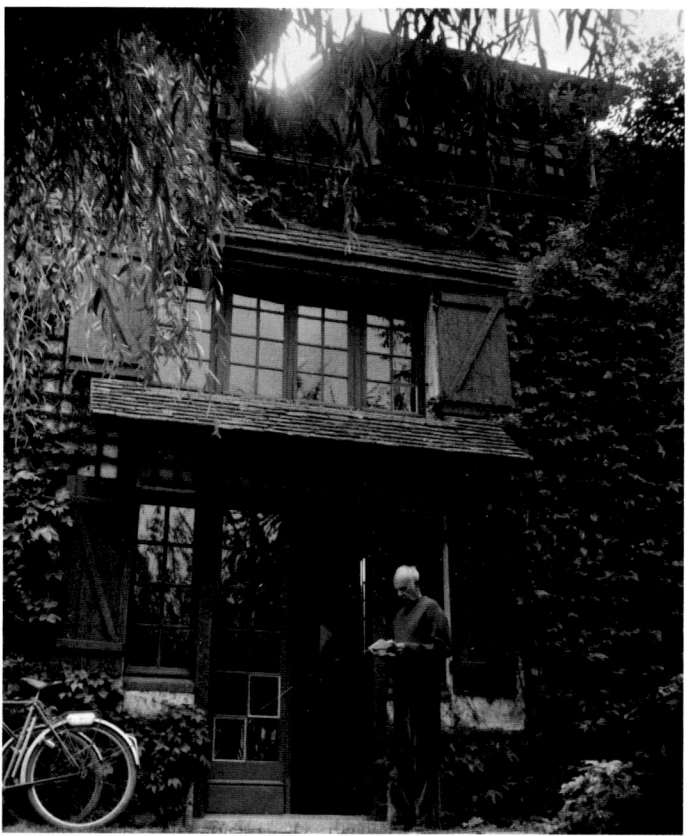

Paul Strand at Orgeval.
Photograph by Hazel Strand

*and Hazel got out a box of prints. He wanted me to sit in the light and tell him what I was looking at. Hazel was in and out, scraggly, with a wonderful smile. She seemed pleased to see we were talking and that I was interested in him instead of coming with my own work to have the master's blessing. I didn't even ask to see his darkroom. I think that pleased him. "Why don't you stay for lunch?" So Paul and I went into the village to buy things and Hazel made a simple, lovely lunch. I told them about my trip to Normandy, and Paul got out maps to show me where to go.*

*About three o'clock, just before I was leaving, he asked if I had any pictures. I showed him the few I had with me, and he said one of them was a good picture but it wasn't printed well. "What do you think, Hazie?" He always deferred to her, and now that he couldn't see well because of the cataract she served as his eyes in the darkroom. She knew all about the mastery of Paul's prints.*

From that first meeting, the house at Orgeval adopted Susan. For Hazel, she was like a daughter. *I'm not so sure about Paul*, Susan says. *The prints were his children. Real children were attracted to him. They clung round his trouser legs. But he was clumsy with them, and his portraits of children are sentimental. Of course, there was Viviane, Hélène's daughter. Paul helped with her education. She was still little when they came to Orgeval, and had to be coaxed out of her shyness with bonbons. Hazel and Hélène made a quilt for her wedding. Later on her boys came—they weren't shy about the bonbons.*

THE LIGHT-YEARS OF MEMORY can be condensed into a few sentences. In reality, those years for the Strands were filled with constant work. I met them first in Paris before they moved to Orgeval, when they had an apartment in the rue Auguste-Blanqui. Marion Michelle introduced me. She had worked with Paul as a still photographer on his film *Native Land* and knew most of the friends who gathered at the Strands' on Sunday. Almost everyone was an exile from different brands of Cold War McCarthyism.

When exiles leave home, they usually take with them books, objects, or projects essential to their identity. Many of these are jettisoned or replaced on arrival. Others need to be integrated into the new context before the exile can feel at home. Paul had brought with him an old dream of making the portrait of a village, where the inhabitants recount their individual histories, a dream caressed since the publication in 1915 of Edgar Lee Master's epic poem on a village, *Spoon River Anthology*. Paul saw the realization of this project as the bridge between his work in America and the work he would do in exile. As soon as Hazel joined him in Paris, they set out together, weaving their way over the roads of France, from Finisterre to the Upper Rhine, from the Vosges to the Pyrenees, through Charente and the Dordogne, always in search of Paul's village.

*It was our fault if we didn't find the village in France,* Hazel recalled. *We could have chosen any one of the fifteen places friends recommended if we'd known better. The village we finally picked in Italy wasn't any more attractive than those in France, but once you sit down in a village and go round the back streets and the back gardens, there's always stuff to photograph.*

Presumably, they also went round the back streets in France, because eventually, Hazel says, Paul began seeing things to photograph *that were very much France—things I'd never seen anywhere else. So although we didn't find the village, I ended up doing a lot of work.*

Indeed, he looked almost aghast at the mounting pile of prints. How could they ever make a book from such heteroclite material?

*Claude Roy has a good visual eye,* Hazel suggested. *If you asked him to write the text he might have an idea.*

Claude Roy not only had one idea, he had so many he took the prints away with him to see how they could fit together. Set side by side, relationships began to form, images calling up old sayings, peasant proverbs about weather and the seasons, inscriptions on sundials and tombstones. There were children's songs and sailors' shanties, as if the photographs released a cascade of voices from the echo chamber of the centuries. Juxtaposing this material with the photographs and his own poems and text, Claude Roy created a visual collage.

*La France de Profil* was published in 1952 by La Guilde du Livre in Lausanne, at a time when books of photographs were still rare. In spite of Daguerre and Nadar, in France no law existed before 1957 protecting *photographic works of an artistic and documentary nature.* Photography remained the poor relation of the arts. Signed by Claude Roy and Paul Strand, *La France de Profil* is the only book where Paul's photographs are listed as *illustrations.*

In his opening text, Claude Roy introduces Paul seen through the eyes of a Frenchman: *A bit like Picasso (minus his passion) with a peasant's walk and a gentleness that sometimes seems sleepy and is only meditative, a slow doggedness which when we were working together often gave us the impression of being at loggerheads with each other, whereas we shared the realities of a complicity that opposed and made us complementary, irritated and enriched us.*

THESE DIFFERENCES OF TEMPO and temperament are evident in the book. The text has a Gaelic verve that leaves the photographs oddly silent. Writer and photographer might be addressing different hemispheres of the brain, so that reading the text we do not see the photographs, and looking at the photographs we exclude the text. There is no *disagreement* between text and photograph for those who have an intimate knowledge of French, but in Paul's case, a text with so many levels of cultural reference and so subtle a play of language was almost impossible to translate, or for him to understand. Before leaving America, he had been among the most fervent of a group of artists, poets, and philosophers in search of a new language to express a potential world of creation and invention. His own play of language, consisting of puns so barbarous even his friends groaned, was perhaps a way of inventing *words which could express something which is our own, as nothing which has grown in Europe can be our own.*

Now, here he was living in Europe, and *La France de Profil* posed in dramatic terms the relationship between text and image.

So far as photography was concerned, Paul found no difficulty in adapting to the new context. Even before leaving America he had been a nomad, traveling to areas with widely different climates and ways of life. Exile in this sense simply extended Paul's way of working. The fact that he would be debarred from language as a means of direct communication meant the photograph would have to bear the full weight of what he had to say, obliging his camera to probe dimensions of the image beyond the reach of language.

Already, in *La France de Profil*, the titles he gave his photographs are no more than laconic statements of fact: *Harness, Countryside, Old Peasant*; or they situate the photograph as *Near Livarot (Calvados)*. Whatever else there is to say is left to the writer. The famous portrait of the angry young man is related in Claude Roy's text to the time of the Revolution and the anger of France against injustice, a specific interpretation dependent on the presence of both photograph and text. But when we encounter the same portrait on the cover of the monograph covering sixty years of Paul's work, the photograph stands alone with no text to tell us anything about it, and we are seized by deeper meaning.

In the fifties, when Paul made this portrait, rural France was still suspicious of being photographed. *Being taken like that I give myself to the camera.* Black magic at work, according to the peasant. Urban sophisticates judged such beliefs to be *a hangover from the prelogic mentality of primitive times, when the image was regarded as a physical emanation of the personality.* It is not sure, however, if the young man glaring into the camera was not right to be wary of the photographer, Paul Strand, who took from him more than a physical representation. *Jeune Gars (Gondeville, Charente)* is a portrait of rage itself, coiled in the archaic substance of our being.

A CHILD COMES INTO THE WORLD biologically programmed with fleeting images, patterns of light and shade, desirable shapes and finds outside himself their material counterparts. These are the strange attractors that beckon him to live, to catch, and to verify the sensual feel of things against the image of his own desire. The image shifts and changes as he grows, yet the primitive attraction for certain shapes continues to inform the way an artist works, and to distinguish what is characteristic in how he sees the world.

No artist has ever adhered more serenely to cer-

tain themes than Paul Strand. *I photograph the things that make a place what it is; which means not exactly like any other place, yet related to other places.*

The *things* by which Paul measures such differences and relationships are not chosen haphazardly. In 1932, on his first visit to Mexico, he reports that he no longer needs to know a region before beginning to photograph, as if *things* had been decided in advance, the themes set, and all he had to do was photograph the same *things* wherever he went for them to reveal automatically their particularities by comparison with those elsewhere.

One of the most enduring of these themes, which he would continue to explore and develop until the last photograph he ever took, was stated when Paul made the photograph of Wall Street: *I became aware of those big dark windows of the Morgan Building on Wall Street, huge, rectangular, rather sinister windows—blind shapes actually, because it was hard to see in.*

From then on windows marked a point of contact between the inside and the outside, a transparency welcoming the eye to see *in*, as with his own house at Orgeval, or a blind shape only to be *looked at* from the outside. Windows became a symbol of his relationship with the countries he visited and the people he met. If they never found a village to photograph in France, it was because at 6:30 every evening all the windows were shuttered. *We had a feeling of being barred from close contact.*

Some of the friendliest windows Paul photographed are in his book *Tir a'Mhurain*, on the island of the Outer Hebrides, where the thatched roofs are weighted by stones against the wind, and windows are set deep into stone walls. In the first place it had been the songs of South Uist and Eriskay that called Paul and Hazel to the islands, eerie echoes of an ancient language and culture, which their friend the musicologist Alan Lomax had collected. But in 1954, when they spent three months on the islands, they came to photograph the *things* that held these Gaelic people so tenaciously to the rocks and parsimonious soil of their homeland. Here, the lacy curtains and pots of flowers in the windows invited Paul to enter, to take his time, quietly interrogating objects on the dresser, pots on the stove, books beside a china dog. The merit of these objects lay not in their beauty, but in the homeliness of their report on what was particular to this place, on how people lived, and what were their chances of survival in the modern world.

For Basil Davidson, who wrote the text of *Tir a'Mhurain*, it appeared paradoxical that a photographer should choose this outpost of an ancient culture and then insist it was a *romantic and unreal view of historical development to say the people can only survive through its continued development*. But Paul had no nostalgia for vestiges of ancient culture as such. He knew technology would change the very structures on which that culture rested. What he sought were the potentials of a *modern* relationship between the place and the people, the old world and the new.

We can trace Paul's mediation as he moves about the islands. Poring over a tangle of knotted roots. Observing cut peat stacked half as high as a house. Ropes lashed shipshape. Or, he remembers, making the photograph of a drowned boot washed up by the tide, its similarity to one made in New England of a woman's slipper stranded among seaweed. He would watch clouds blustering up and photograph the bull against them, steadfast as granite, eloquent of the stand made by the Gaelic people to keep their culture and their way of life.

The iris is another emblem we find on the islands, and again and again in his work. But instead of the New England iris in voluptuous acquiescence to the wind, on *Tir a'Mhurain* the wild iris resists, lacing its fronds in a buttress against the elements.

To appreciate how Paul worked and the scope of his vision, it would be necessary to set side by side the emblems he photographed wherever he went, comparing them for their likeness and for that nuance of difference conferred by the particularities of a region. The windows in *Tir a'Mhurain* tell us a great deal about a climate and way of living. The same is true of the window with the child's doll, the floor cloth, and scrub brush in the Italian village of Luzzara. There, camera and photographer no longer huddle in the lee of the wind, they share a luminous transparency traversed by the image. Certain shop windows and café windows could be found nowhere else except in France. In Egypt windows are shuttered against the heat with palm baskets leaning against the wall; in Italy shutters are framed by vines or wisteria. The black and white window in Ghana, with its closed shutters, withholds the mystery of a mask, no longer a sign of exclusion for the photographer but an engagement of regards between his own and the hidden force inside, looking out. Sometimes I think Paul didn't photograph an external image at all. He simply appropriated fragments of reality that coincided with a yet unrealized image within himself, an image never fixed, forever in flux, but guiding his choice of what to photograph by an imperative desire.

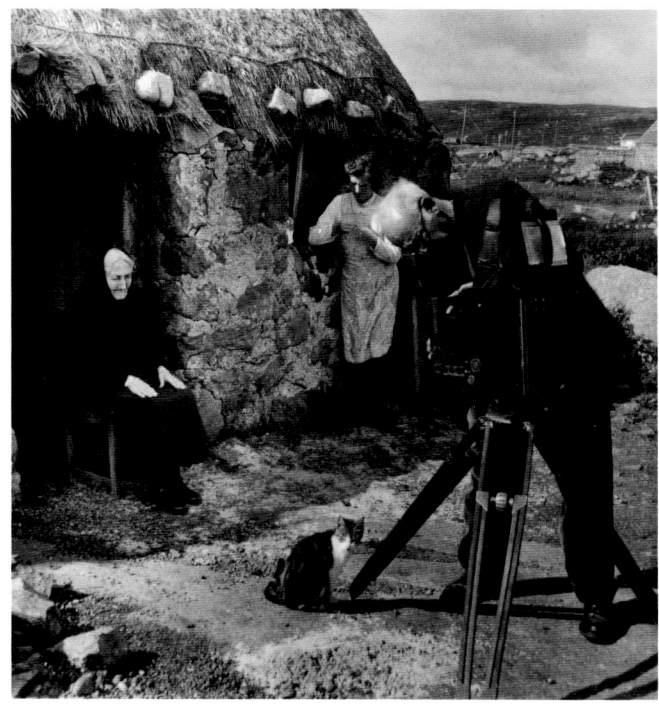

Paul Strand at work in the Hebrides, 1954. Photograph by Hazel Strand

ONE OF PAUL'S OLDEST FRIENDS, the photographer Walter Rosenblum, and his wife, Naomi Rosenblum, author of the invaluable *World History of Photography*, stayed on several occasions with the Strands in Orgeval, where Naomi worked on Paul's letters and papers. She and Walter weren't always in agreement about Paul.

*An extremely difficult character to grasp,* Naomi felt.

*A very special person,* countered Walter. *The greatest photographer I ever met.*

They both described him as serious, retiring into himself if the conversation turned to tittle-tattle. Walter added that when Paul wrote in his beautiful round hand, it was always *as if history were looking over his shoulder.*

Talking to him however, Naomi detected a twinkle in the seriousness. *You were never bored or felt you wanted to strangle him as you do with some heavies.*

WEEKDAYS IN ORGEVAL followed the same pattern, with work in the mornings for Paul and his forays down to the village or to St. Germain-en-Laye in the afternoons. Paul did all the shopping, as Hazel had never learned to drive. *He tried to teach her,* Naomi recounted, *but I have a feeling he was a terrible teacher.*

On this point, Walter leapt to Paul's defense. *Whenever he was around you learned something. After the war I had a little money saved and wanted to buy one of his prints. He chose a couple, and I wondered why those two pictures when there were so many others I would have liked better. He was teaching me, because at the time I didn't understand what he was doing in those pictures. I never learned so much as from looking at those two photographs.*

Paul always treated young photographers with respect, setting their prints up in a good light to be studied, as he did his own. He never criticized unless he could be helpful. *The fence doesn't work here,*

Hazel Kingsbury at Sag Harbor, New York, 1949. Photograph by Paul Strand

he told Walter the first time they met. *The shape doesn't go with the other shapes.* Walter stared at his print. He had never noticed before that there *was* a fence.

Marion Michelle also remembers showing him a photograph of children in Mexico. *It's out of focus but full of life.* Marion photographed Paul and Hazel's wedding, and he liked showing her his prints because she had a professional eye. Most of their regular visitors were writers, filmmakers, musicians, doctors, architects, or artists. Marion's husband, the French painter Jean Guyard, described Paul as his idea of an American sheriff, a man to be respected, even if he didn't understand Jean's painting! Paul's interest in modern painting had been sparked off by the Armory Show in New York and artists exhibited in the Stieglitz Gallery. His two-room apartment in New York had been full of paintings by O'Keeffe and Marin, but I don't remember any painting on the walls in Orgeval. Or perhaps they were overshadowed by his photographs and I didn't notice them. Once I suggested his overall flower photographs were doing what Jackson Pollock did in his paintings. Paul denied flatly any resemblance between himself and "Jack the Dripper."

His recognition of Piero della Francesca's kindred world had been immediate. The same emblems. The same portraits turned inward on an intense and subjective vision. And in Piero's landscapes stretching to infinity, Paul focused on that point where, in parallel, their worlds met.

Less predictable, perhaps, was Paul's admiration for Picasso. Claude Roy had described Paul as looking like Picasso, which, in Paul's case, might not have facilitated their meeting. Nor the portrait he had come to make of Picasso for an album on French celebrities—another idea suggested by Claude Roy—a series begun and then abandoned, not only, I suspect, because the editor wanted to impose his choice. Paul had no real interest in photographing celebrities, and in several portraits of distinguished writers his Medusa glare tended to unhinge the public mask. Picasso met Paul's challenge with an equal gaze. Each time I see this portrait of Picasso I imagine Paul, the two in one and face to face.

THERE IS MUCH UNSEEN MUSIC in Paul's photography. When he gave me Vivaldi's *Four Seasons*, I heard the leitmotif of *The Garden Book*. The old, frail voices of my Gaelic ancestors are like the sound of the sea on the lonely coastline of *Tir a'Mhurain*. There are the drums in *Ghana*, reedy flutes in the desert, hurdy-gurdy tunes of an Italian fête. Paul took me to *Boris Goudonov* at the Opera to hear Boris Christoph. This, too, belonged to Paul's music, a dark and tragic violence still smoldering under other ashes.

But even in music, Paul had his lighter moments, surprising me one Sunday with a record by Elvis Presley! Sunday, of course, was his day off.

On Sundays, the papers, books, and correspondence encumbering the long country table in the living room gave place to Hazel's traditional American lunch. Roasts, vegetables from the garden, and, of course, an American pie! Hazel was a stressed cook, and Marion one of the few people allowed in the kitchen while she was getting lunch. Their New England and Chicago accents could be heard swapping recipes or talking gardens. Outside the kitchen door Marion broke off flowering thyme, sweet basil, and tarragon from the herb garden to take home. Hazel usually added a pot of jam or dill pickles at the last moment. *With Hazel*, Marion said, *everything was real and homespun. Her way of showing affection was to make food or useful objects for others.*

In summer, Ruth Lazarus from UNESCO arrived early so she and Paul could go swimming in the pool at Pontoise. Paul had been a Polar Bear in his youth, and he still loved to swim. Afterwards they sat in the sun and talked politics. *He was very concerned about pol-*itics, Walter confirmed. According to Naomi, *absorbed by politics* would be a more precise description.

But whatever he was, or whatever he did, Paul liked to be the center of attention. If anyone monopolized the conversation or beat him at *boules*, he had a way of disappearing. Hazel would find him sulking in the bedroom, waiting for her to plump up his rumpled ego.

*Rather childish, like his jokes*, Naomi considered.

*He was a great man*, Walter objected. *He deserved to be the center of attention!*

And so he was on Sundays, presiding at the head of the table, sure of getting a second helping of Hazel's pumpkin pie without her watchful eye on his girth. The French, who eat their pumpkin as *soupe au potiron*, preferred the season of her aerial strawberry shortcake puffed with cream.

When there wasn't a strawberry left and we'd drunk two cups of coffee, we all crowded into the little sitting room seldom used except to show the prints. This gave it a rather formal atmosphere, with upright chairs and black boxes to store the finished prints. Hazel took them out of their tissue-paper wrappings, one at a time, and Paul presented them without hurry, letting us study each print. He rarely talked about his work because *talking about it shattered the illusion.*

I often pondered over this word *illusion*. It seemed strangely paradoxical for the realism of photography. Yet the power of the image is ancient and mysterious, a rite of passage between two worlds, performed since the beginning of time in caves and grottos, in temples and churches, and here, once again, in the little sitting room at Orgeval.

IN 1949 PAUL MET THE FILMMAKER Cesare Zavattini at the Congress of filmmakers in Perugia. The two men liked each other and found they shared the same approach to film and photography. Once again, Paul spoke of his elusive village—could it be found in Italy? If so, and they made a book, would Zavattini write the text?

Zavattini thought of all the suitable villages he knew, and the Strands set out on another journey of prospection. But although life continued long after sunset in Italian villages, Paul still hesitated. Finally, Zavattini proposed that no village had the same music on his tongue as Luzzara, the village on the Po where he was born. *All right,* Paul said, *we'll go and see.*

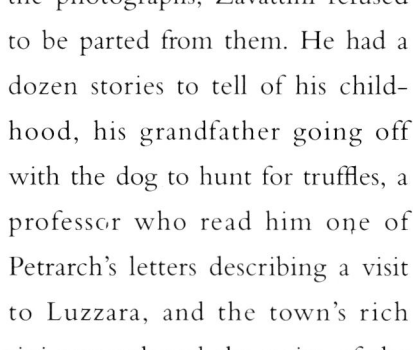

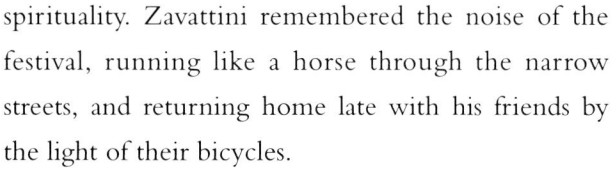

Cesare Zavattini, October 6, 1952

When they came back with the photographs, Zavattini refused to be parted from them. He had a dozen stories to tell of his childhood, his grandfather going off with the dog to hunt for truffles, a professor who read him one of Petrarch's letters describing a visit to Luzzara, and the town's rich spirituality. Zavattini remembered the noise of the festival, running like a horse through the narrow streets, and returning home late with his friends by the light of their bicycles.

In his text, Zavattini lets the people Paul photographed tell their own stories, lives and memories strung along fourteen kilometers of the river Po, always the same river, never the same water flowing under the two bridges.

Paul's emblems are all in place. Windows open, windows shuttered, windows barred. Ropes of ancient, interlocking vines. Even more explicit than the people, objects report on how life is lived in the village. Hats come from the hat factory, milk from the Latteria Cristo. Umbrellas because it rains. A fertile soil with oxen plowing, scythes for mowing, forks for haying. Boats on the Po, where German soldiers drowned in borrowed clothes, trying to escape after the Occupation.

In *Un Paese*, Paul's photographs are not even titled, so we vision them with the unimpeded flow of a film, to the rhythm of a film text. We know life in Luzzara has already changed. Yet for us, the old lady who served the great during forty years is still there long after her death to tell her story: On the whole she had been well treated by her patrons, and felt more at home with them than with her own kind.

Was it the village Paul dreamed of making? Perhaps. Or perhaps he discovered in Luzzara that his village could be contained in a single photograph. With the consummate economy of a Samuel Beckett, he made a set piece, grouping a woman and her five sons in the doorway of their house. It is one of his great emblematic photographs.

THE CONCEPT OF *LIVING EGYPT* arose from a visit to Orgeval by the writer James Aldridge and his Egyptian wife, just returned from a year in Egypt. Their enthusiasm for changes taking place since the 1952 revolution was so communicative that Paul and Hazel were soon studying maps and reading books, sure signs of a forthcoming journey.

*Egypt?* queried Hélène. *Will you photograph the pyramids?*

Hazel laughed. *I doubt it. We'll leave them to the tourists. Where Paul likes to go there aren't many tourists.*

On their journeys together, Paul and Hazel had their separate roles. Hazel did the background research. A fast reader, she could sift and communicate information most likely to interest Paul. He studied the maps, planning the itineraries they would follow. In practice, these were flexible. After a couple of hours on a highway, Hazel would propose turning off. *Let's see what's over there. It looks interesting.* The only problem was that others also found it interesting. As soon as Paul set up the camera people materialized out of an apparently empty landscape, demanding to be photographed. When the curious pressed too close to the camera, Hazel enticed them away with her own little camera, taking hundreds and hundreds of photographs, with the names and addresses of where to send them, as send them she always did after her return to Orgeval.

Meanwhile, Paul made his portraits undisturbed. There are many portraits in *Living Egypt*, people they met along the way as well as portraits painted on buildings and private houses. Ancient Egyptians invented the comic strip at about the same time they invented a written language, and today their descendants still decorate their walls with the pictured account of journeys to Mecca, marriage festivities, or family portraits. So Paul borrowed from the same tradition, setting his portraits against walls chalked by weathering and the hieroglyphics of time, the same people thousands of years later as pictured in popular frescoes. Only the chalk marks changed. Behind the portrait of Rushdie Abdul Salan in the Halen steel mills, the chalk drawings on the wall are plans of technique and construction.

Paul has sometimes been accused of presenting only the positive side of Egypt, where so many people are victims of disease and impoverishment. For him, the victims bore witness to the power of negative forces hidden behind black windows. The tension existing between the actual state of things and Paul's belief that human beings had the potential to change them is the motive behind all his work. *I like to photograph people with strength and dignity in their faces. Whatever life has done to them, it has never destroyed them.*

DRIVING ALONG THE ROAD, Hazel sometimes pointed out things of interest. Usually Paul grunted and drove on. Where the car skidded to a stop in some arid landscape and Paul piled out, setting up his camera with feverish proficiency, always surprised her. What had he seen that had to be photographed with such urgency?

To capture reality, a distance had first to be established between himself and the object by structuring the image with the lens. Paul, even as he worked, an-

ticipated every fluctuation of light that might fill the object with his ardor. He knew there was only one instant of isomorphic coupling between the real and the image, an instant so vertiginous that when the shutter clicked and light entered laying traces on film, he would be absent. His participation in the event could be restored only when the print emerged and the black vertigo of absence was transformed into light. For this moment he would have to wait until they returned to Orgeval and work began in the darkroom.

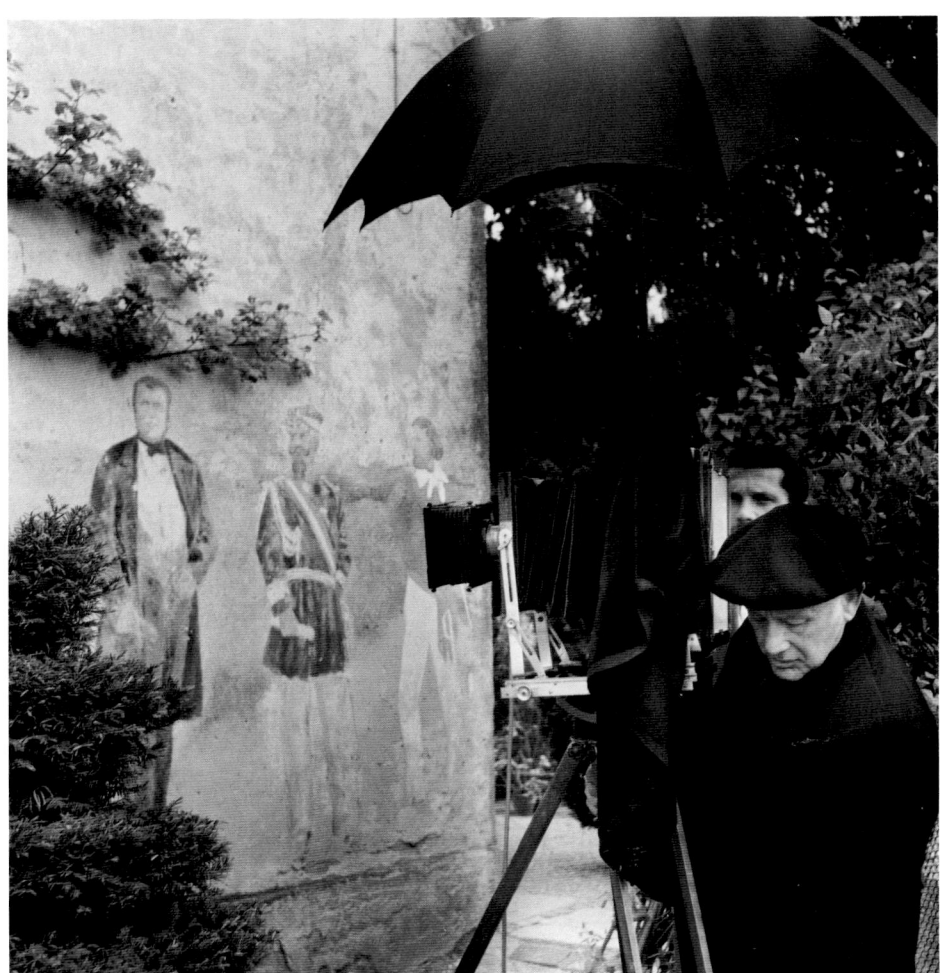

Paul carried the print, still damp, from the final wash.

*What do you think, Hazie?*

For the first time Hazel saw what he had been so impatient to photograph.

The ruins of a village, stained by black shadows of courtyards among the rocks.

Paul Strand at work in Italy, 1953. Photograph by Hazel Strand

What was the name of that place?

Hazel, who kept account of every photograph, checked her notes on the map.

*El Shadida el Manaab. In Upper Egypt.*

Paul touched the print to test the reality of El Shadida el Manaab now that time had stopped for all time in the village. Had the photograph captured that instant when the object became the image, the reality became the illusion? Had the print an integrity of being which restored the village to his touch? He let the mobility of his eye travel to include the imaginary world beyond the frame, making sure none of the essentials had been lost when he pressed the shutter. Then, with the gesture of recognition Hazel knew so well, he caressed the print, feeling under his fingers the dust of those disintegrating walls.

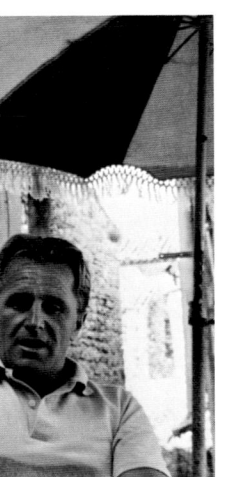

Paul Strand and James Aldridge, 1965

*LIVING EGYPT* IS DEDICATED to Hazel, and at times, Paul's sensual delight in tactile recovery could be almost indiscreet. His friends thought him to be something of a prude, and certainly reticent about his personal relationships. But he showed no reticence when handling a certain photograph of Hazel made at Sag Harbor on their first weekend away together. Hazel said it had been very hot and she'd got terribly sunburned lying on the beach. The photograph shows us only her smile and her youth, and each time Paul caressed the print, the grains of sand and the sunburned skin responded to his touch.

One morning I had gone out early to work on a text with Paul and found both Paul and Hazel sunning themselves over coffee in the living room. The atmosphere seemed unusually relaxed and communicative.

*You're up early, Hazel.*

*We were making love,* Paul said, *and I had a blackout. It was so unexpected I could see they enjoyed my confusion.*

*What do you mean—you had a blackout?*

*For a moment I wasn't there.*

I turned to Hazel for help. *Has this happened before?*

She gave her brief, gurgling laugh. *First, last, and always a photographer.*

The Hazel of Orgeval wasn't always so responsive as her beach photograph. She suffered from chronic insomnia and was often depressive and abrupt, going to earth in the garden, grubbing away on her knees behind the laurel, smoking savagely in secret. In such moods, Paul's plaintive call of *Hazie?* usually got a tart reply. Even when guests were there she could be embarrassingly sharp with Paul, irritated by his slowness or his obvious need of her. *What can I do?* he begged Hélène to tell him. *Let her alone,* Hélène said. *She'll get better.*

*She was never like that with me,* Hélène recounted. *We did everything together. She taught me how to weave and to make quilts. I learned how to retouch prints. I loved doing that, the photographs were so alive. Sometimes I'd arrive in the mornings to do the housework and she'd come downstairs and say, "Not today, let's work in the garden." And how we worked! It was crazy. We'd go to the woods and trundle home barrow-loads of humus and little plants to fill up the shady corners. Paul didn't like changes in the garden. We finally persuaded him to let us take out the pear trees, but he never allowed us to touch the willow. He said he'd come to France to discover the difference between an American and a French tree, and the willow could never be lopped however much Hazel insisted.*

DURING THE SIXTIES, those questioning years for the whole of Europe, Paul and Hazel were almost always traveling. In 1960 they went to Romania, where Paul had heard of a center reputed for its rejuvenating cures. He also planned a book, and returned in 1967 to continue photographing. But the book was never completed. Nor was the book on Morocco, where Paul began to photograph in 1962. *How can I make a book when there are only kings, bitterness, and serfs?* For Paul also, it was a time of questioning, and only in the young republic of Ghana, to which he traveled at the invitation of President Nkrumah in 1963-64, did he find a positive answer. The book that resulted would not be published, however, until 1976.

There had been an exhibition of rotogravure prints taken from his books at the Kreis Museum in Germany. He received the Swedish Archives Award for his films, a recognition of past work rather than his place in the present.

On Paul's return from Sweden, Hélène noticed a change. She was always there to meet them when they came home, the house full of flowers, the garden impeccable, and the gate wide open. She knew the first thing Paul would do was make a tour of the garden. It had almost become a game between them, for her to preserve an equilibrium between the inevitable change and his desire to find the garden as he remembered it. Afterwards, she would make tea. They would all sit round the fireplace while they told her about the trip, and she told them what had been going on in Orgeval during their absence. This time it didn't happen that way.

*I know it was summer because I was picking raspberries. Paul seemed so—bizarre. He didn't look at the garden, just went straight inside and up to his room. The house changed after that.*

Friends also noticed the change. There were health problems, the cataracts that made him increasingly dependent on Hazel to assist him in the darkroom, and omens of bone cancer in his shoulder, which prevented him from traveling. Paul became withdrawn, his energy concentrated on the world on his doorstep, shrunk to the dimension of the garden.

From the time they came to live in Orgeval, Paul had photographed his emblems. A lupine here. There, a cascade of flowers falling over the rock garden. Or the magical path under Hazel's window leading to some imagined Cytherea. He began to talk to me about a garden book, using a selection of photographs made over the years and completing them with new work.

As summer passed and the leaves began to fall, he kept urgent watch from his upstairs studio. Nothing must be touched. The leaves must lie where they fell, the yellowing stalks allowed to rot in the ground. Hélène and Hazel could hardly venture into the vegetable patch without Paul arriving to see what they were doing.

For the first time since he made *The Garden of Dreams*, on his first visit to Versailles in 1911, he began giving titles to photographs, as if the simple naming of their reality ceased to be appropriate. For him, they had become *signs*.

Winter came. In the woods he photographed *Things Past on the Way to Oblivion*, searching in the disintegration of forms and devouring creepers some intuition of a new order. The threat he saw advancing through the undergrowth clutched at his heart with the tentacles of *The Great White Wood Spider.*

ESCAPING FROM THESE SATANIC twilights, he turned for reassurance to the emblems so often photographed and cherished, the willow and the iris. But the garden had lit its *Last Candles to a Dying Sun.*

How long did Paul doubt and question before the spent lilies offered him their *Revelations?* Before he learned to interpret *The Oracle* of the ivy? Not until, perhaps, the brittle stalks had dressed for him their *Arc de Triomphe.*

*Paul had been working alone so long,* Hazel said, *he'd been forgotten. Nobody knew what to make of him. Young people were either crazy about his work or found it too finicky and precious for words. Finding a publisher wasn't easy. "Is he still alive?"*

THE POLITICAL CLIMATE in America had changed after President Kennedy's election, and in 1966 Paul and Hazel returned to New York, Paul with a letter in his pocket from an unknown young man, Michael Hoffman, recommended by Nancy Newhall, who had worked with Paul on *Time in New England*. He wanted, this young man wrote, to relaunch the moribund photographic review, *Aperture,* and create a book-publishing program, which had never existed. Nancy had a genius for getting people together at the right moment, and she must have thought Michael and the "forgotten" photographer could be mutually helpful.

On Paul and Hazel's arrival in New York they went to lunch in Michael's Brooklyn apartment, where he lived with Misty Carter before their marriage. It could have been a difficult encounter without Misty's charm and intelligence to put everyone at ease. The Strands liked her at once, and some of Paul's reserve dissipated.

The apartment overlooked the ocean, and during lunch clouds rolled in, piling up as they once had done behind the bell towers of New England and the church of Taos. Paul felt his life had come full circle. There were the skies he loved, sharing that moment of supreme suspense before the storm broke and the clouds scattered into new formations.

They were discussing the possibility of reediting *The Mexican Portfolio*. Michael knew of a press where a man of eighty-four could make by hand the twenty thousand gravure prints required, a redoubtable task that of course Paul would supervise. Michael had also discovered another man who made lacquer for religious objects, and tests proved it to be the purest lacquer available. The hand-molded paper for the portfolio could be imported from France.

Paul liked the sound of the old printer and his way of working. But he was still wary. Only Hazel knew of the prints and negatives locked away in the vault in Versailles or hidden in a box under Paul's bed. A life's work waited to be discovered, and Paul was determined it should not become the feast of crows.

Over the next five years, beginning with the reedition of the *Mexican Portfolio*, Paul and Michael undertook several projects together, but the real turning point in their association came in 1971. During the intervening period Michael had helped to found and direct the Alfred Stieglitz Center at the Philadelphia Museum of Art, and he looked forward to reacquainting the American public with Paul's work within the same context. As one of the world's great museums, famous for the Annenberg collections and exhibitions presented under the inspired direction of Evan H. Turner, the Philadelphia Museum's recognition of Paul's place in American photography would establish his reputation at an international level. This prospect became reality when the Philadelphia Museum scheduled a major retrospective of Paul Strand's work for 1971.

Michael flew to Orgeval, where he and Paul could select prints from sixty years of photography for the exhibition. After two days of working on a single sequence, Paul taking his time as always, never allowing prints to be eliminated, Michael became frantic. The third morning, when Paul came downstairs, he found Michael, up since five, laying out prints on the floor with a reckless disregard for Paul's meditative eighth-of-an-inch moves to which these precious prints were accustomed. Michael looked at Paul, and Paul looked at the prints. Shorn of their tissue-paper wrappings and precipitated into new unexpected relationships, they revealed unsuspected dimensions. Paul realized that with other eyes, in other contexts, people would see his prints as he had never seen them. This way of working opened abruptly on such a vast perspective, he needed time to adjust his focus. Almost grudgingly, he said: *Go ahead. Keep on with what you're doing.*

GIVEN PAUL'S CARTE BLANCHE, Michael prepared the great retrospective exhibition that opened at the Philadelphia Museum in 1971, a major artistic event all over America, which later traveled to great museums in Europe. When the photographs were on the walls, Paul and Hazel traveled to be present at the opening.

Slowly they walked together through the gallery, where Brancusi sculptures and other works of art evoked the original exhibitions that they and Paul's prints had shared in the early Stieglitz "laboratory centers." Without speaking, Paul and Hazel looked at every detail, at every one of the four hundred and forty prints. At the end, Michael waited for the verdict.

Paul said, *There is only one picture that isn't properly hung. It's upside down.*

Issued as a catalog for the exhibition, the two-volume monograph on Paul Strand—then the most expensive publication ever devoted to a photographer—immediately attracted book collectors and sold out. Encouraged by the growing interest in Strand, Aperture listed a forthcoming edition of *Ghana: An African Portrait*, which, ten years before, Paul had laid out with a text by Basil Davidson. Michael insisted on reviewing the original version and making changes. Paul, having suffered what he described as the Dresden editor's *attempted violation of the unity and integrity of Tir a'Mhurain*, the first book made with Davidson, bluntly resisted editorial demands. Michael, equally intransigent, matched Paul's stubbornness in knowing how things should be done. Hazel remembered a former dispute in Orgeval when both men stormed up separate staircases, each followed by the other's wife to coax the unyielding partners down again. This time, an underlying issue had to be reconciled. Both Paul and Michael recognized the Ghana book as a test of their relationship.

Paul needed someone he could trust if he were to continue working, and perhaps he chose this occasion to be the proving ground for his decision. He capitulated, but with the worst possible grace. *All right, have it your own way. I want nothing more to do with the book.*

Another project met with unexpected opposition from Hazel. For a long time Michael had worked with a young American printer and photographer, Richard Benson. Knowing his outstanding qualities, Michael proposed the publication of two portfolios

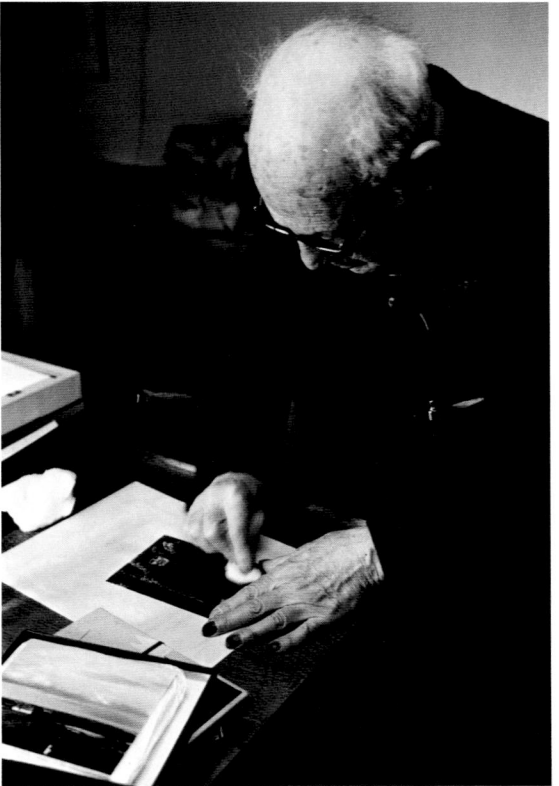

Paul Strand varnishing prints.
Photograph by Paolo Gasparini

of Strand prints, in an edition of fifty. Hand-printing fifty faithful reproductions of each photograph was an unimaginable task for Paul, who had never printed a negative more than twice on the dwindling stock of sixteen-year-old Illustrated Special, the paper he loved best. Michael suggested that Richard Benson come to Orgeval and work in the darkroom under Paul's supervision. To this suggestion Hazel opposed an outraged veto: *Over my dead body.*

After further discussion Paul agreed, since he and Hazel were in New York, to meet Richard. He chose a negative for Richard to print, giving him his own print as guidance, but no instructions. When Richard returned he told Paul it had required every skill he had to make the print, but that he had been unable to tone it. Paul nodded, examining the results.

*I never said I was a straight photographer,* Paul remarked, examining the results. Then he added: *Once toned it wouldn't be a bad print. Do you think you could make fifty of the same quality under my direction?*

IN 1975, PAUL AND HAZEL returned from the United States to France and we began work on a book of photographs of the Strands' garden at Orgeval, to this day unpublished.

We set up the prints round his bed upstairs, replanting the garden in his bedroom. Columbine days and the sunshine of marigolds. Happy families of buttercups and bachelor's buttons, the garden as he had photographed it when they first came to Orgeval. In retrospect, Paul preferred the later, more austere prints, when winter laid bare the structure of the willow and the dark whorls of its bole. For hours Hazel and I shifted prints as he tried out different relationships to reveal their attractions and antipathies. Not until they combined to make a third dimension did Paul give the imprimatur of his approval:

*Very handsome.*

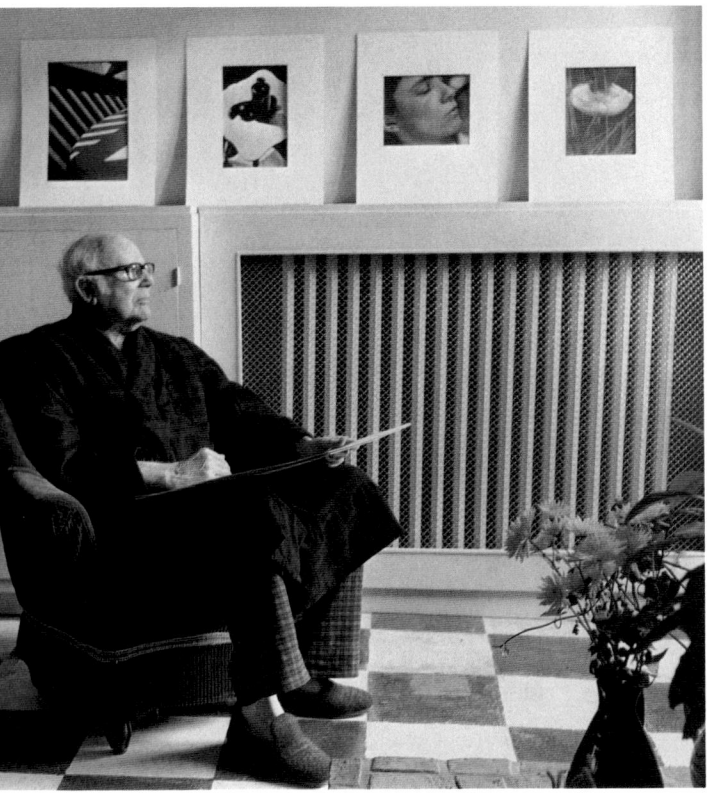

Paul Strand inspecting prints from Portfolio One. Photograph by Richard Benson

There were other hours when he couldn't work and the pain came back. On one of his visits, Michael Hoffman saw that Hazel was exhausted and suggested sending someone over to help her.

THE HOUSE FILLED with young people. Downstairs, Susan Barron and Ann Kennedy sorted prints while Naomi Rosenblum worked on the papers and correspondence for the archives. Richard Benson arrived to work on the two portfolios, "On My Doorstep" and "The Garden." In this atmosphere of activity Paul's optimism revived. Like Methuselah he wanted to live nine hundred years, even if he set his claim on eternity more modestly at a hundred

and fifty. Each day he announced a still-to-be-accomplished project. He showed me magazine photographs magnifying monsters in a drop of water and spoke about the astronomic discoveries of galactic space. The house resounded with a recording of Beethoven's Ninth Symphony.

As boxes of negatives came out of storage and were excavated from under the bed, images of a lifetime confronted Paul. He astounded Michael by dismissing the *experimental period* of 10-by-13-inch platinum and palladium contact prints with its magnificent *Bowls* and *Porch Shadows* as "not worth keeping." Other negatives, stored since the twenties, he had never printed nor shown to anyone. They belonged to that tempestuous period with Stieglitz when the two men photographed their wives, Georgia O'Keeffe and Paul's first wife, Rebecca. To immobilize Rebecca while he photographed, Paul had used a steadying device known as the Iron Virgin, and now he suggested Richard should use an old Hollywood trick with cheesecloth to soften the print. Even then Rebecca's torso in its strange and shocking nudity gave us the ghostly shiver of voyeurs.

Although I was often in Orgeval during those last months, working with Paul on text for the portfolios and preparations for the presentation of his retrospective exhibition that Michael Hoffman had organized with the National Portrait Gallery in London, I was not there the day Michael arrived with *Ghana: An African Portrait* in its published form. Michael described what happened in a letter written to me after Paul's death.

*I remember bringing the Ghana book to Paul from New York. After what seemed to me an interminable wait and his careful looking from image to image, checking and rechecking every nuance, I left the room not being able to bear the tension. As I returned and sat down, he took his hand and passed it over the front of the book and then through the pages. He said, "Very handsome." His eyes filled with tears and he said, "It couldn't be better." His statement seemed an affirmation that his work could go on even without his direct involvement—an affirmation of the strength of his work, his nurturing of others, and that the work might take on new meaning without his physical presence.*

During those poignant hours when Paul and I worked together, Paul dictating texts out of a fog of drugs and pain, word followed word with infinite slowness, but never losing the coherence of his thought. Waiting for the next word to come in this struggle for clarity and expression, I felt I had never been admitted more closely to knowing Paul Strand, for each word, when it came, seemed to rise from the darkness of our origins, on the long haul upwards toward a humanity Paul had always believed possible.

HAZEL TOLD ME that one night, alone in their bedroom, she and Paul drew up the balance of their life together. Neither of them looked back nostalgically on a grand passion. Right from the start, Hazel said, *we were too old to jump into things.* They weren't romantics. *Come over,* Paul proposed when he left for France, *and we'll see how it works.* They had made it work because they could work together.

Of Paul, she said: *He was a kind and thoughtful man.*

Of her own life: *Doing what you like to do is what matters. I can't understand just pleasuring yourself.*

Paul made his own summing up when we were trying out relationships between photographs for his garden book. Looking round for the photograph made at Sag Harbor, he said:

*Give me Hazel. She goes with everything.*

AS THE TWO PORTFOLIOS progressed toward completion, so Paul's strength diminished. At first he had been able to work with Richard in the darkroom, later Richard went backwards and forwards between the darkroom and Paul's bed, where he mas-tered the prints. The friendship between the two men took its source both at a professional level and at a profound level of trust. At night they talked, sharing the sleepless hours when Richard washed and lifted Paul, changed his position to ease the pain. In so intimate a proximity, Paul felt that Richard touched the inner image of himself, that fluctuating image he had matched with fragments of reality from the outside world to become his photographs. The final print of Paul Strand he himself would never see, never be able to touch as he had touched the print of *El Shadida el Manaab,* feeling under

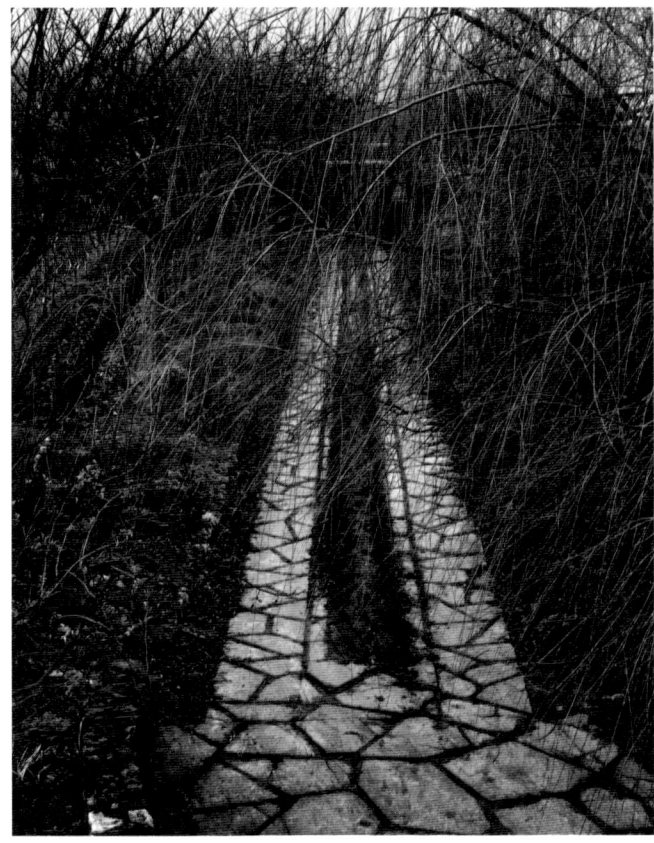

The driveway at Orgeval, 1973. Photograph by Paul Strand

his fingers the reality of his own creation. How could he verify what he had done? That must be left now for others to decide, for others to interpret. In those moments of doubt and discouragement, Paul's only consolation lay in Richard's touch. The same tact and tenderness conferred on his inner image Richard would bring to the understanding of his prints.

Three nights before he died, Richard kept watch in the shadowy bedroom where Paul lay. Once the fourth portfolio had been approved, Paul refused to eat or drink. For over a week he had been in a semi-coma. The house slept and no sound came from the garden. Suddenly, Paul sat upright in bed, his eyes wide open, and cried out his final words: *All my books!*

Catherine Duncan
Paris, 7 July 1993

Strand went his way on a road full of musings, capriciousness, meditation and reveries, a road whose unharried curves and bends he enjoyed like a child playing hooky with no purpose other than that of observing and absorbing as much of humanity's simplest, most naked truth as possible. He avoided with royal nonchalance almost everything the "foreign" photographer feels obliged to investigate from top to bottom. Paul Strand never photographed Notre Dame or Mount St. Michel, Versailles or Chartres. Nor did he feel compelled to take a shot of the inevitable bottle of Pernod, the ladies in black coif, the men in mustache and beret nor anything in France that might appear singular or sublime to a person from the other side of the world. One of Strand's characteristics was that he never chose a subject at first sight, no matter where it was. He was a stranger who was drawn to that which might habitually appear "strange" to foreigners and Frenchmen alike.

If he had something to teach us about our country, its inhabitants, its way of life (which at times is slow-paced, parsimonious and dull as to be no way to live at all) it was not due to the innovative candor of his way of seeing it. The fact is that Paul Strand did not enter life in France like someone who came from the outside. The harvest reaped by this ambulant photographer is disconcerting only insofar as it takes us to the center of that which we no longer see and forces us to stop and take a look. Strand did not try to rediscover or renew France's image through the artful tricks and inventions of his craft. He simply tried to penetrate it by descending into the country's taciturn depths with the unhurried docility of a pebble making its inevitable way to the bottom of a well.

From "Paul Strand," by Claude Roy,
translated by Helen Gary Bishop.

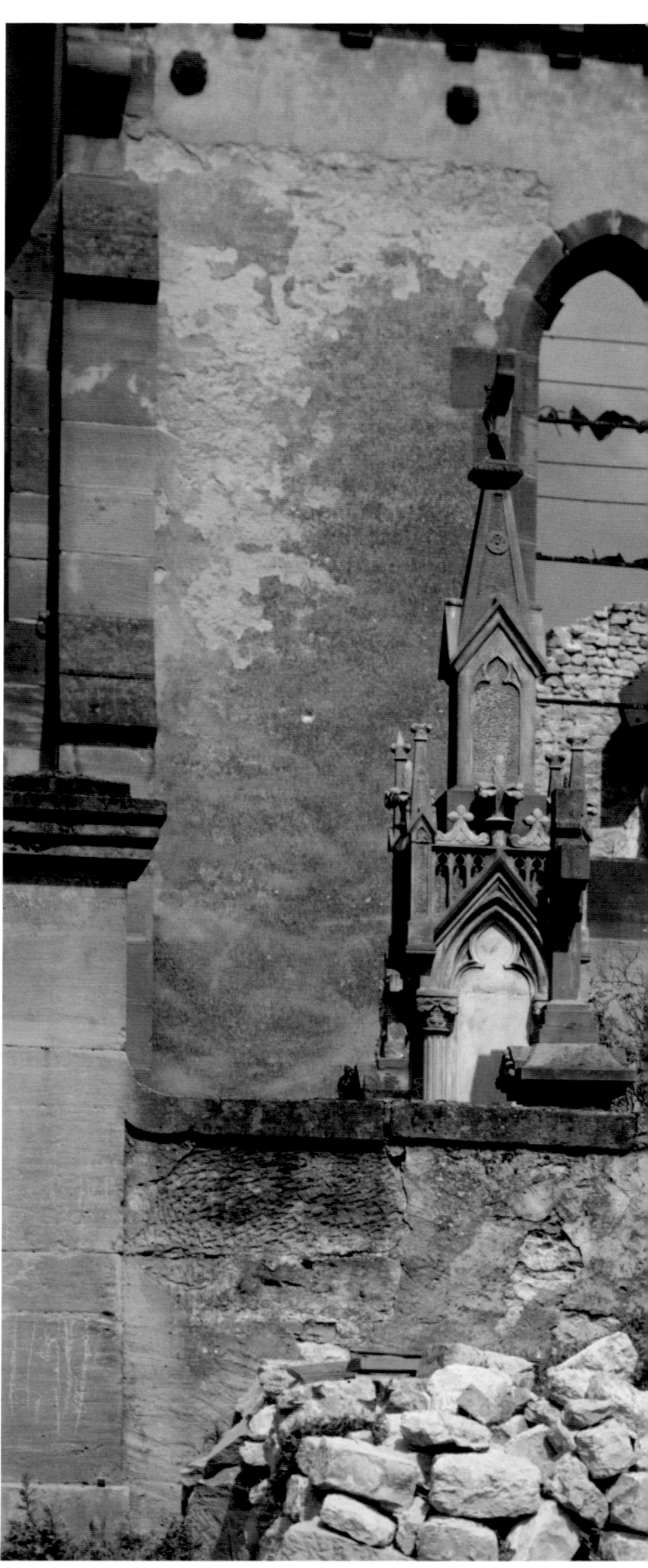

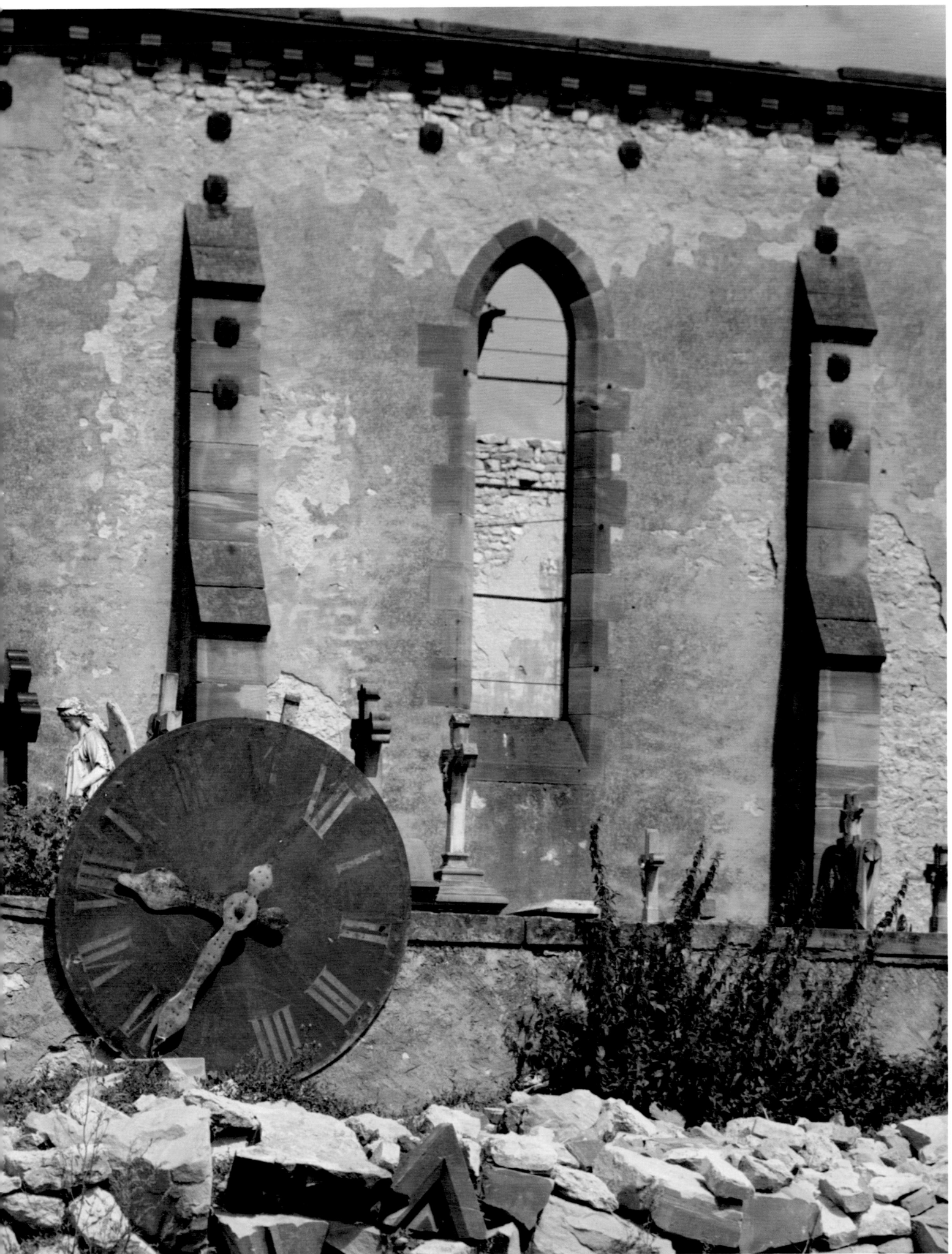

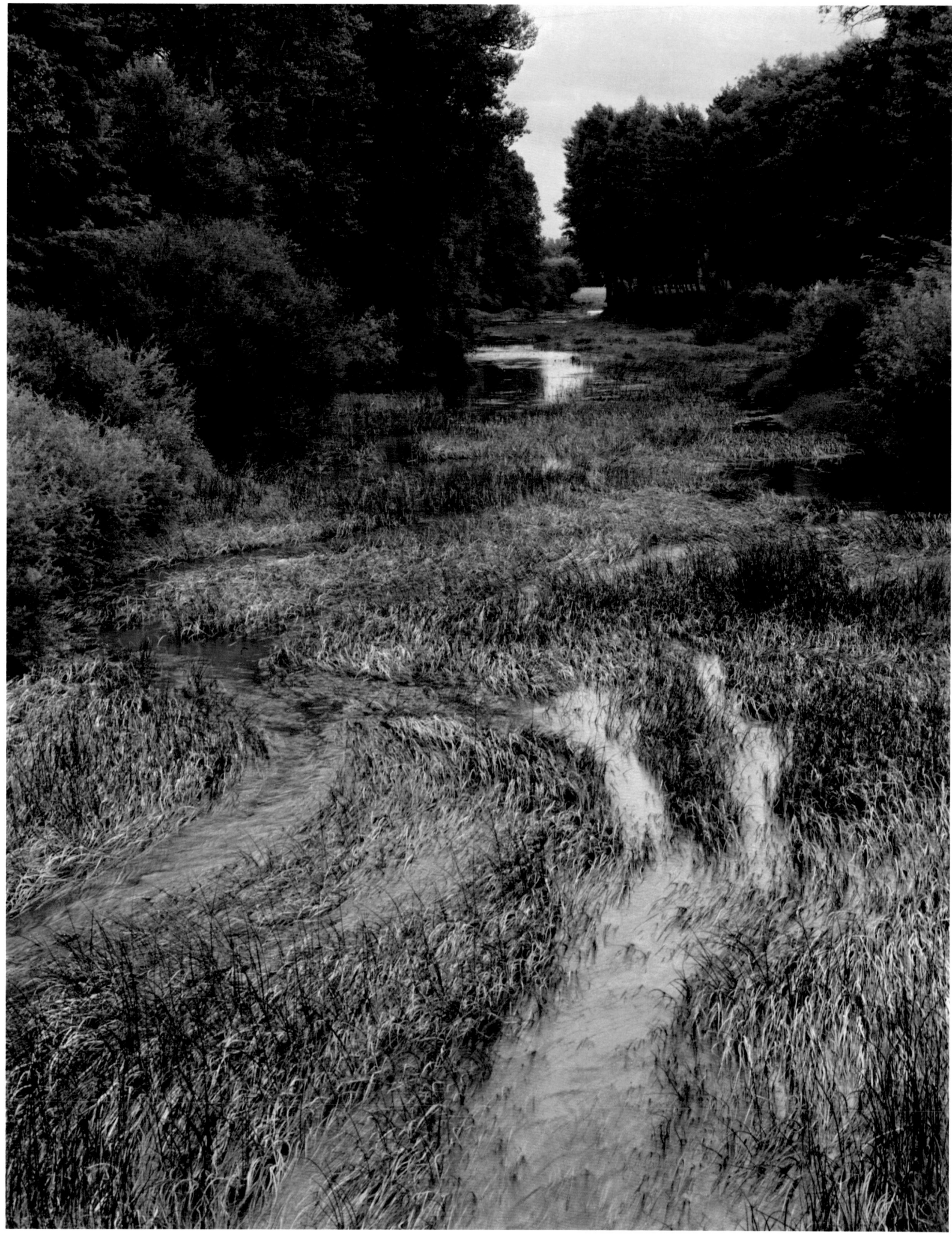

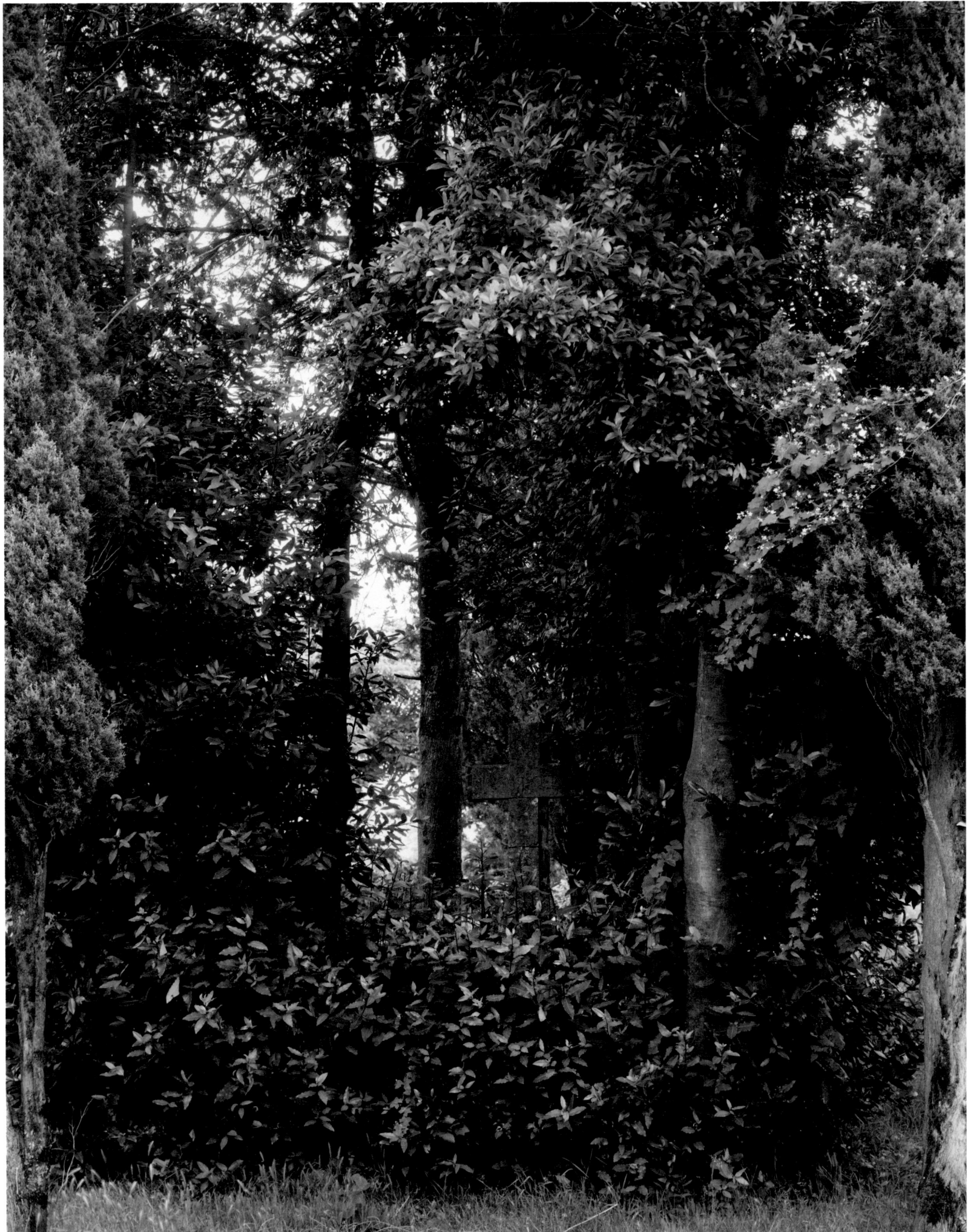

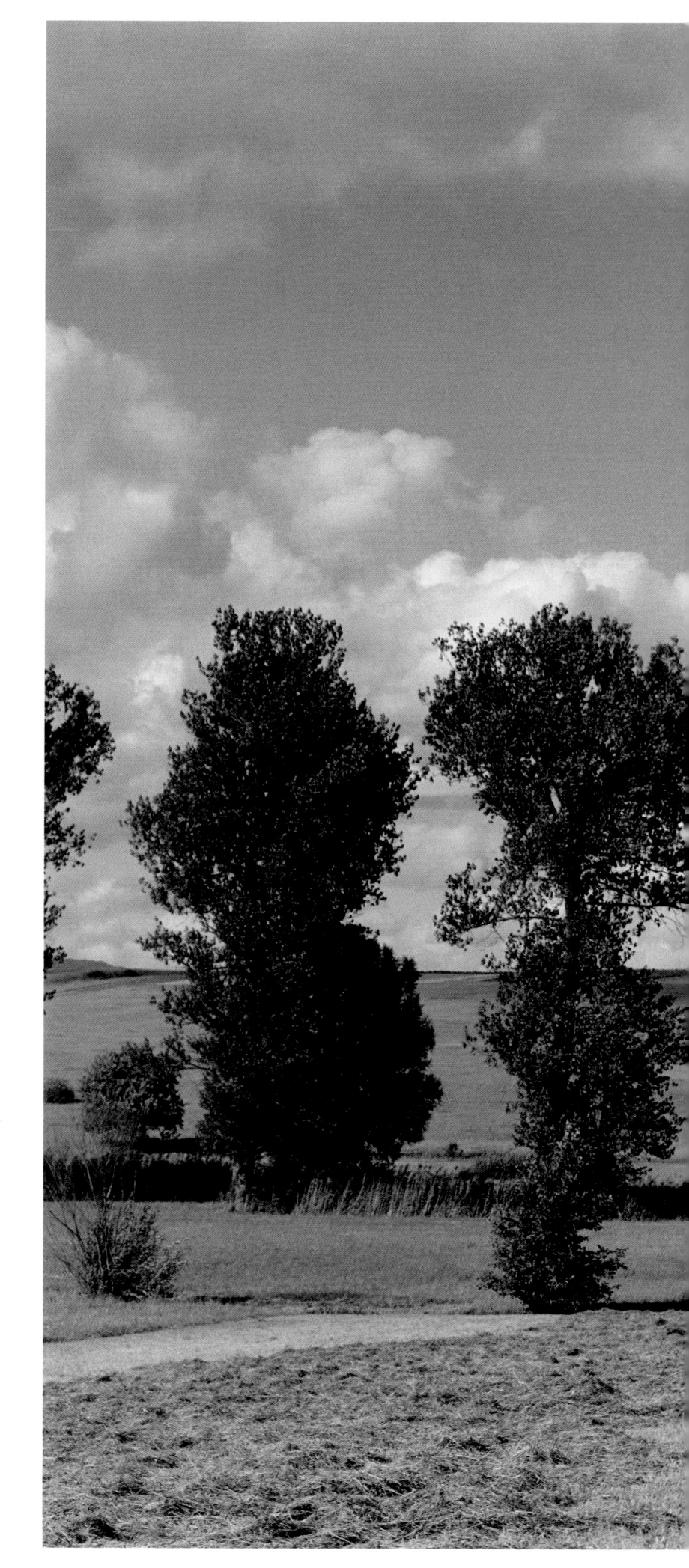

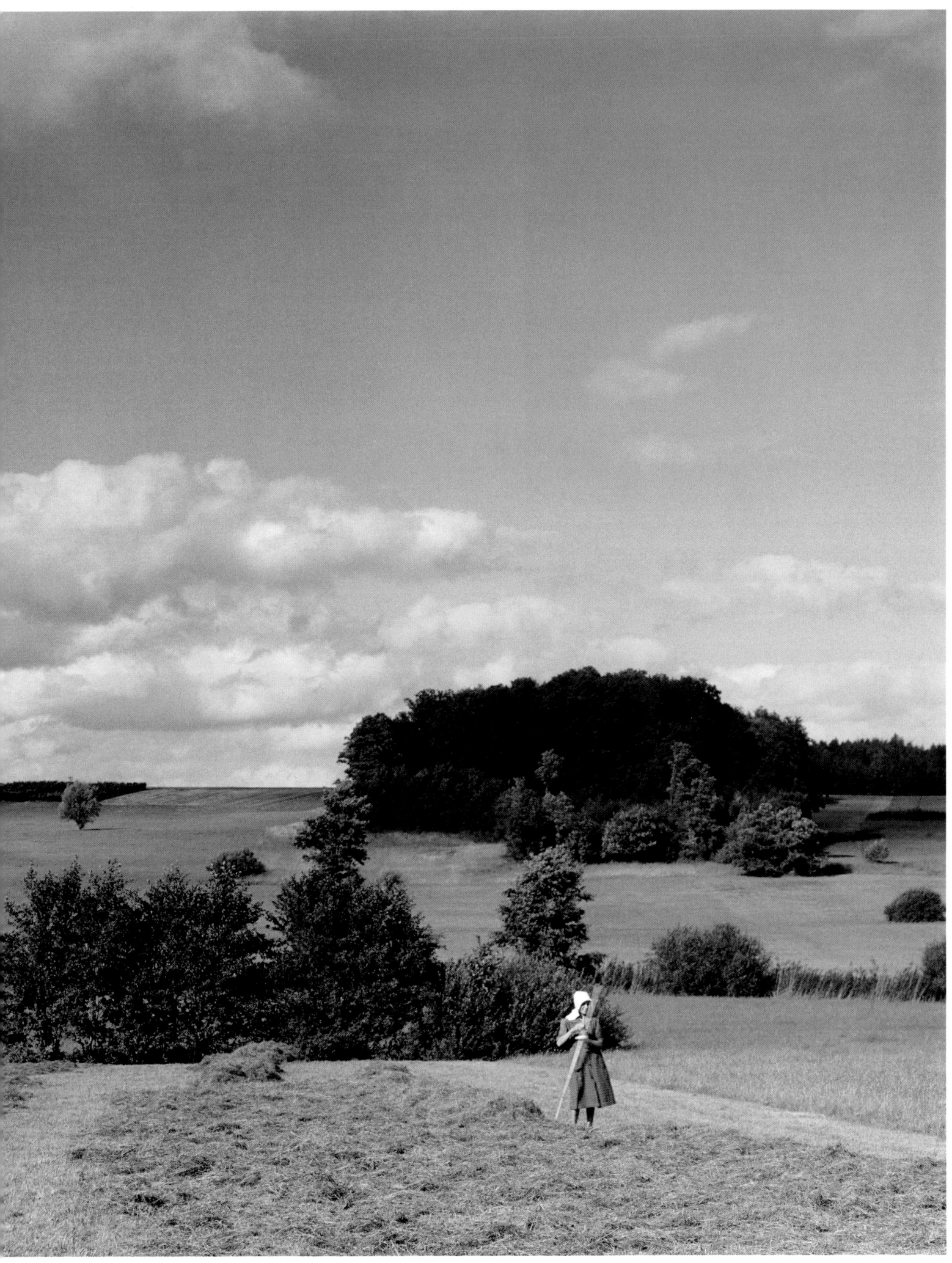

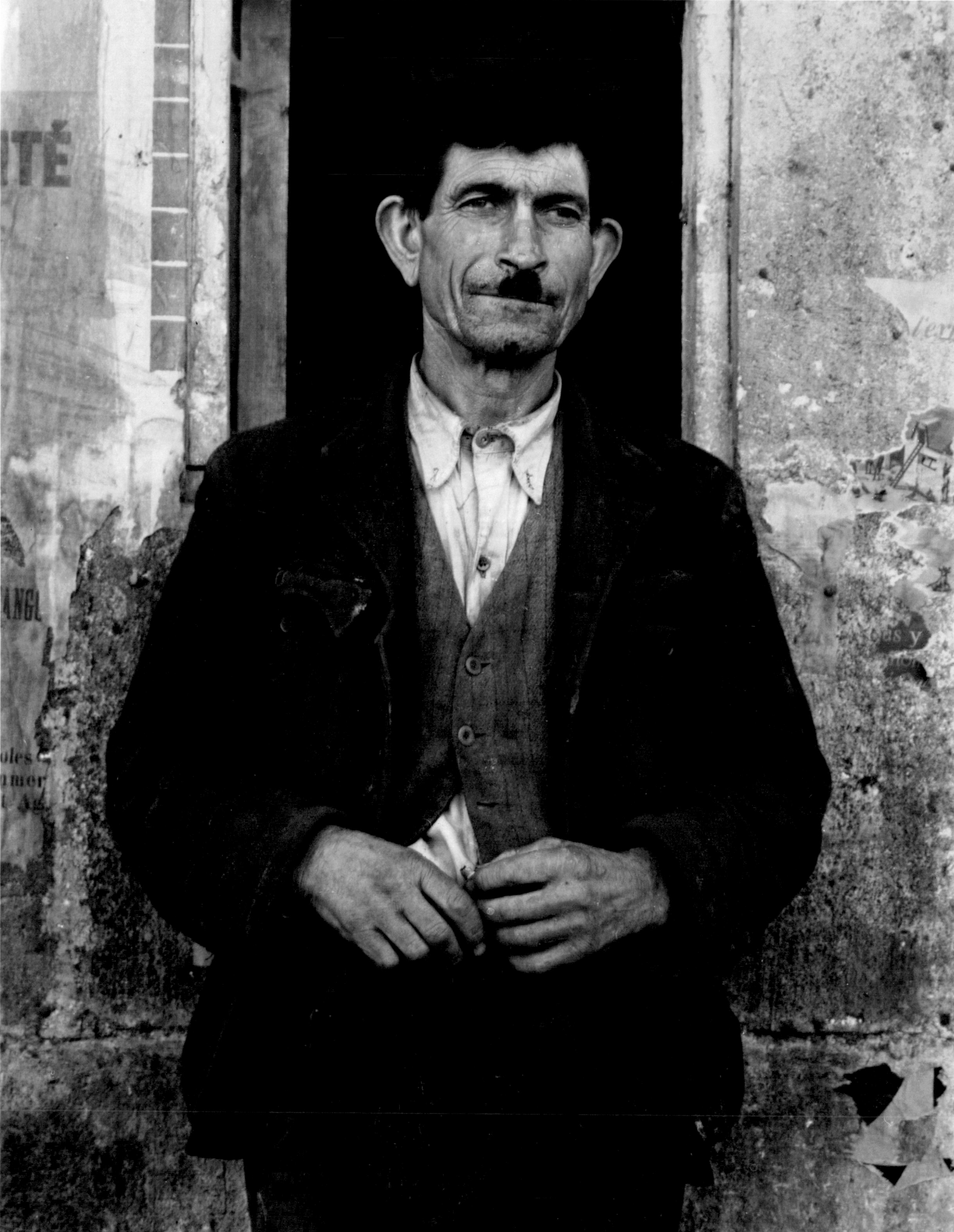

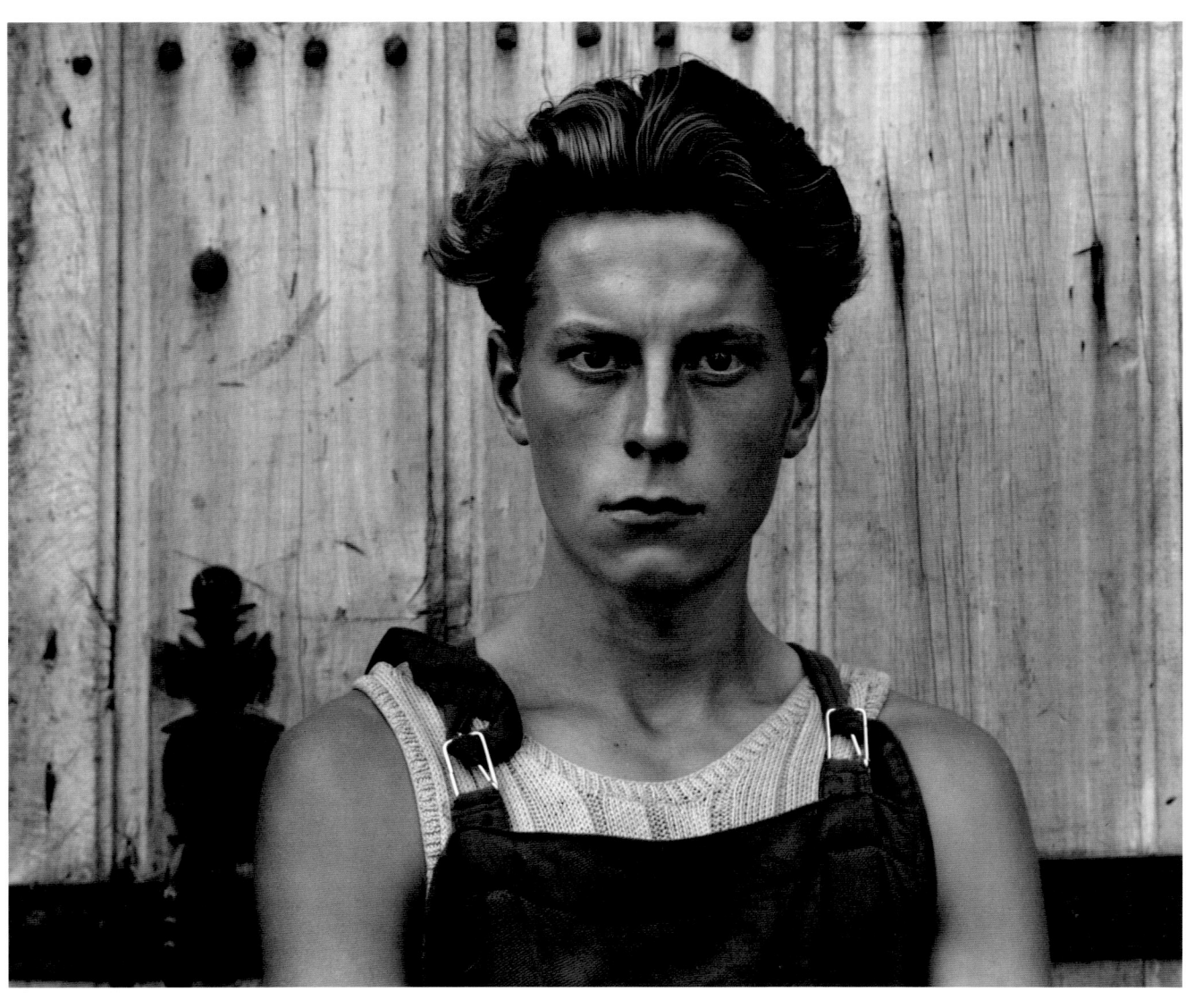

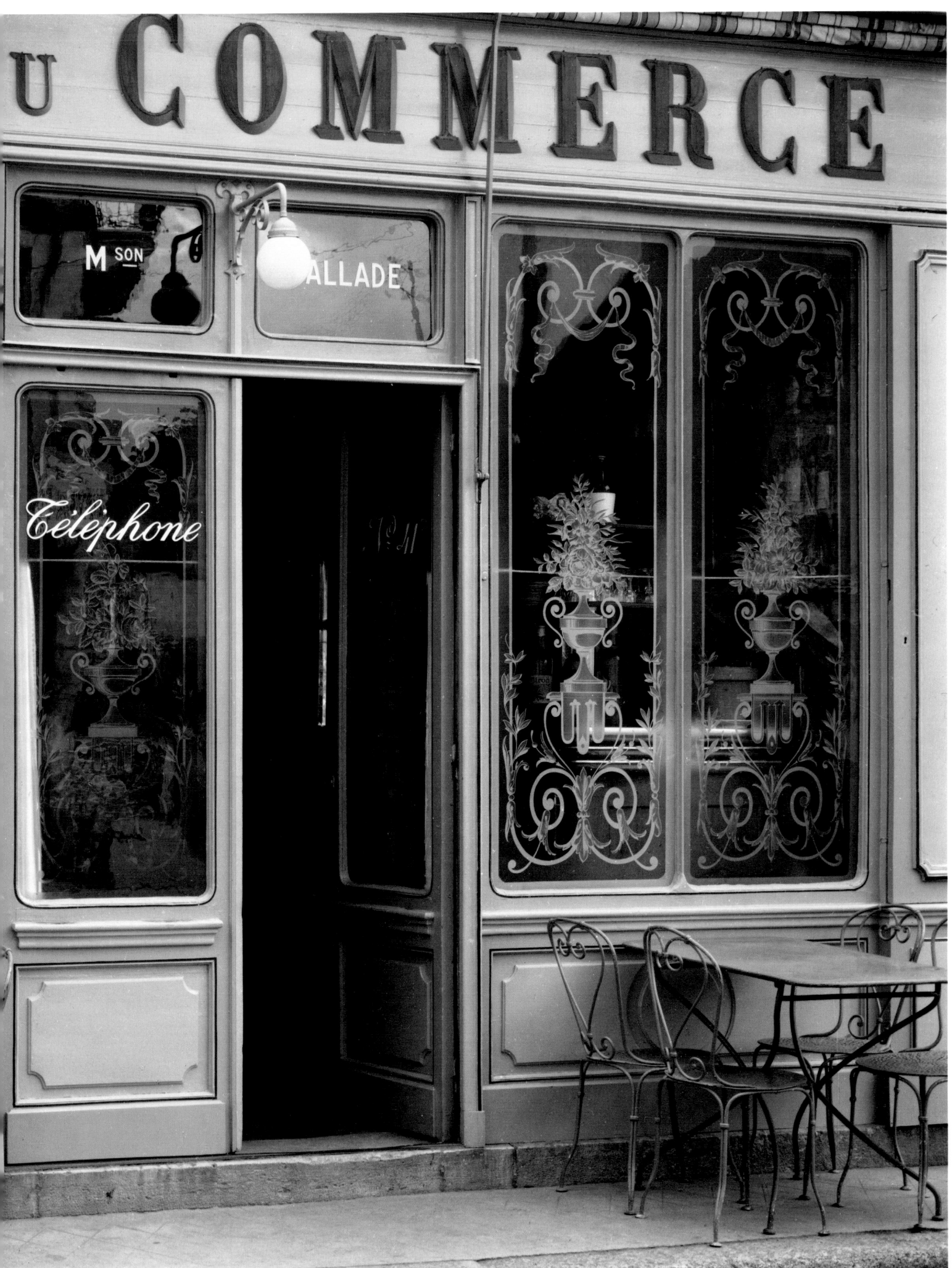

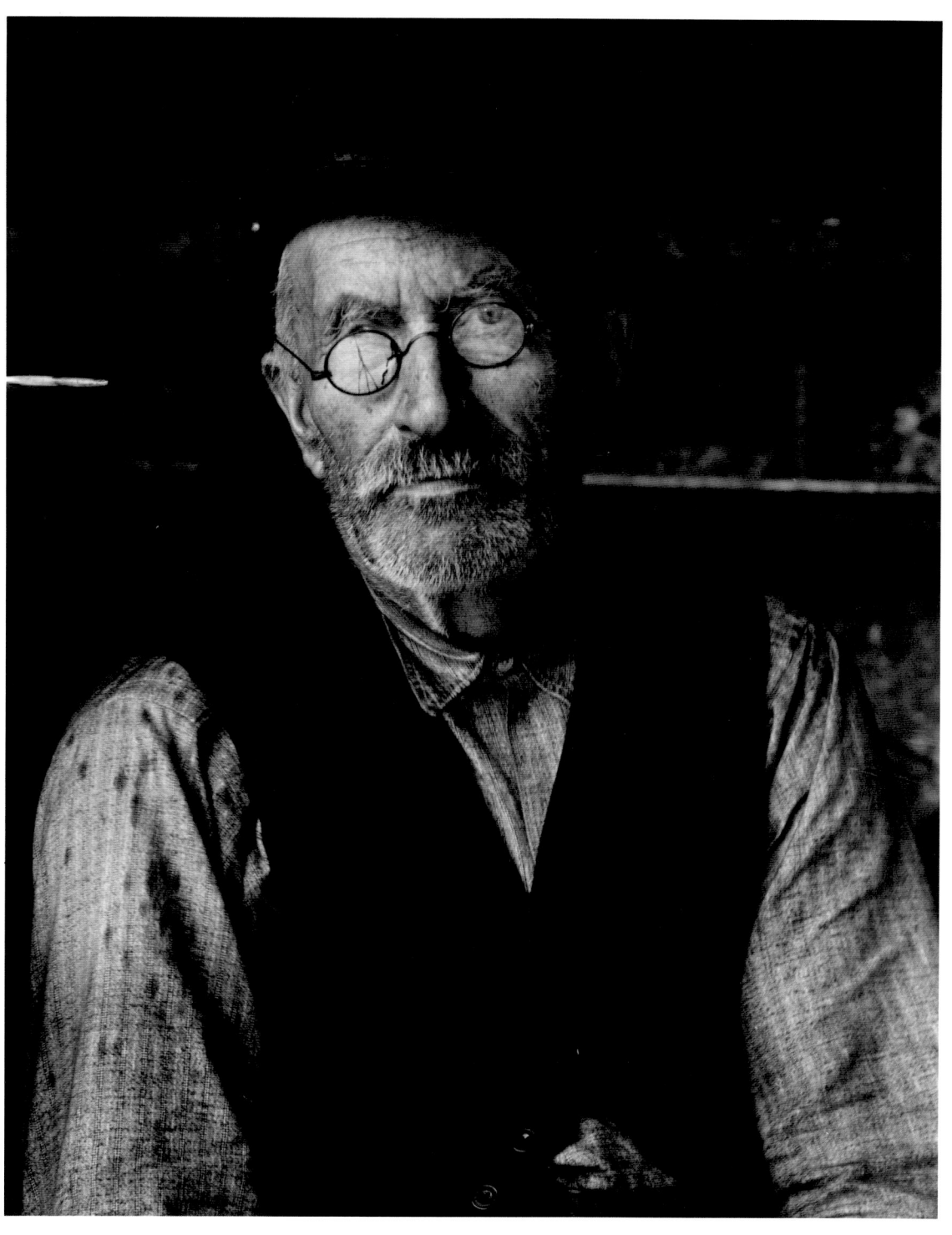

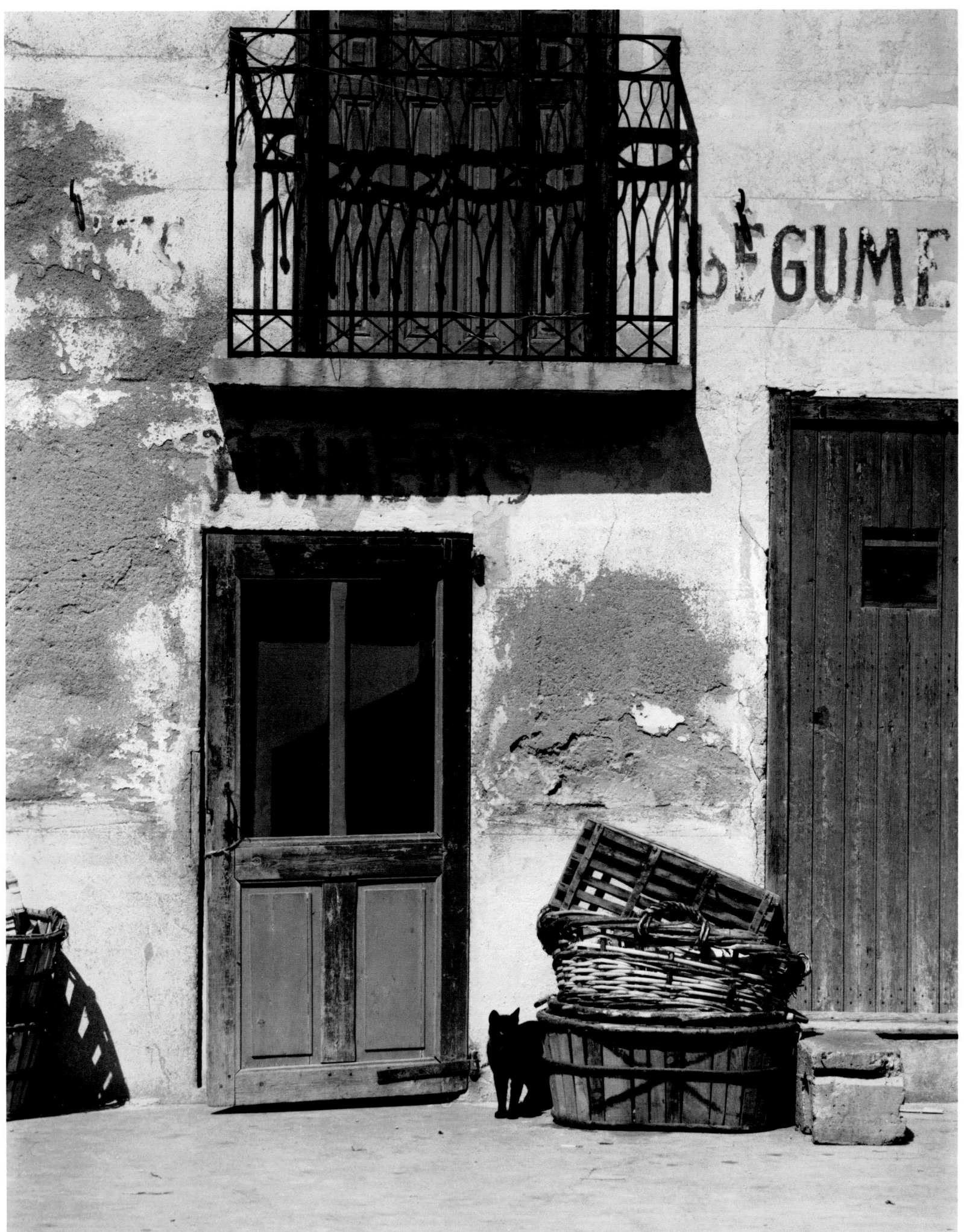

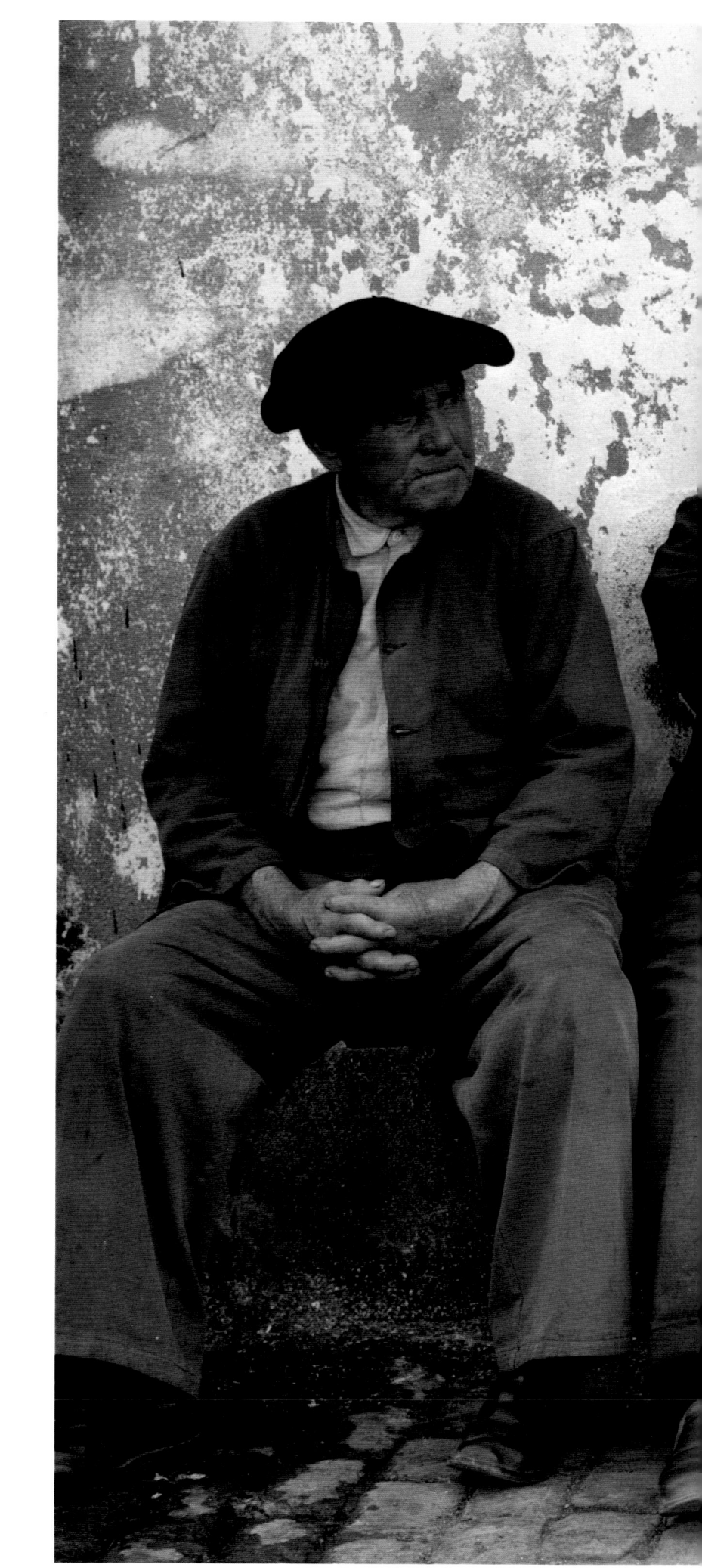

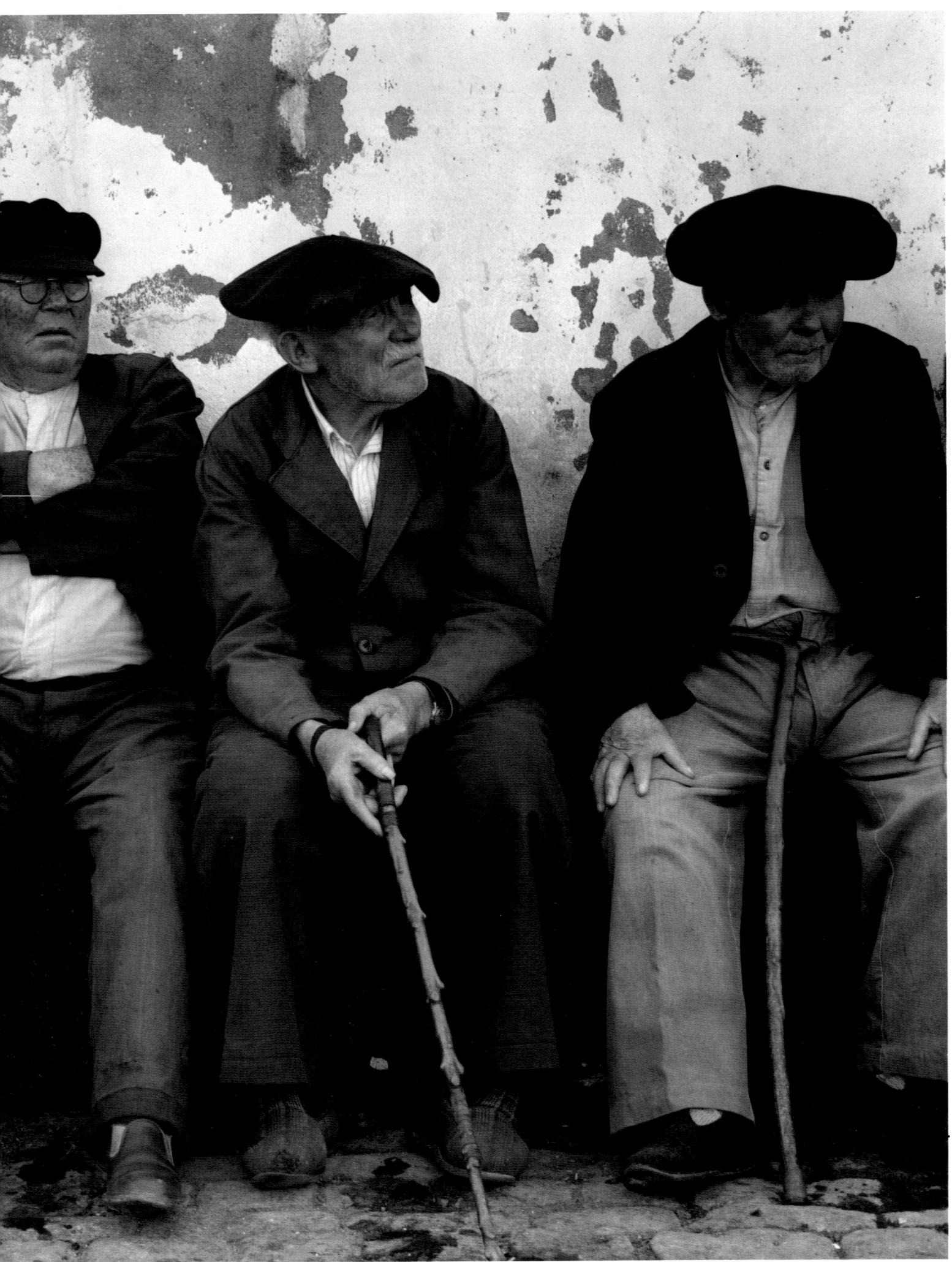

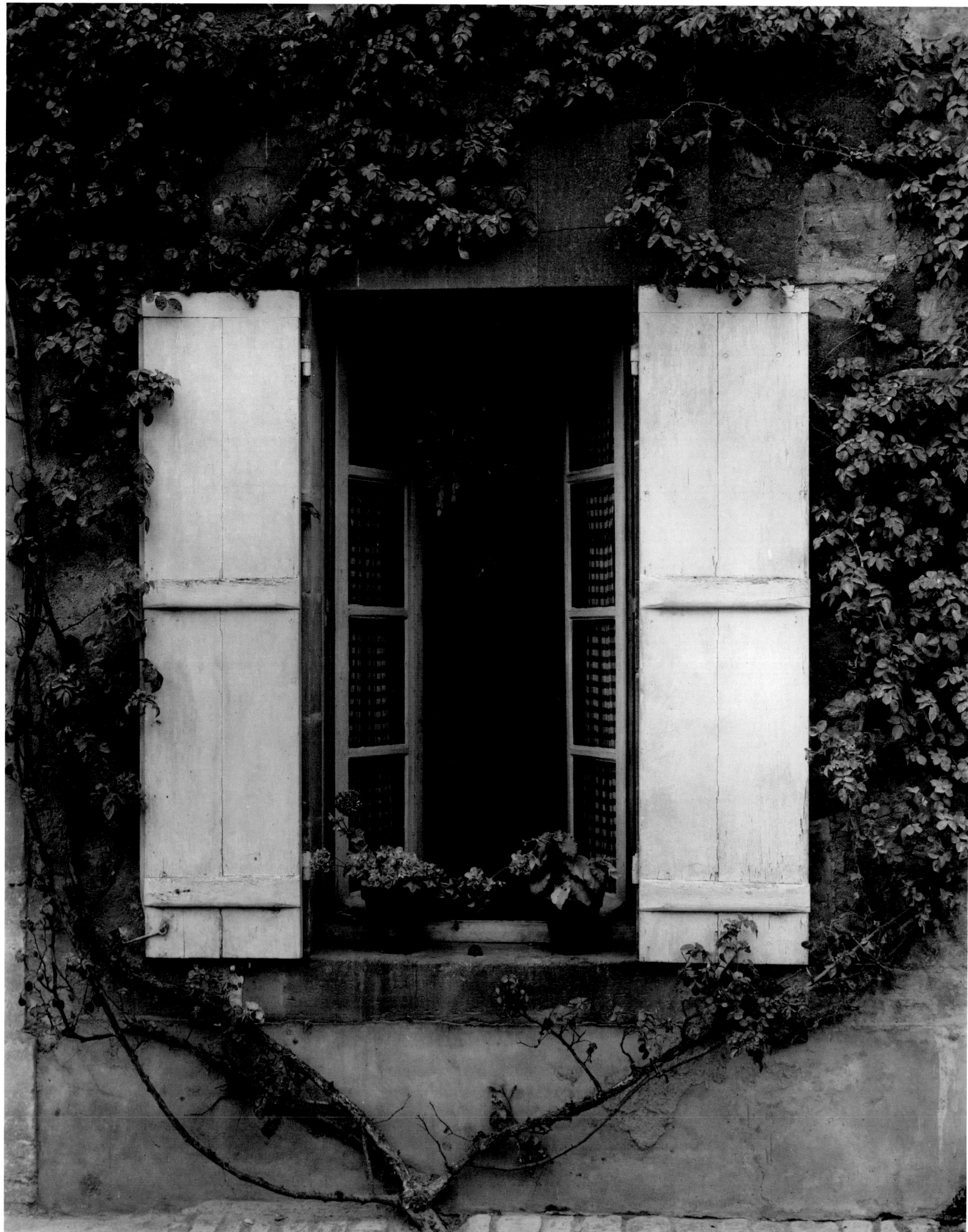

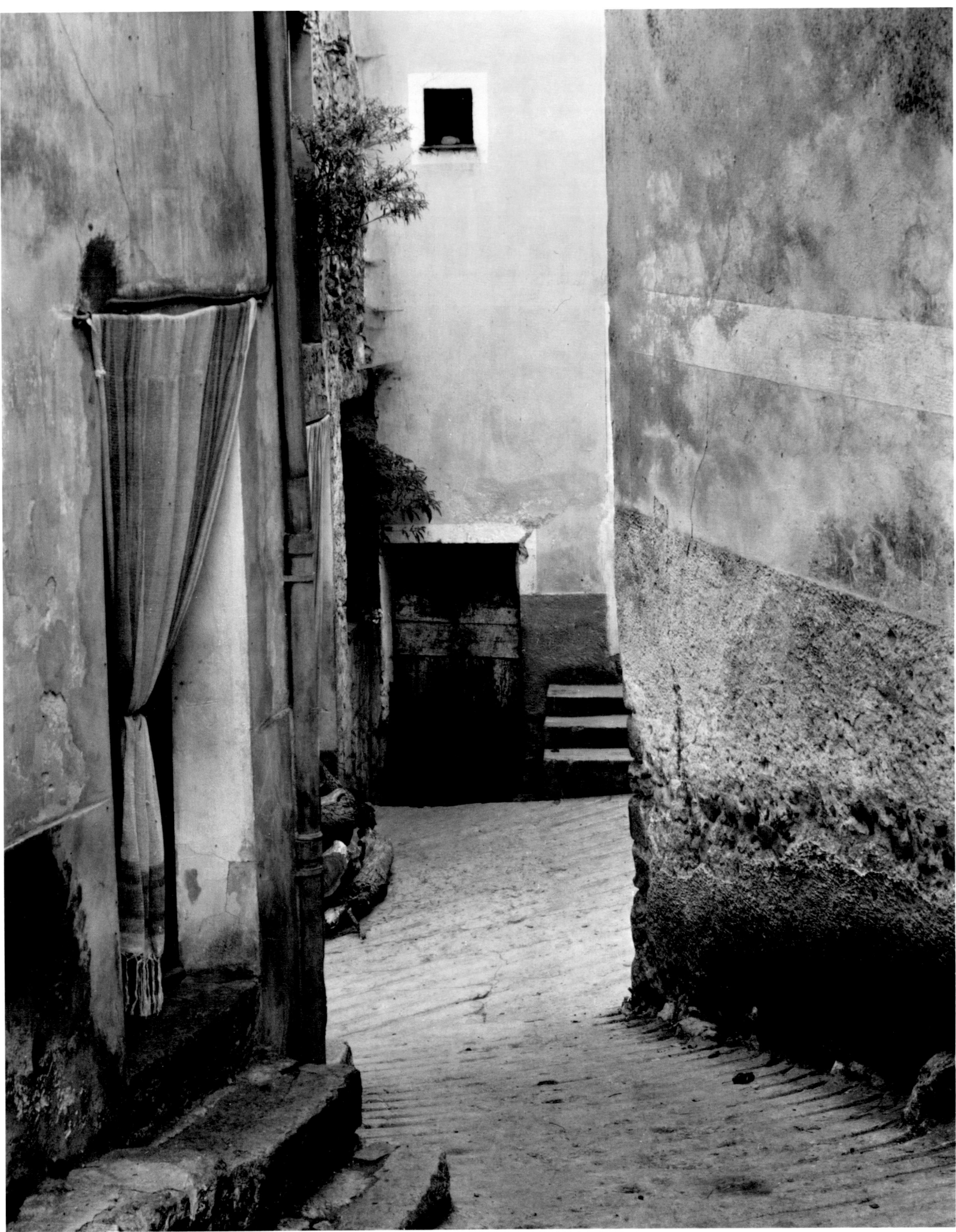

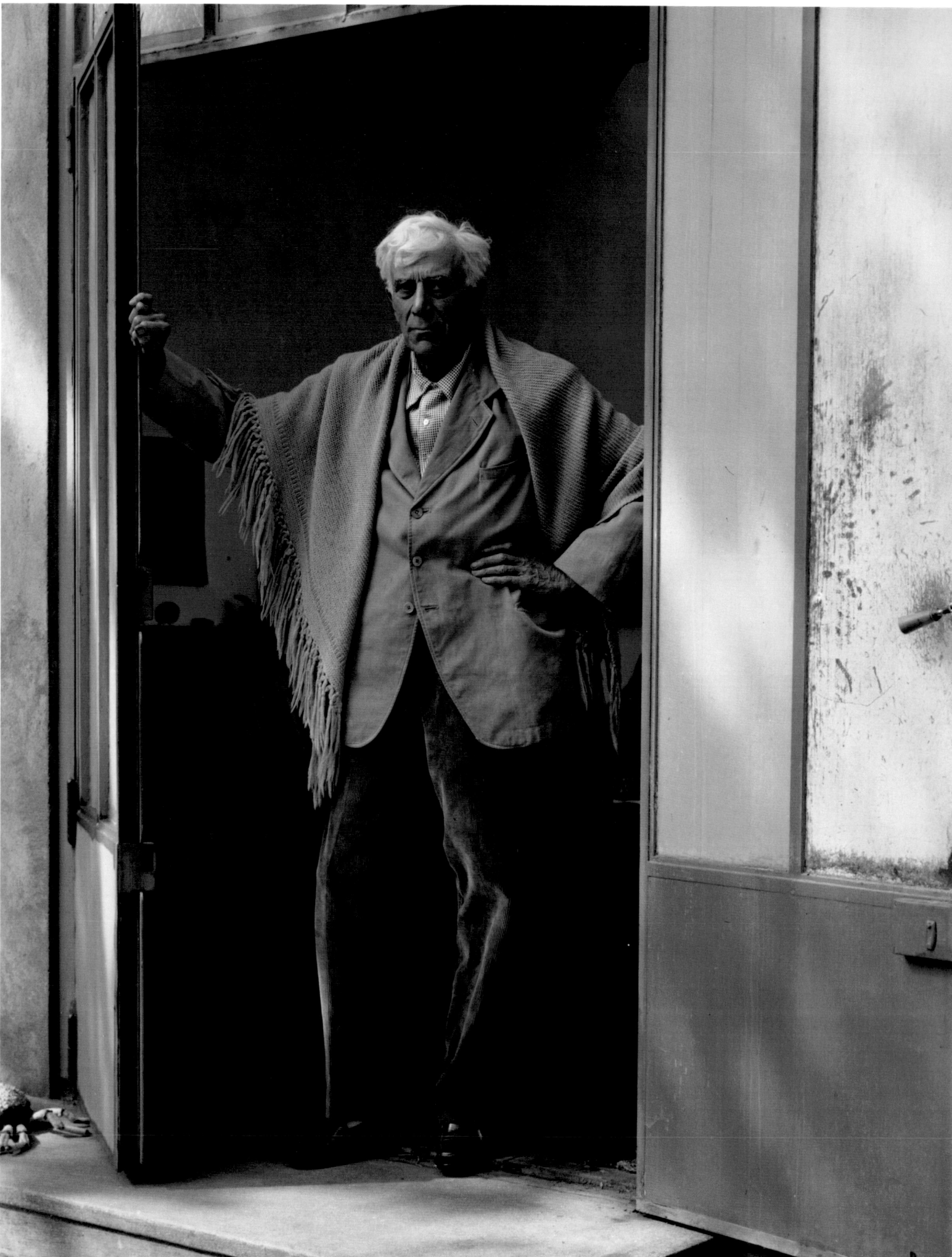

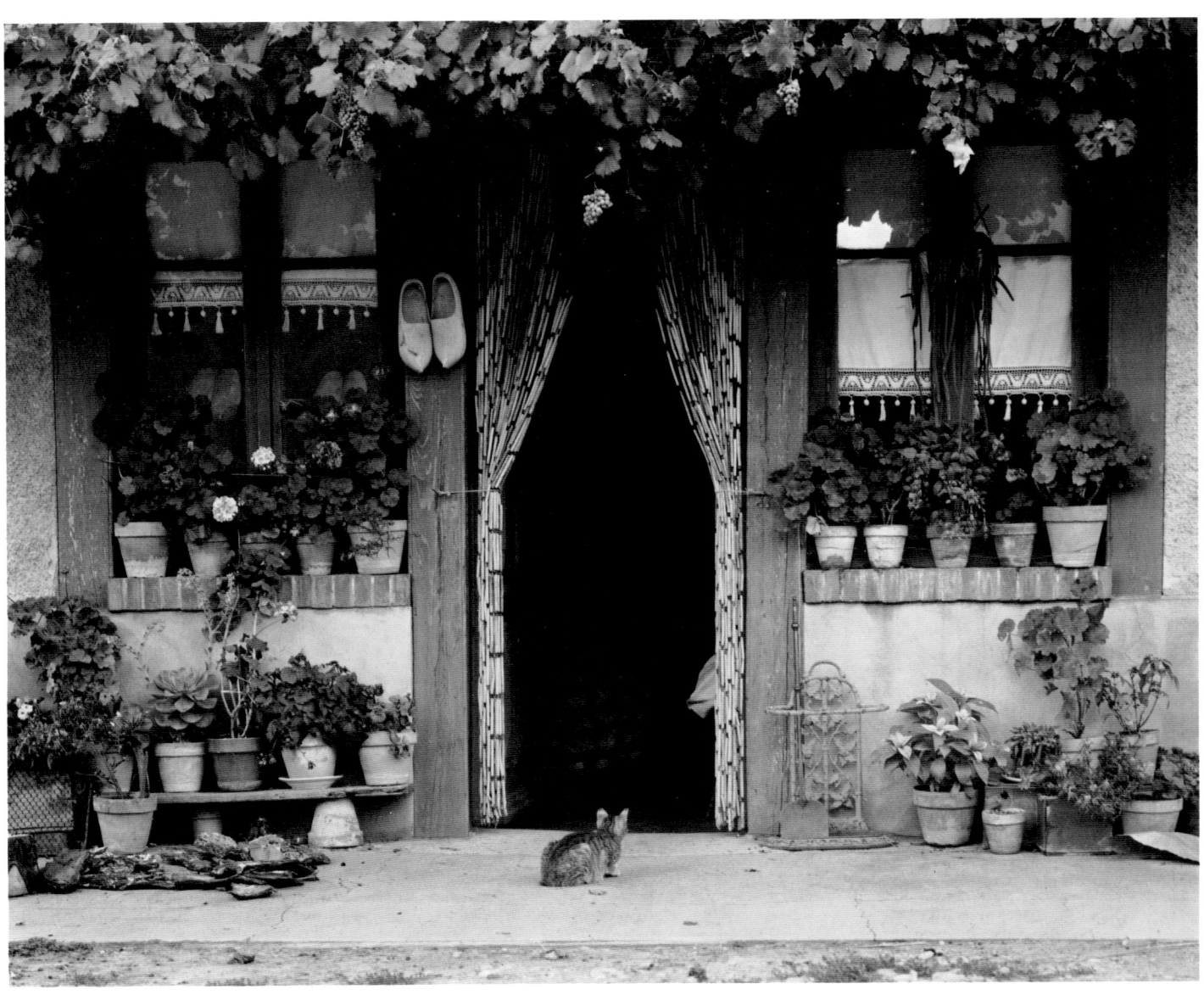

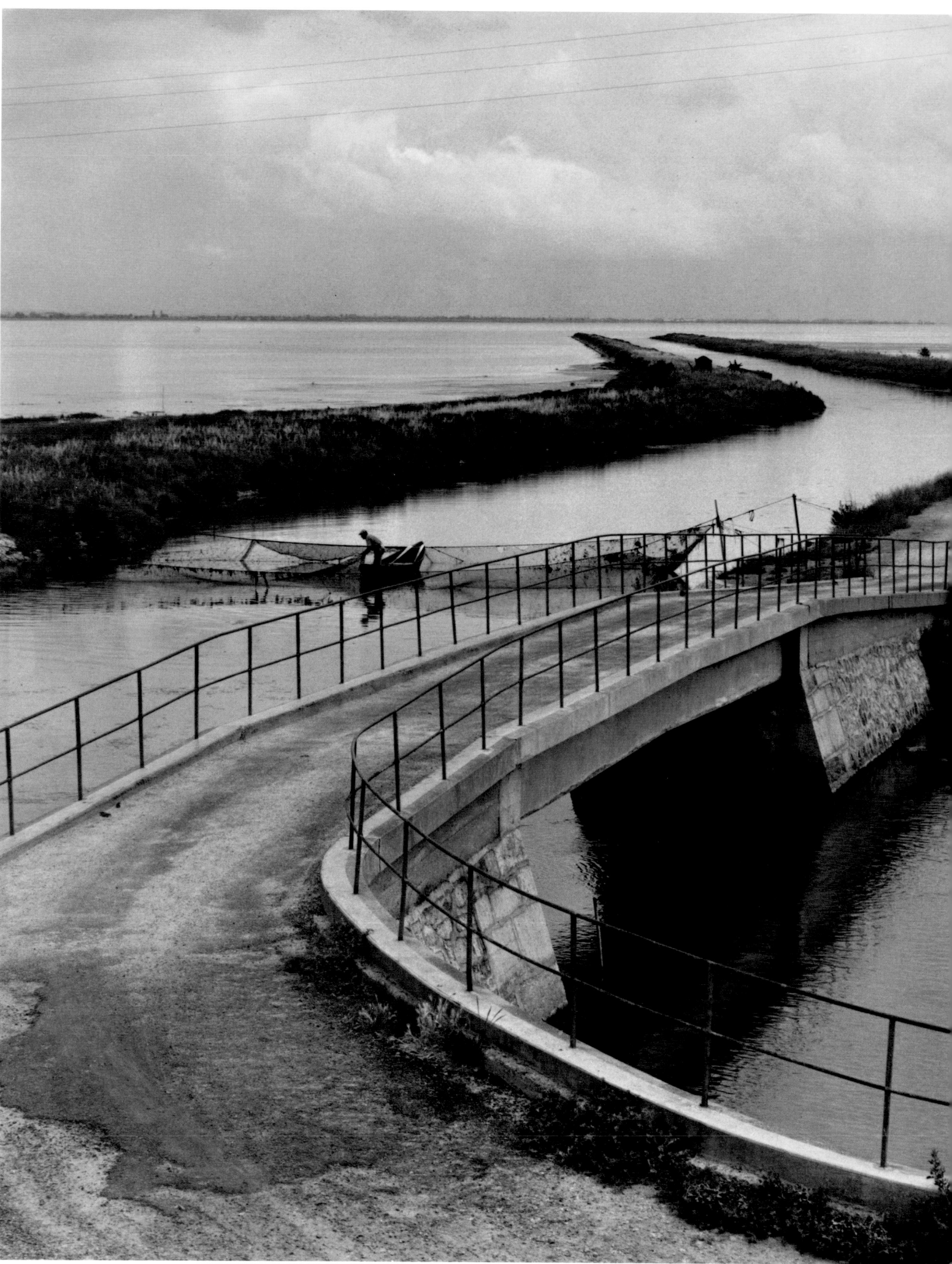

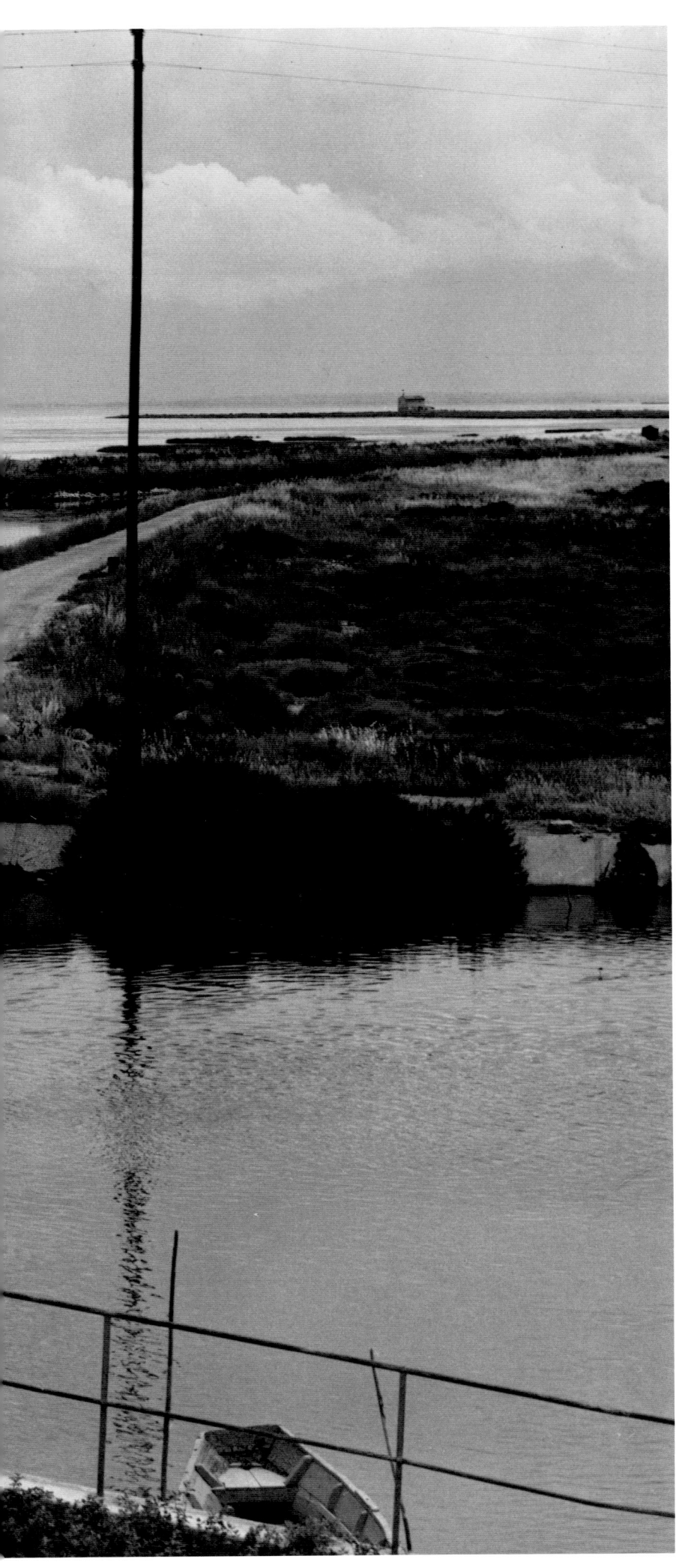

# ITALY

I first shook hands with him in 1949, in the intense atmosphere of Perugia, where filmmakers like myself were trying to give neorealistic cinema a sociopolitical structure that would reach beyond Italy and combine with the most recent advances in motion-picture art. I never could have imagined then that this quiet, self-contained American would within a few years become one of the people I most loved and respected.

Our mutual friend Virgilio Tosi helped us get better acquainted, and I felt honored when Paul Strand later wrote to ask that we do a book together. The pictures and text, he said, would issue from the same impulse, the same need. So, after a few false starts, we settled on a project called *Un Paese (A Village)*, based on Luzzara, where I was born, which Strand immediately made *his*. (The book was published in 1955.) We made the decision to begin work together in a small Roman trattoria in Via degli Avignonesi, called, not coincidentally, Emilian Hills. I had been there before with other great men such as Jean Renoir and Roberto Rossellini.

Paul Strand has since become a legend to me (and to others, I am sure), with his silence, his integrity, his independence, and his extraordinary energy. I heard him raise his voice only once. He and his wife Hazel were boarding ship for Sardinia, when a sailor urged him forward saying, "Old folks first." Strand responded, practically shouting back, "Old? *Me*?" Then he repeated it, a little astonished, a little sad.

He was ageless really (the records say that he was sixty-five that year—1955). The eye never ages. Strand's certainly didn't; he always engaged the two dimensions of things: being and becoming, conversing intimately with time and space, even when he slept, so that his camera might capture sleep itself. Was there anything he did not claim and use?

His serenity was merely an appearance. He in fact quarreled intensely with those tricky movements of time and space that sometimes concealed his own primary reason for existing. His way of working was deliberately casual; he always acted "like a native," bound up with the very subject whose presence he wanted to capture and fix. People thought him careless, I suppose, or too trusting, when they saw him set up his camera only to walk away, leaving it on the street as if he were more concerned with the random and commonplace than with the exceptional. It was a calculated absence though, and upon returning he reaped the rewards. He knew what he would find: the bonding of a particular time with a particular space. Sometimes he dealt with simpler problems: a fraction more or less of exposure time. Secretly he swung back and forth between infinity and the ticking of his watch, which whispered the language of mortality....

I will always be grateful to Strand for what he made me see about my own townspeople. He could always capture that moment of light and line when things have absorbed our presence and our hard work....

Strand was reserved, but he was also human. In an almost biblical way, he always journeyed down from the heights into the valley, losing himself among configurations of dust and human shapes. If then he climbed back up to the summit, toward his own Sinai, this too was part of the mystery with which he struggled so powerfully for as long as possible so that he could communicate directly and immediately with his fellow man.

From the Introduction to Portfolio Four,
by Cesare Zavattini,
August 18, 1981,
translated by W. S. Dipiero

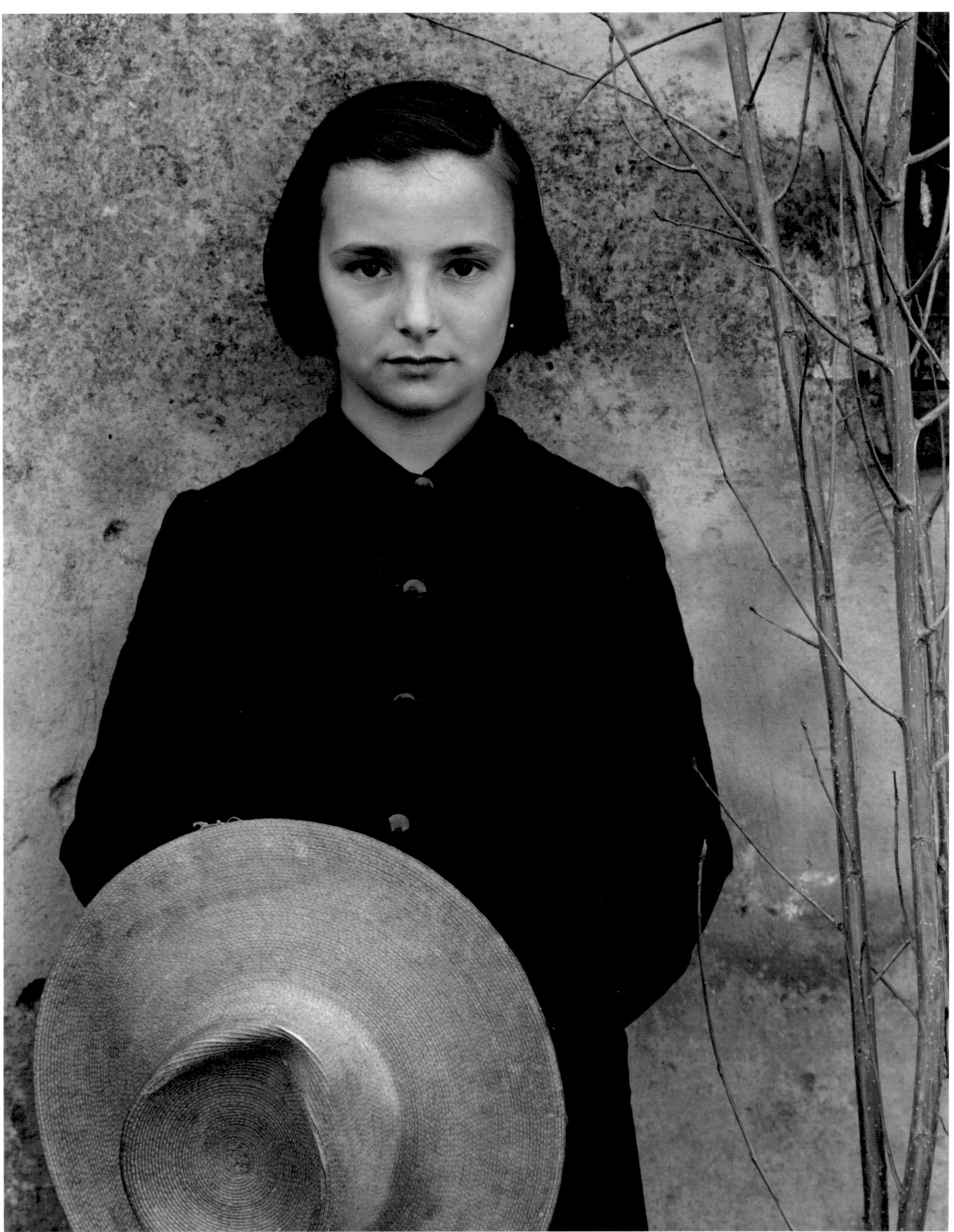

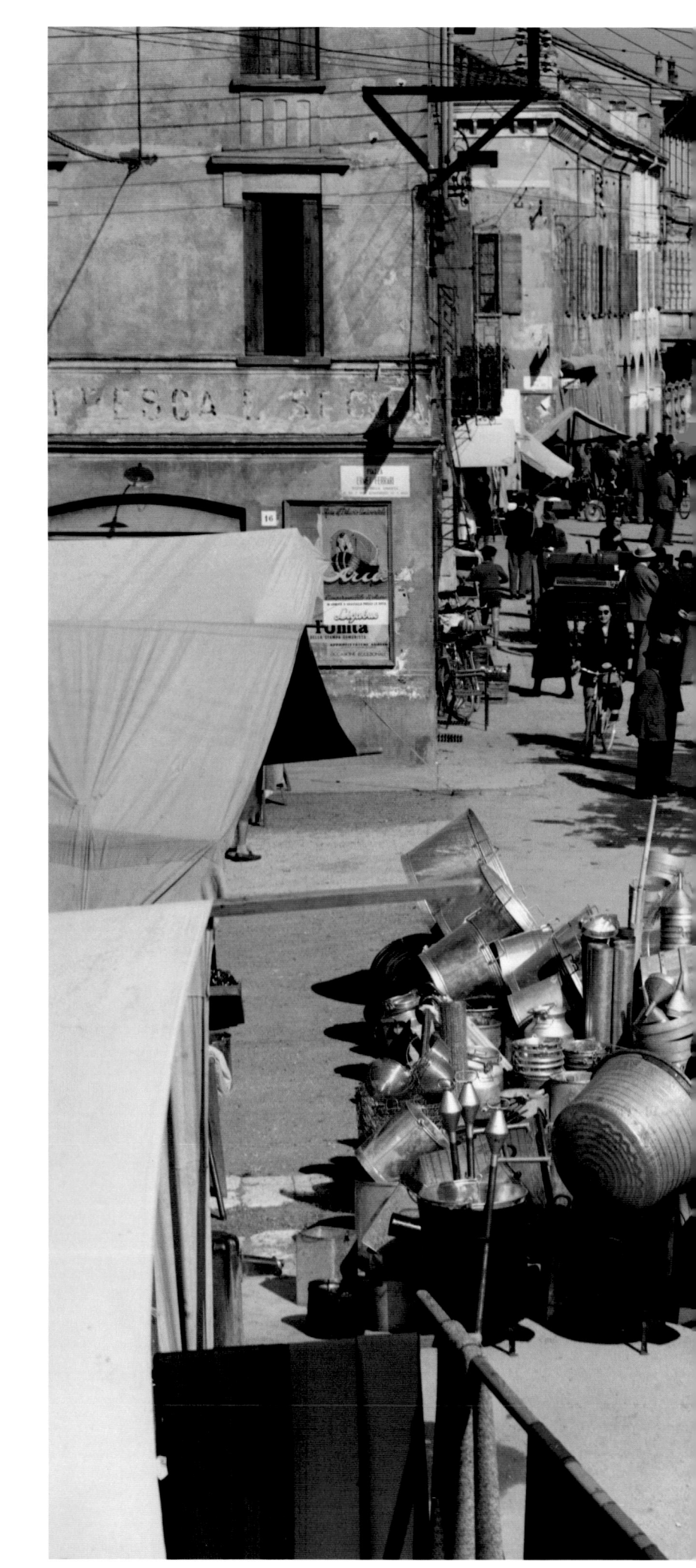

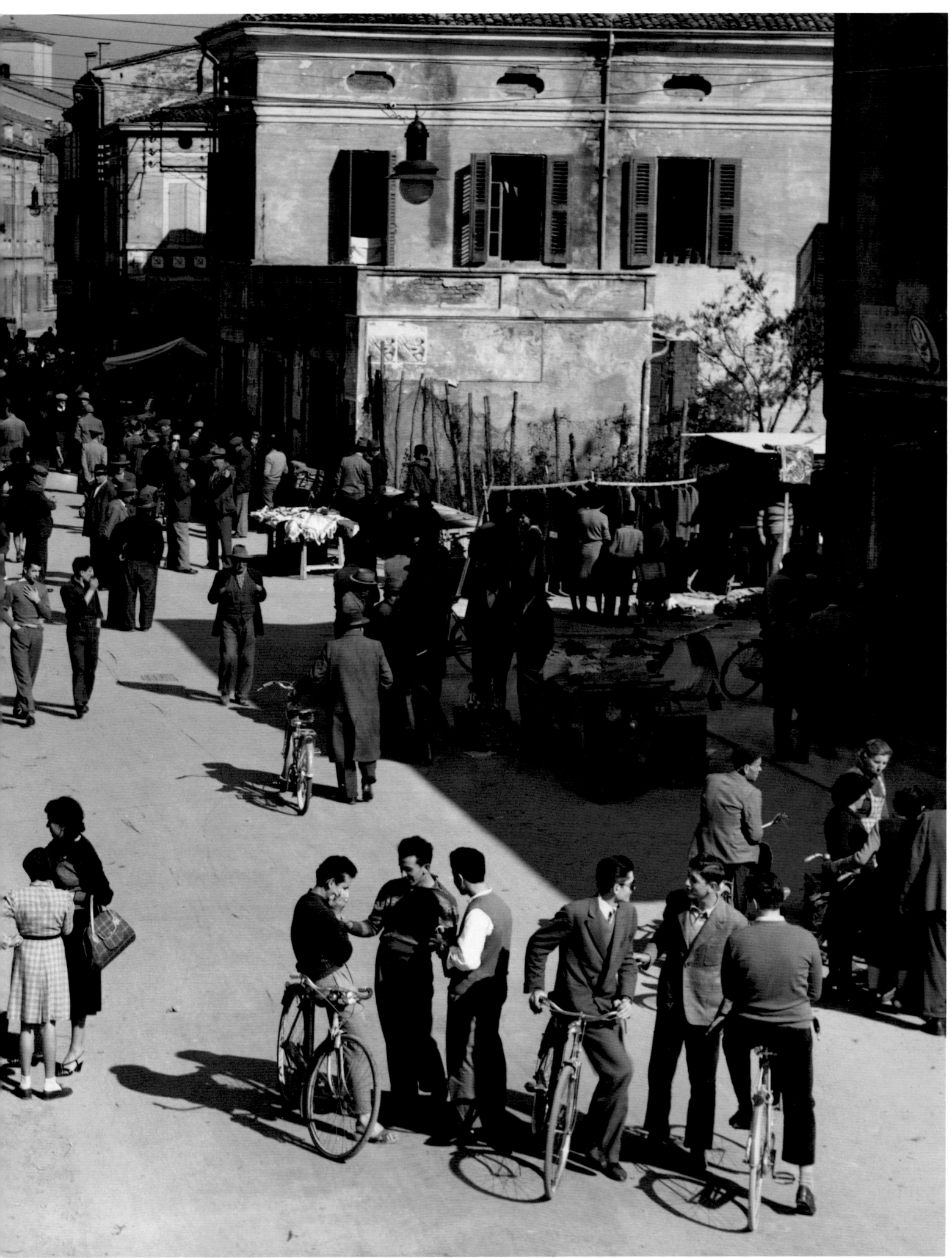

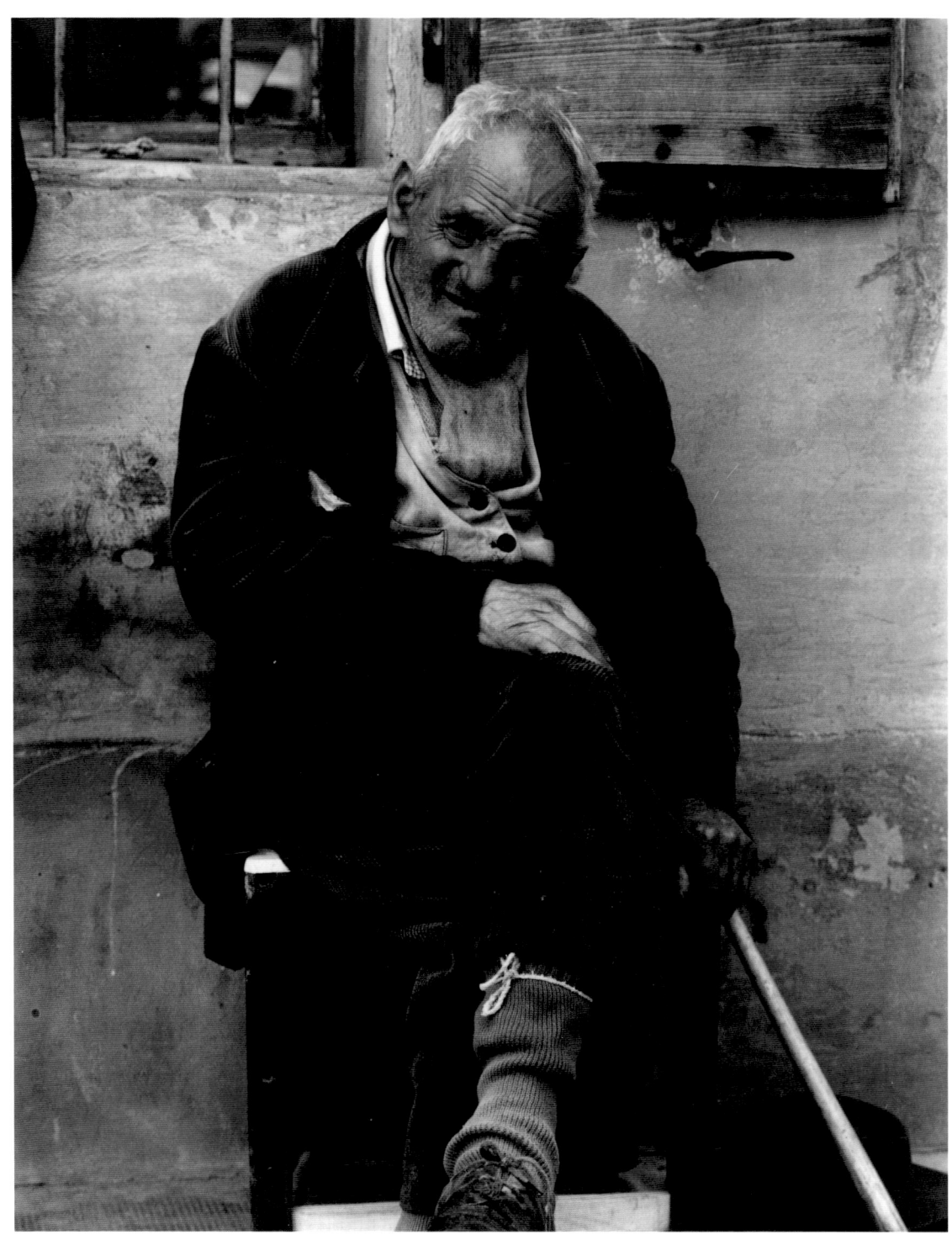

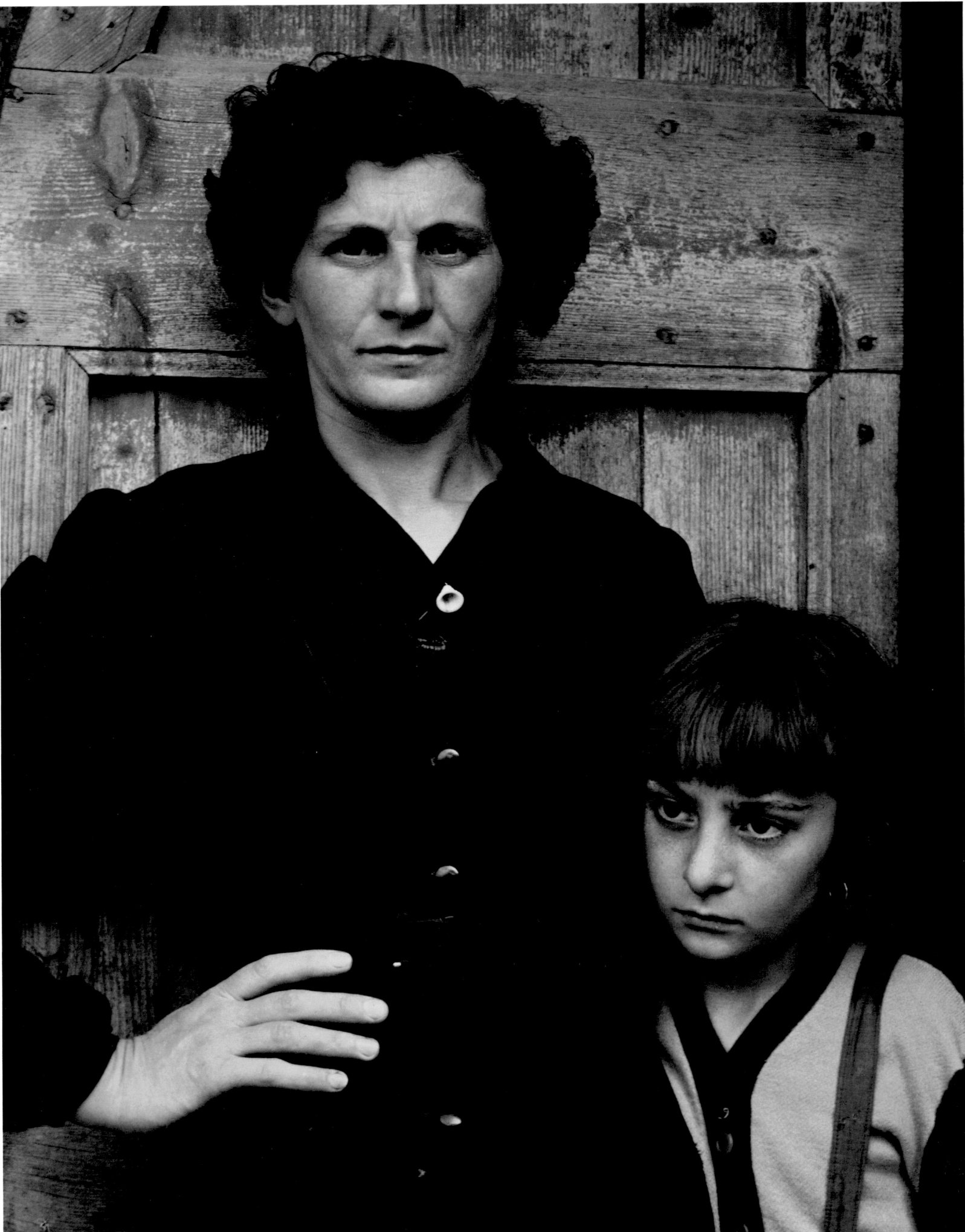

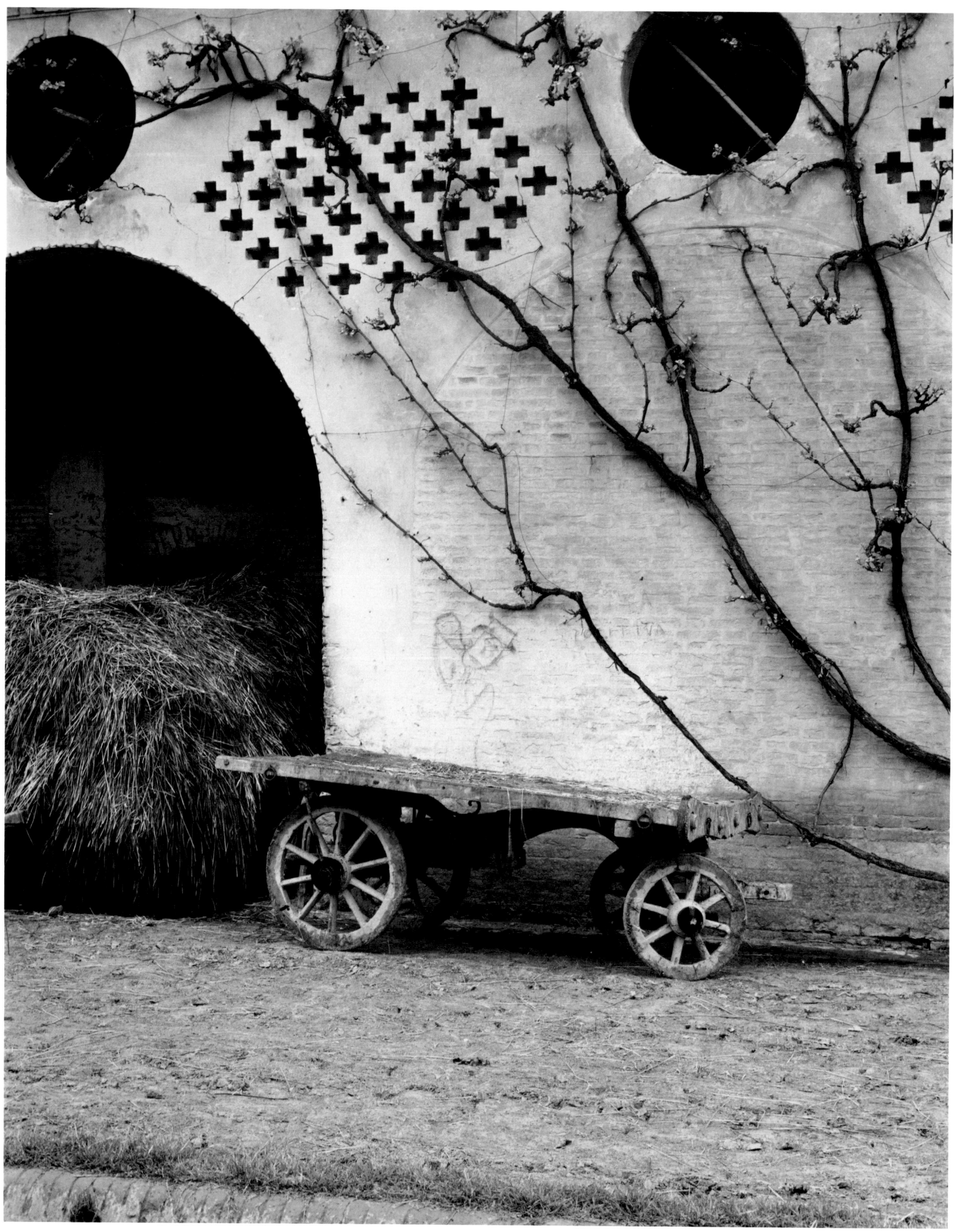

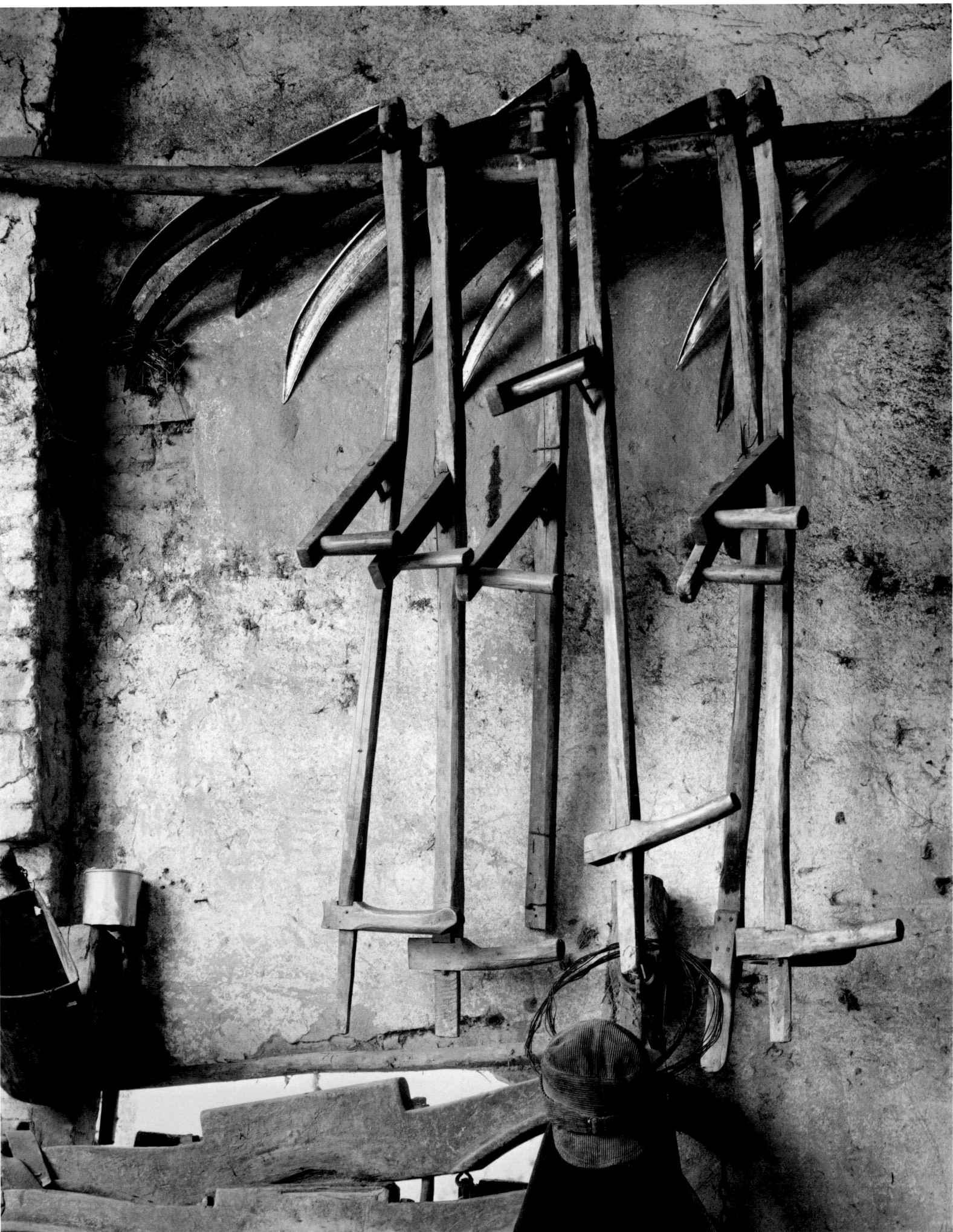

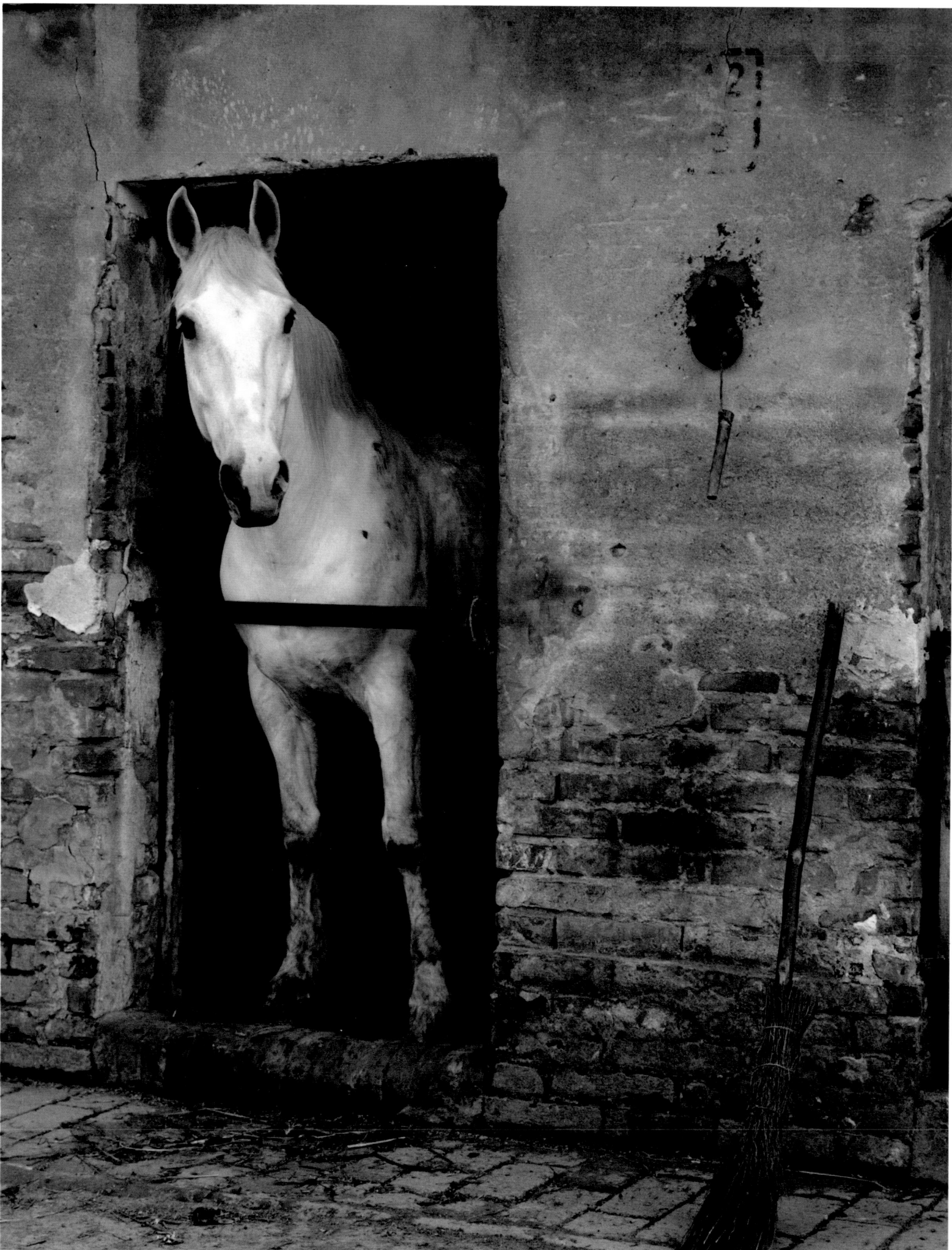

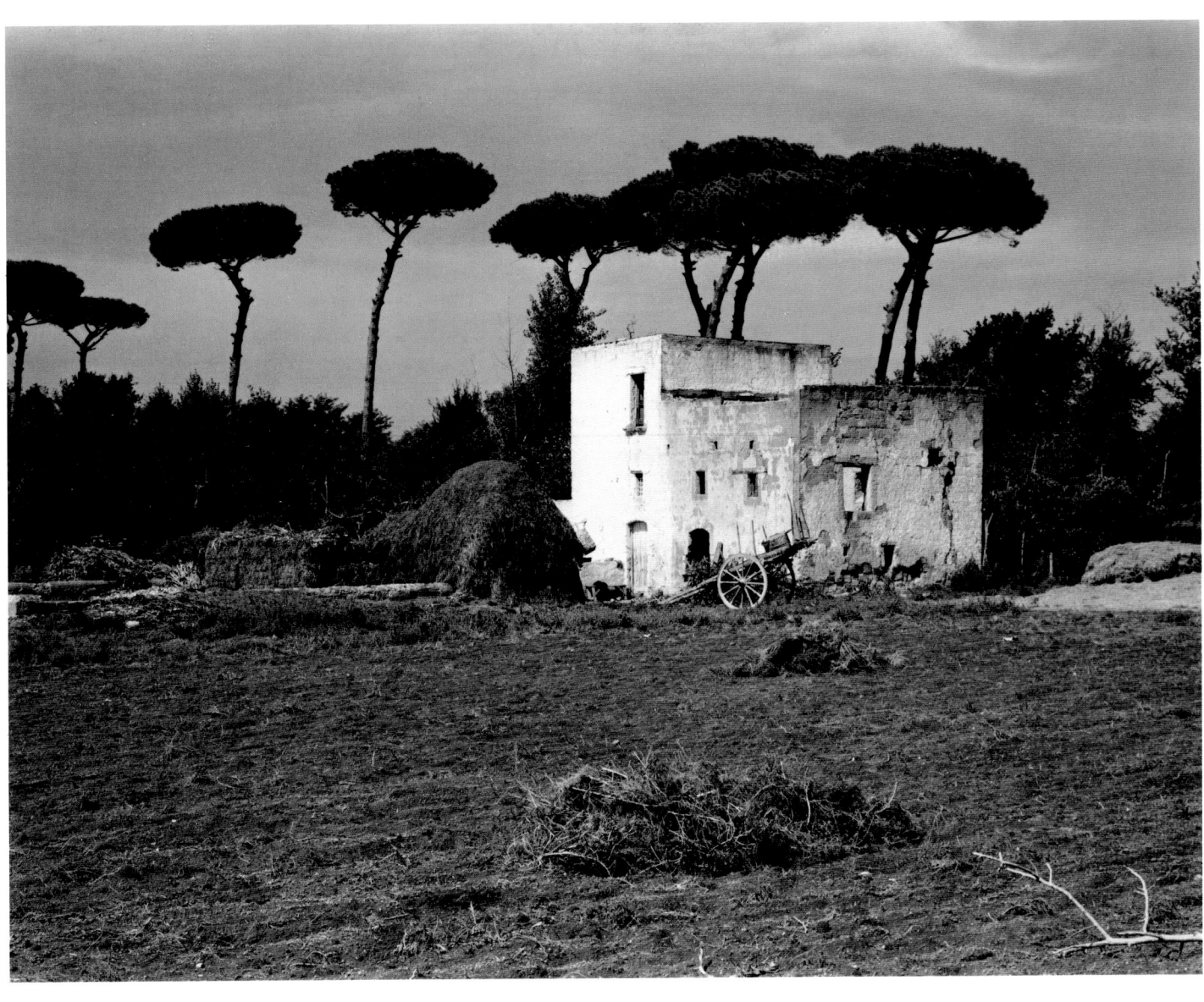

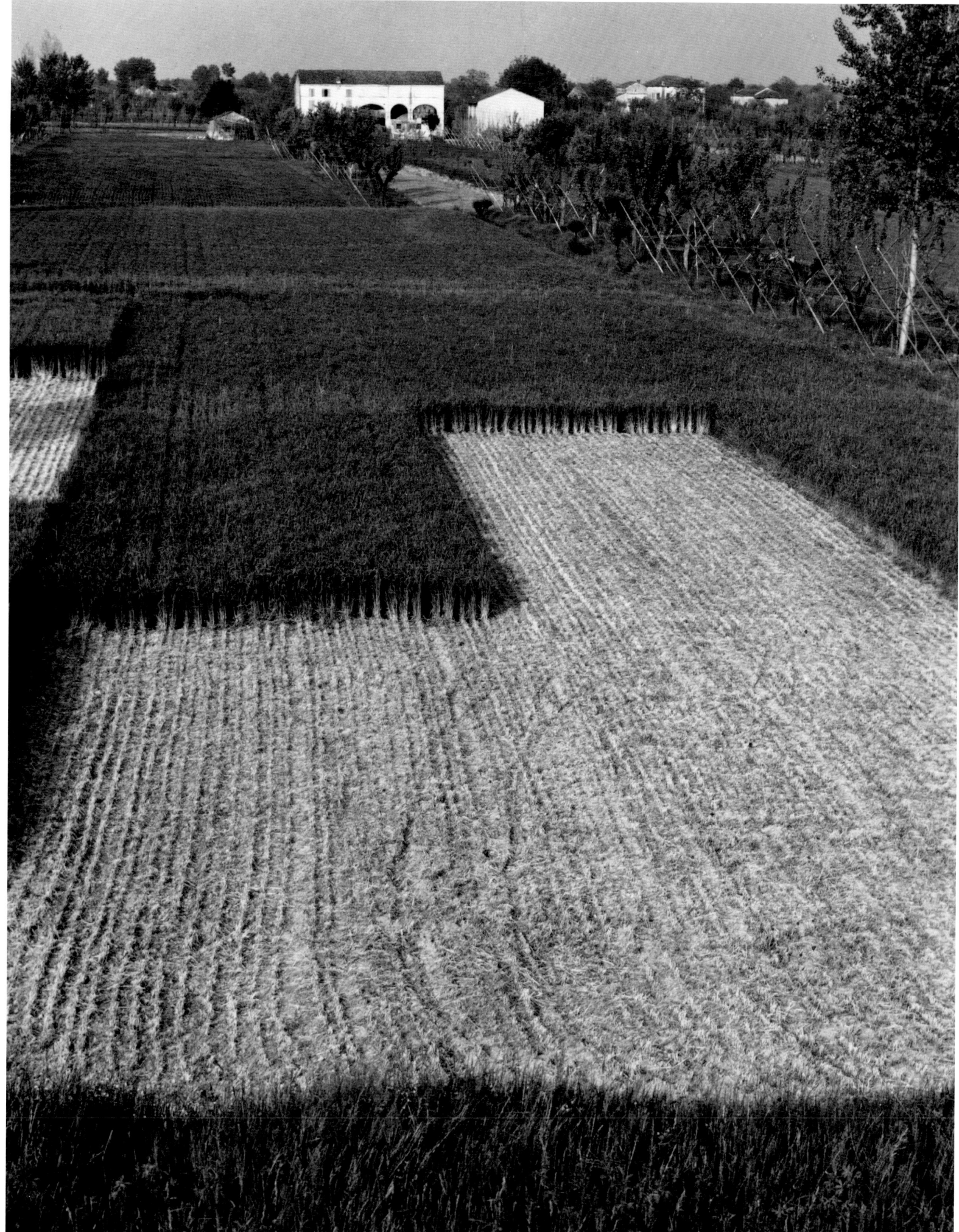

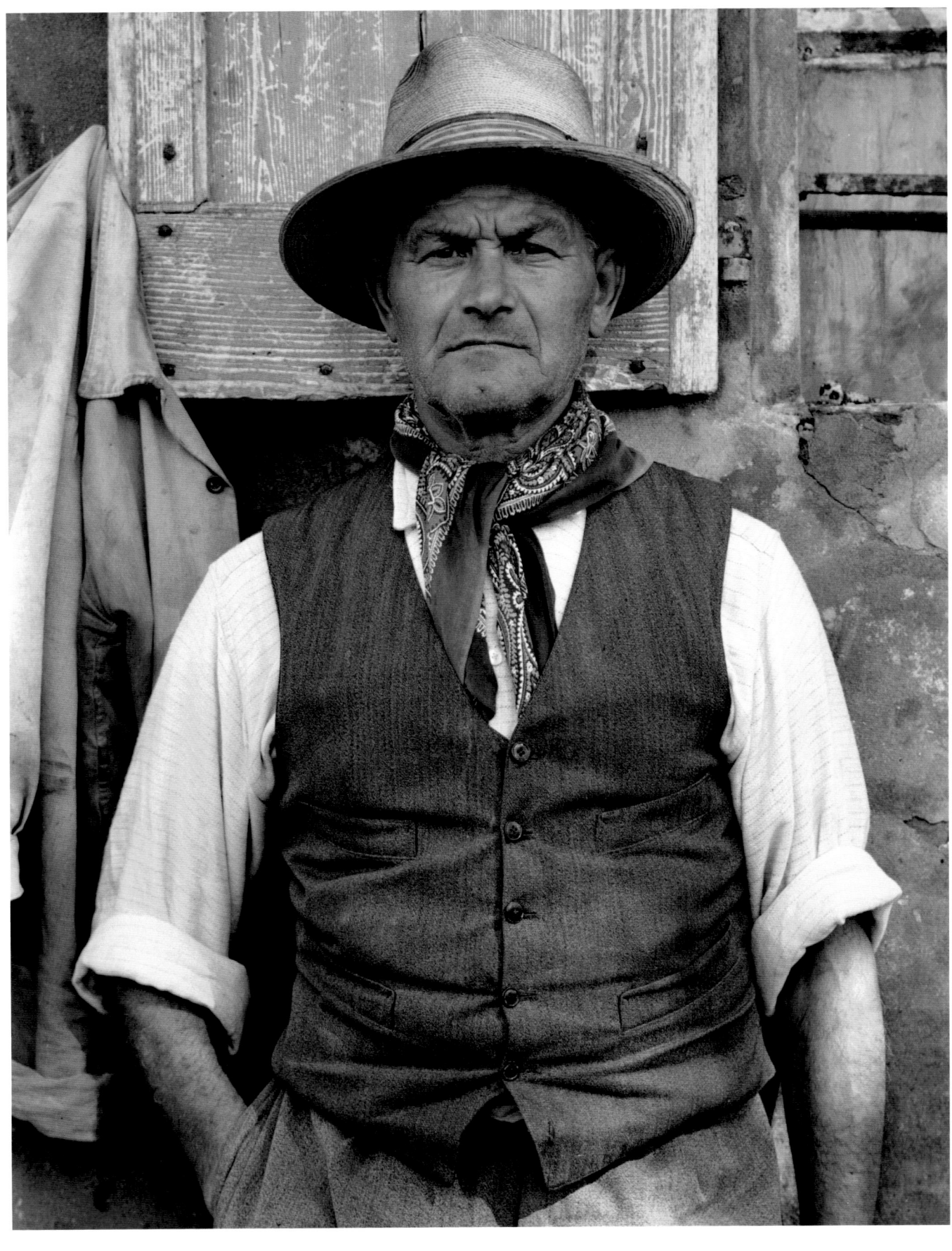

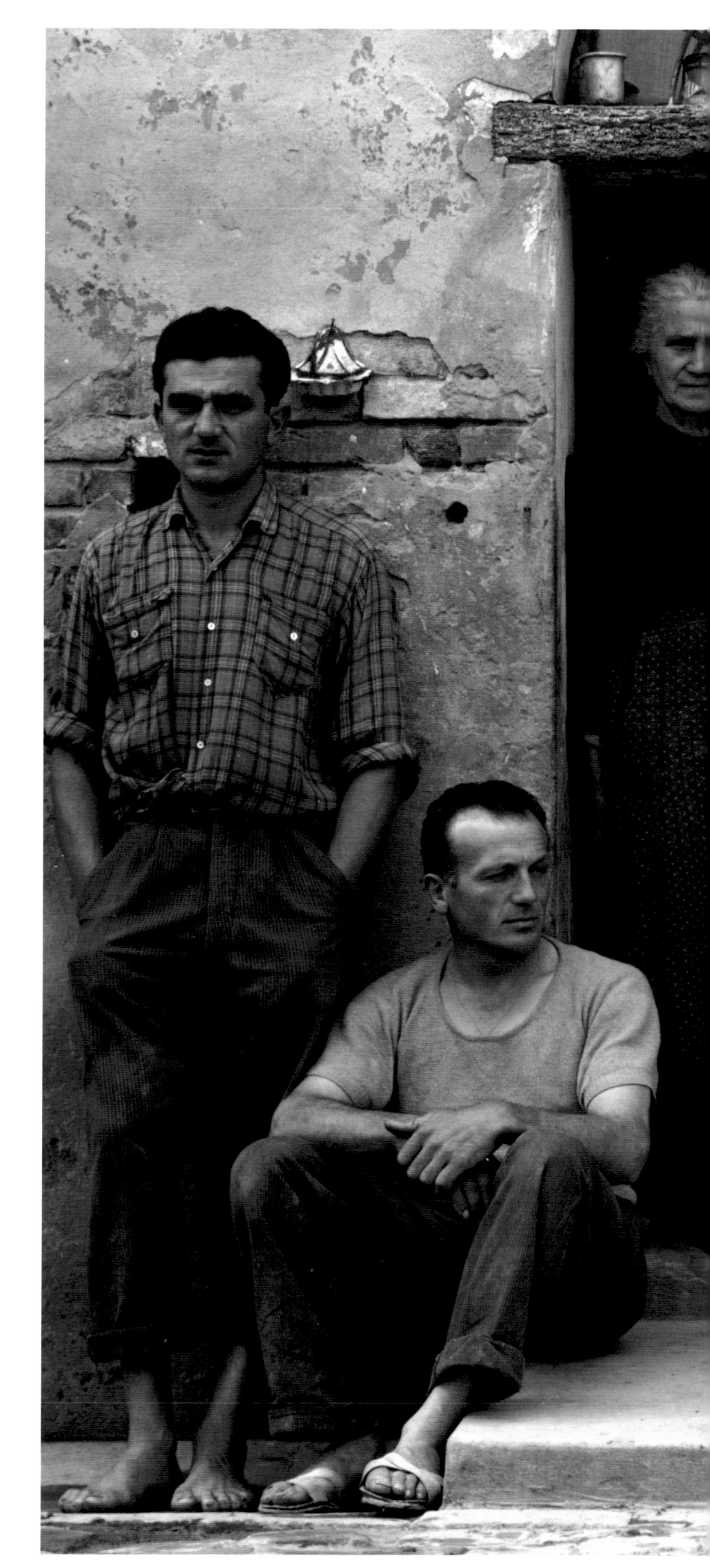

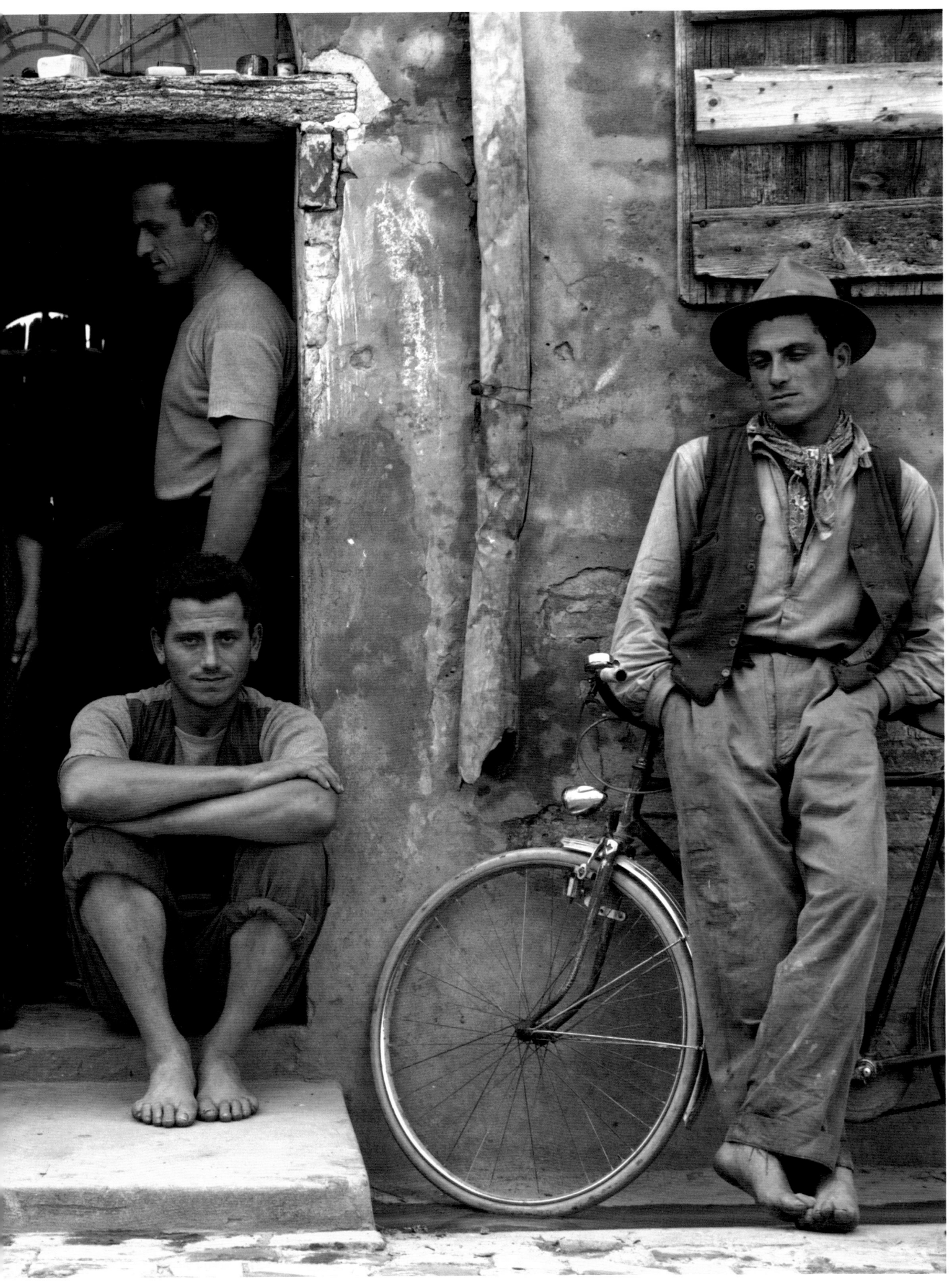

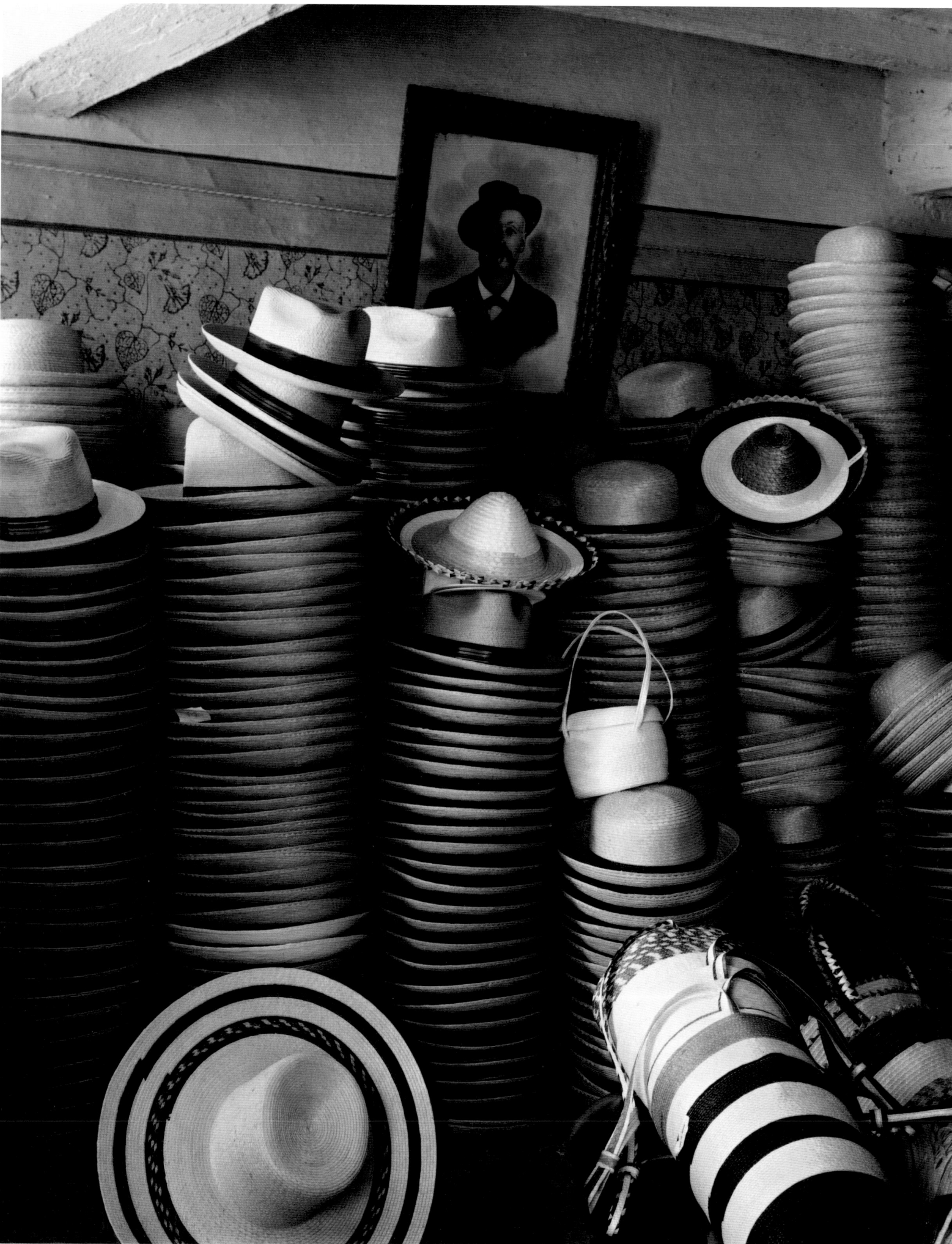

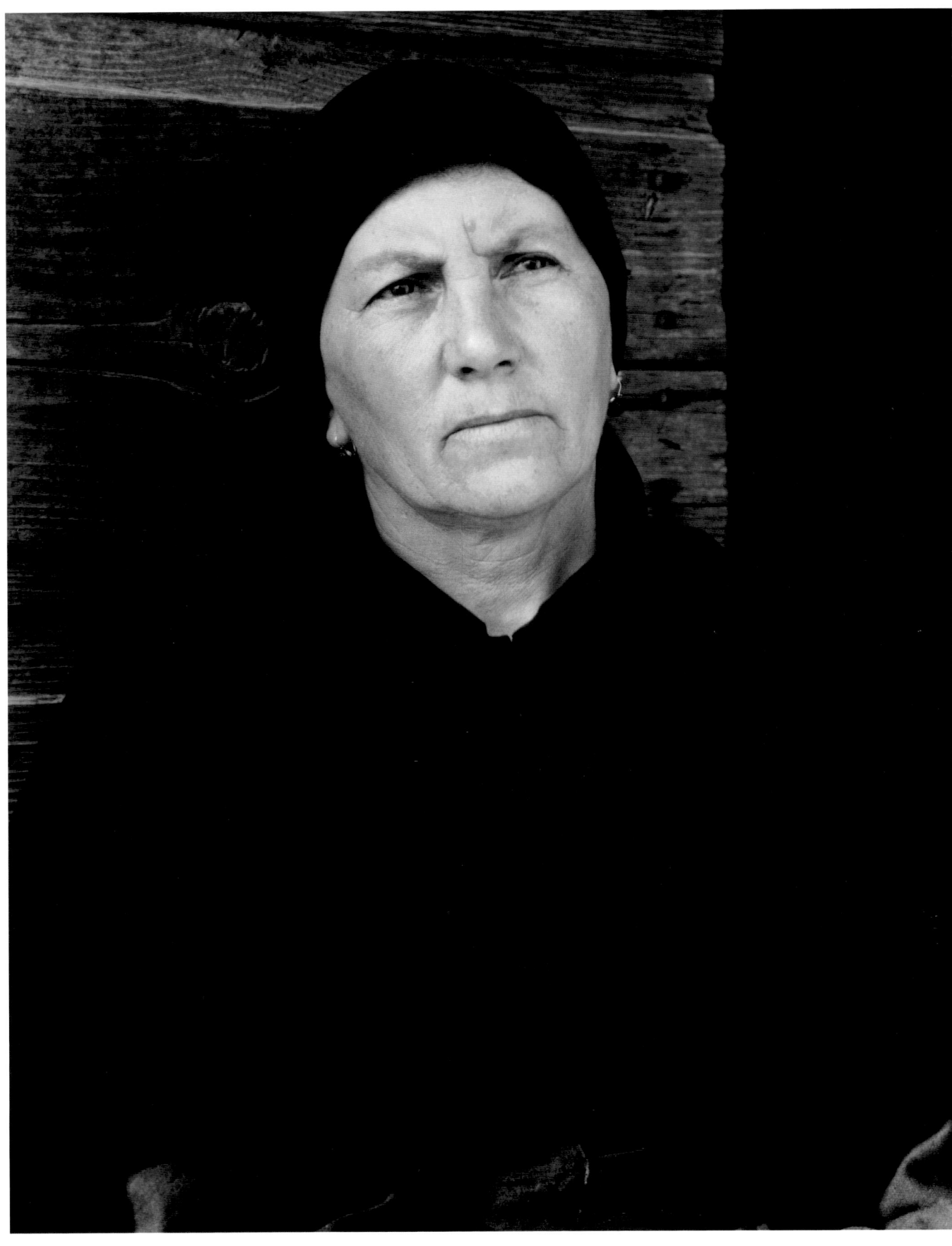

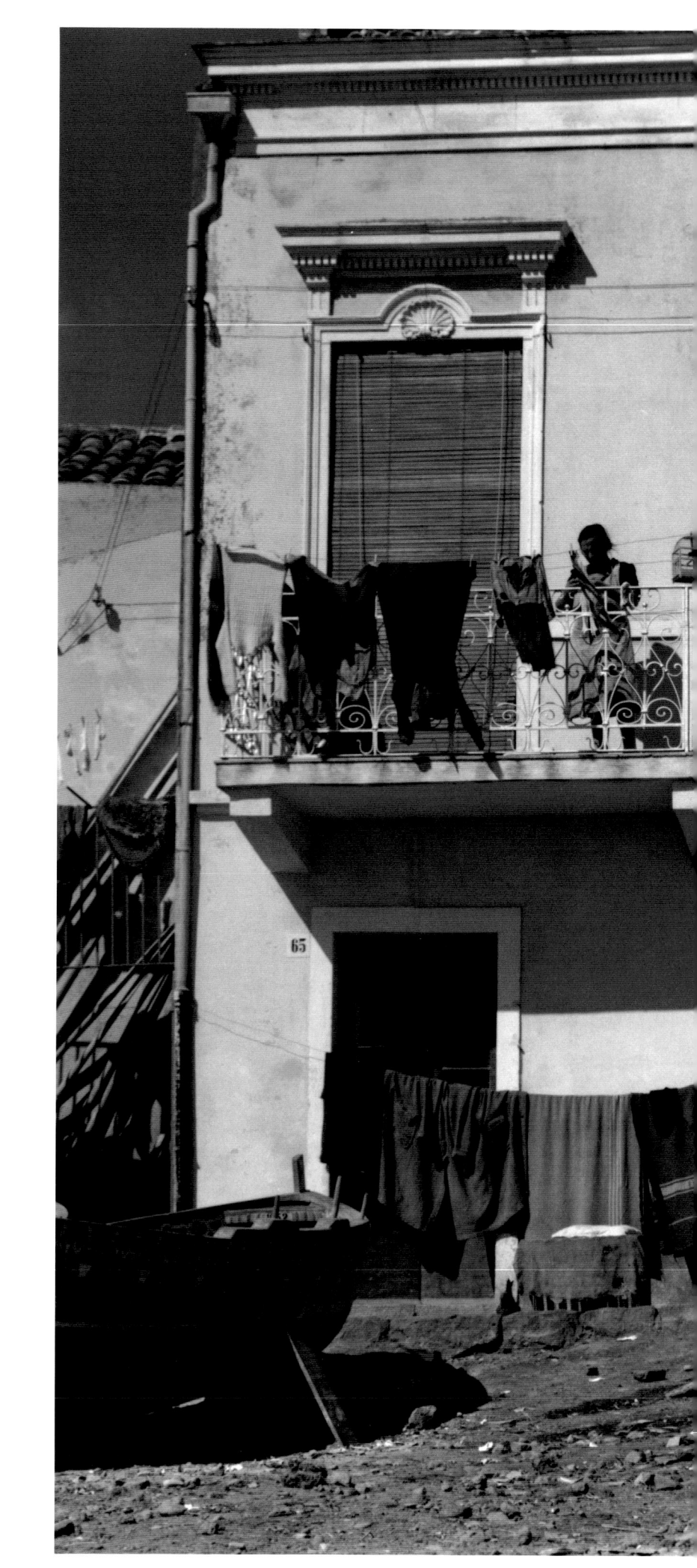

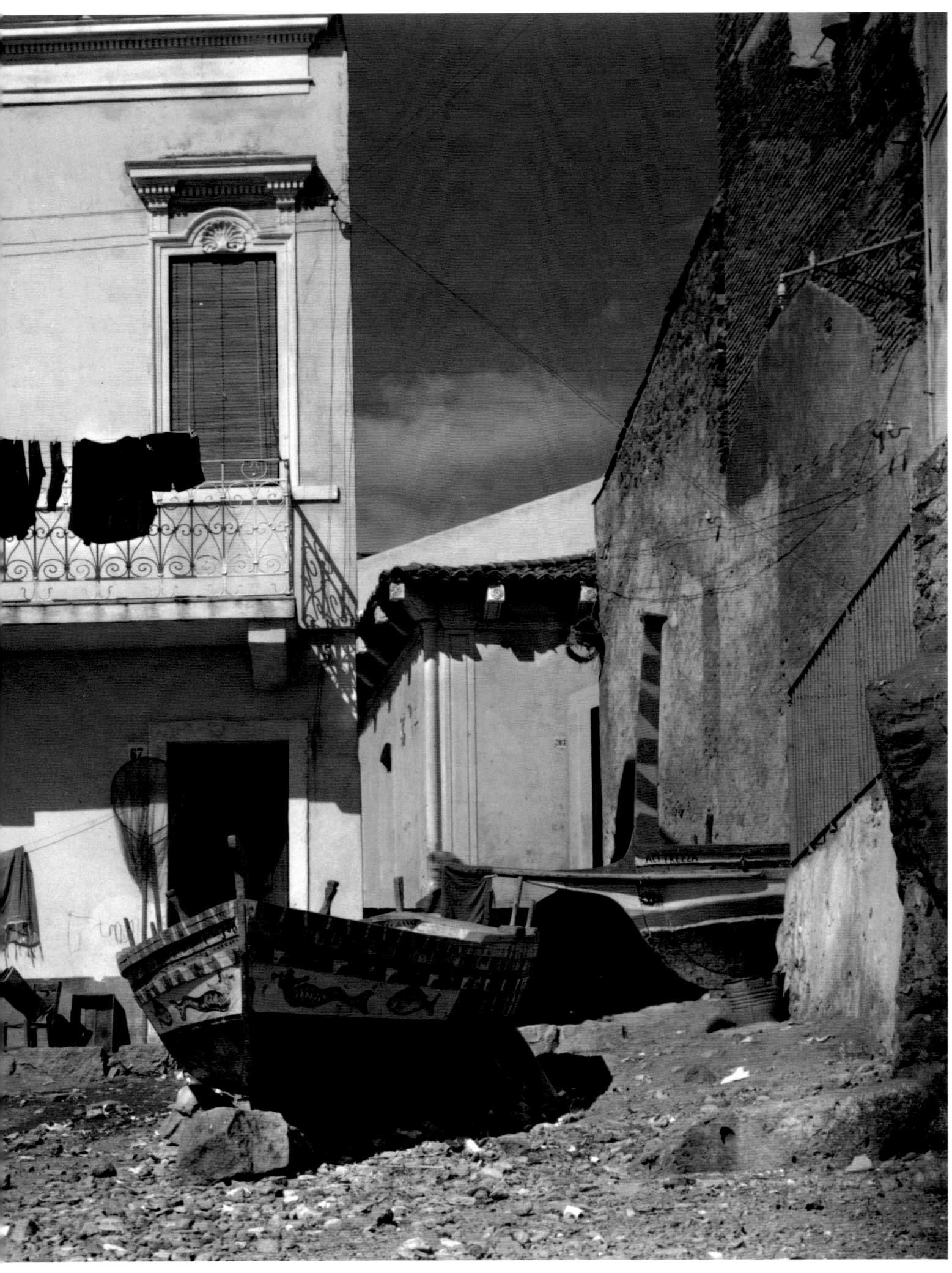

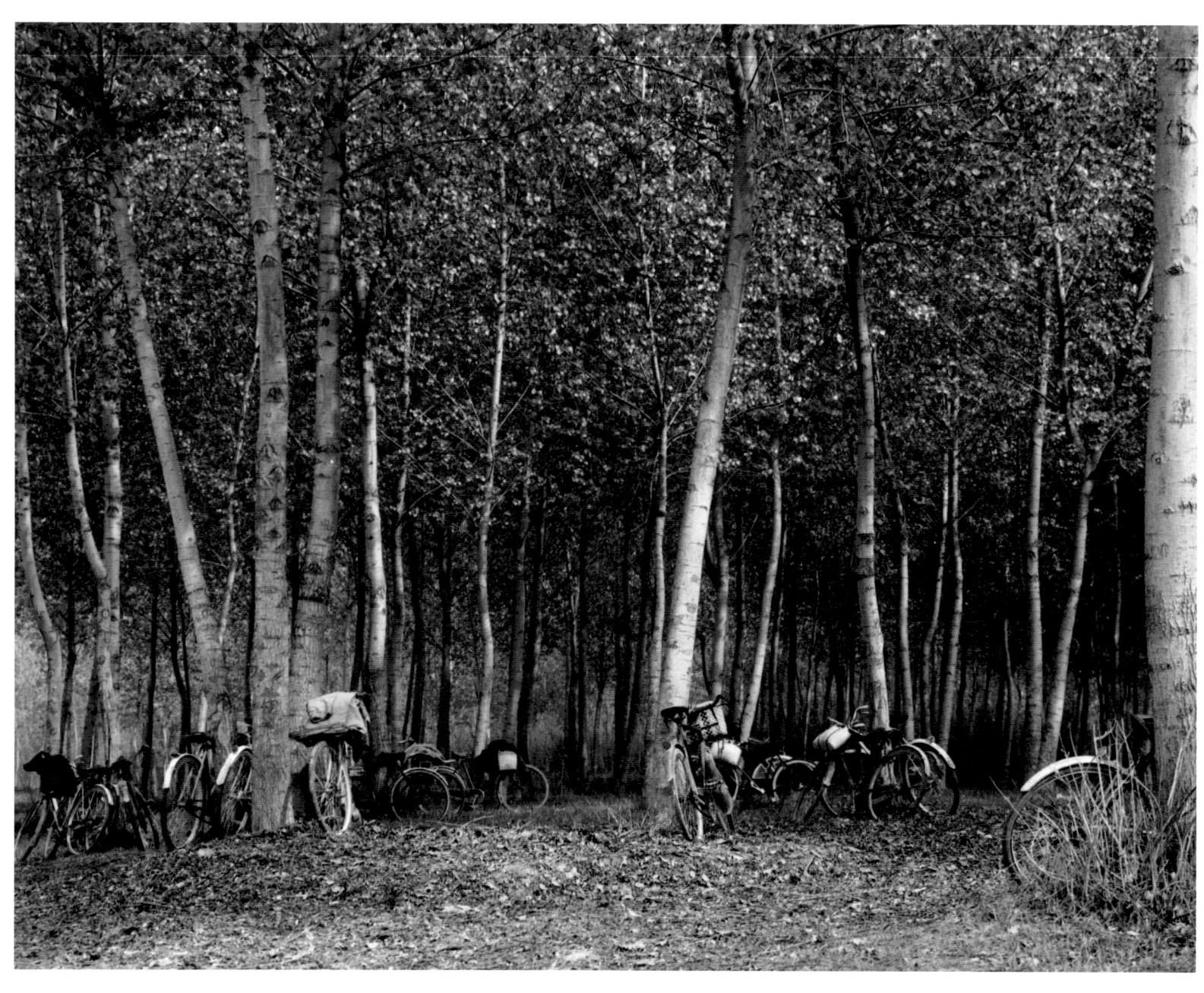

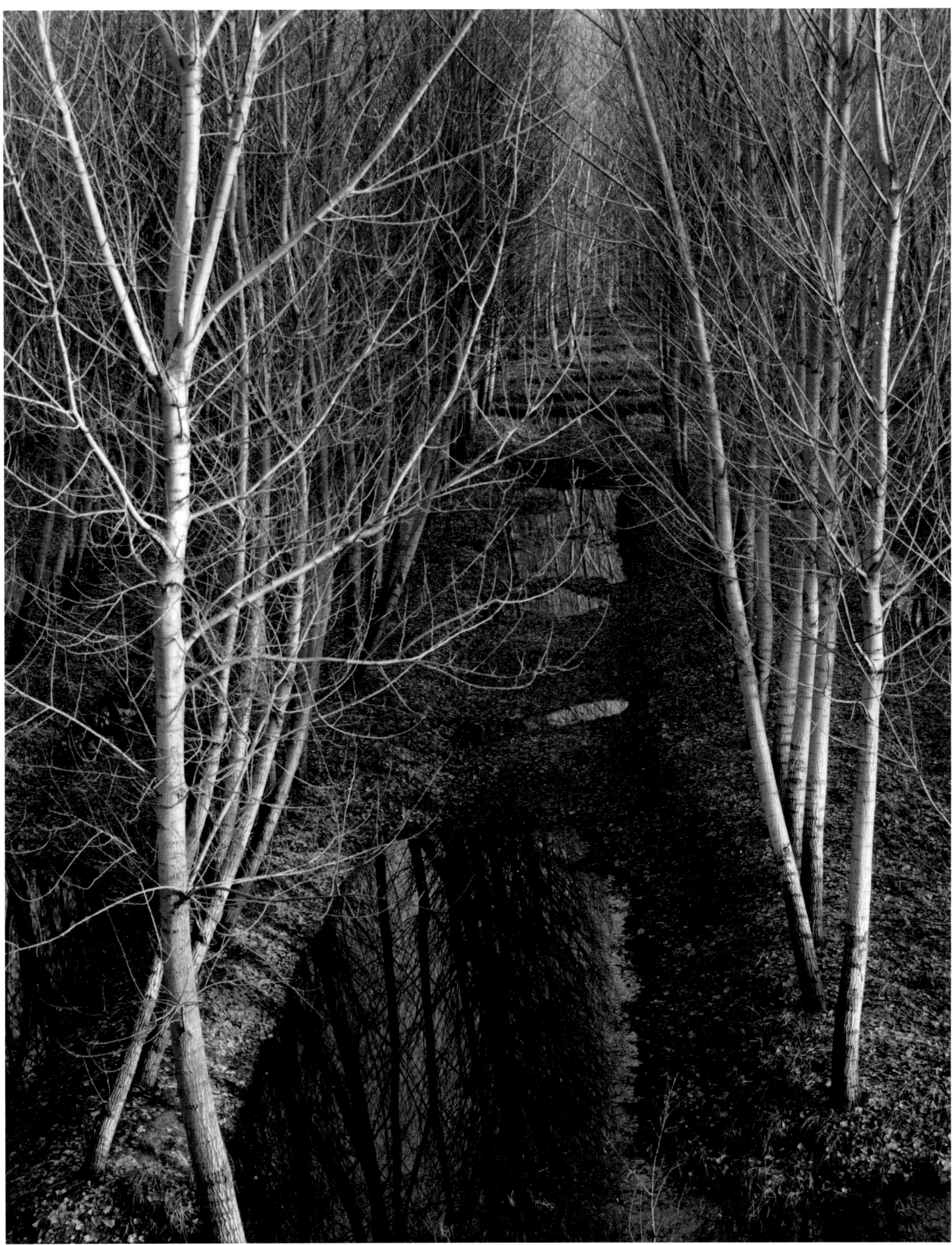

# THE HEBRIDES

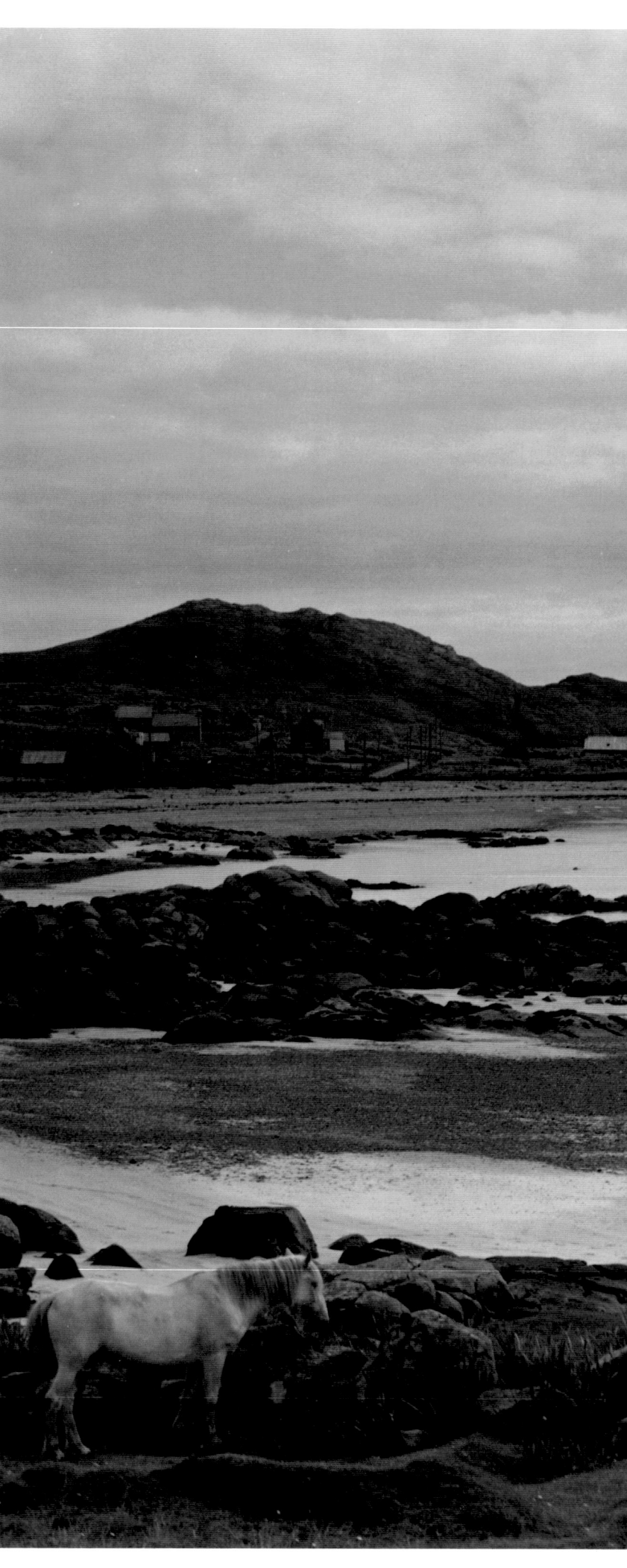

The name of Paul Strand is honored by everyone who believes that photography can be more than a superficial trick of light and chemistry and mirrors. Thirty and forty years ago his early work had the quality of pioneering vision into the art of photography; and throughout his life since then, passed mostly in the United States where he was born, Strand has worked exactingly at raising the standards of photographic art to higher levels....

Working at a slow pace, at his own exacting pace to his own exacting standard, Strand lived in South Uist for three months of 1954 so that he could take the photographs that he felt he wanted. He and Hazel Strand, who is also an experienced photographer, wandered for long weeks up and down the southern islands of the Outer Hebrides, waiting until they felt they understood the nature of the place, before he was ready to begin work.

But once he was ready the photographs seem to have come into existence without the camera; for the great gift and genius of this artist, it will appear, is to be able to place reality before you without demanding that you "see" the cameraman as well. Perhaps that is why his photographs achieve an intimacy that is always without embarrassment, a depth of purpose that is never pretentious, a truth that is momentary but is also universal. These islands of the Outer Hebrides deserved a great photographer: it can be seen, in this volume, that at last they have got one.

From the Foreword to *Tir a'Mhurain*,
by Basil Davidson, 1962

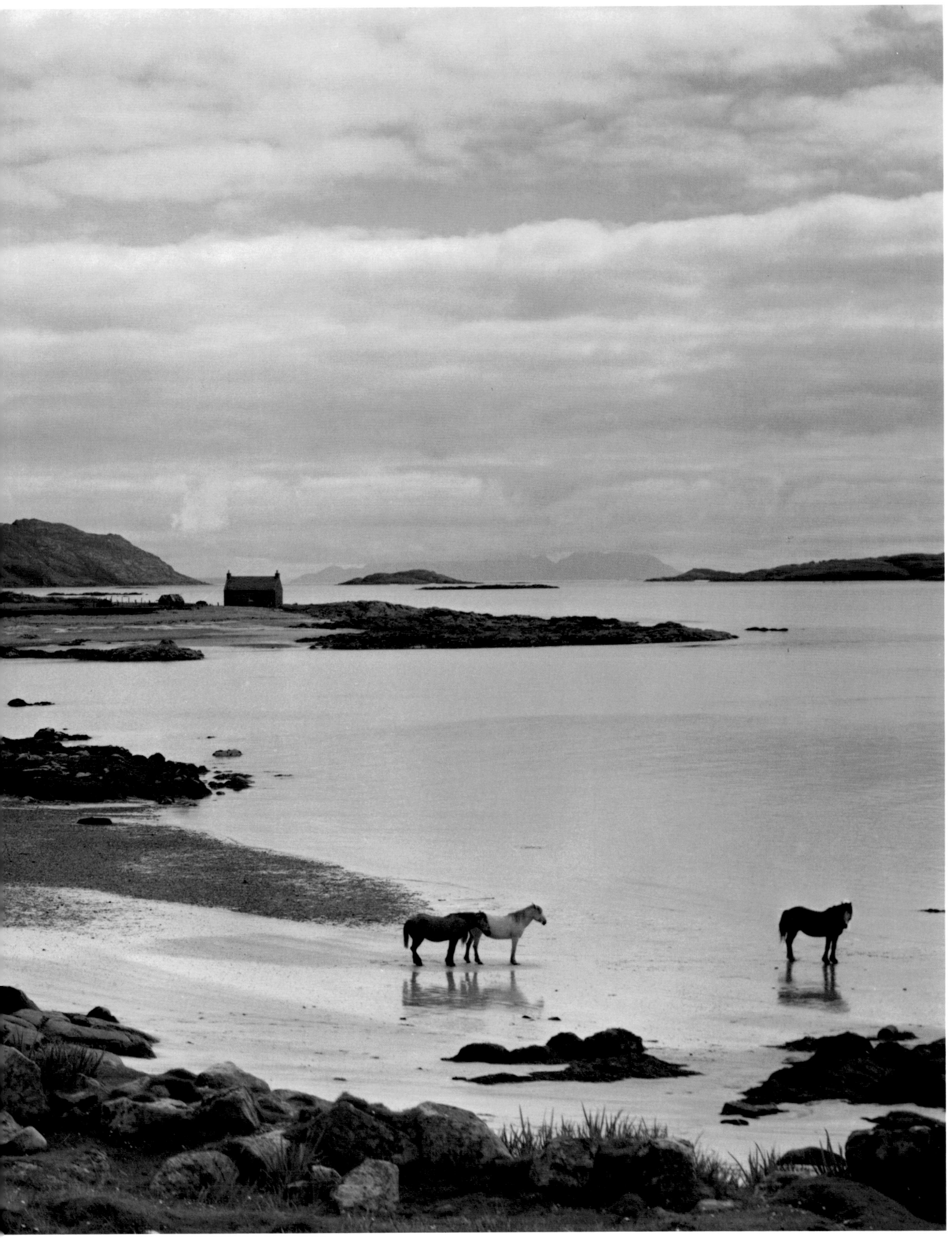

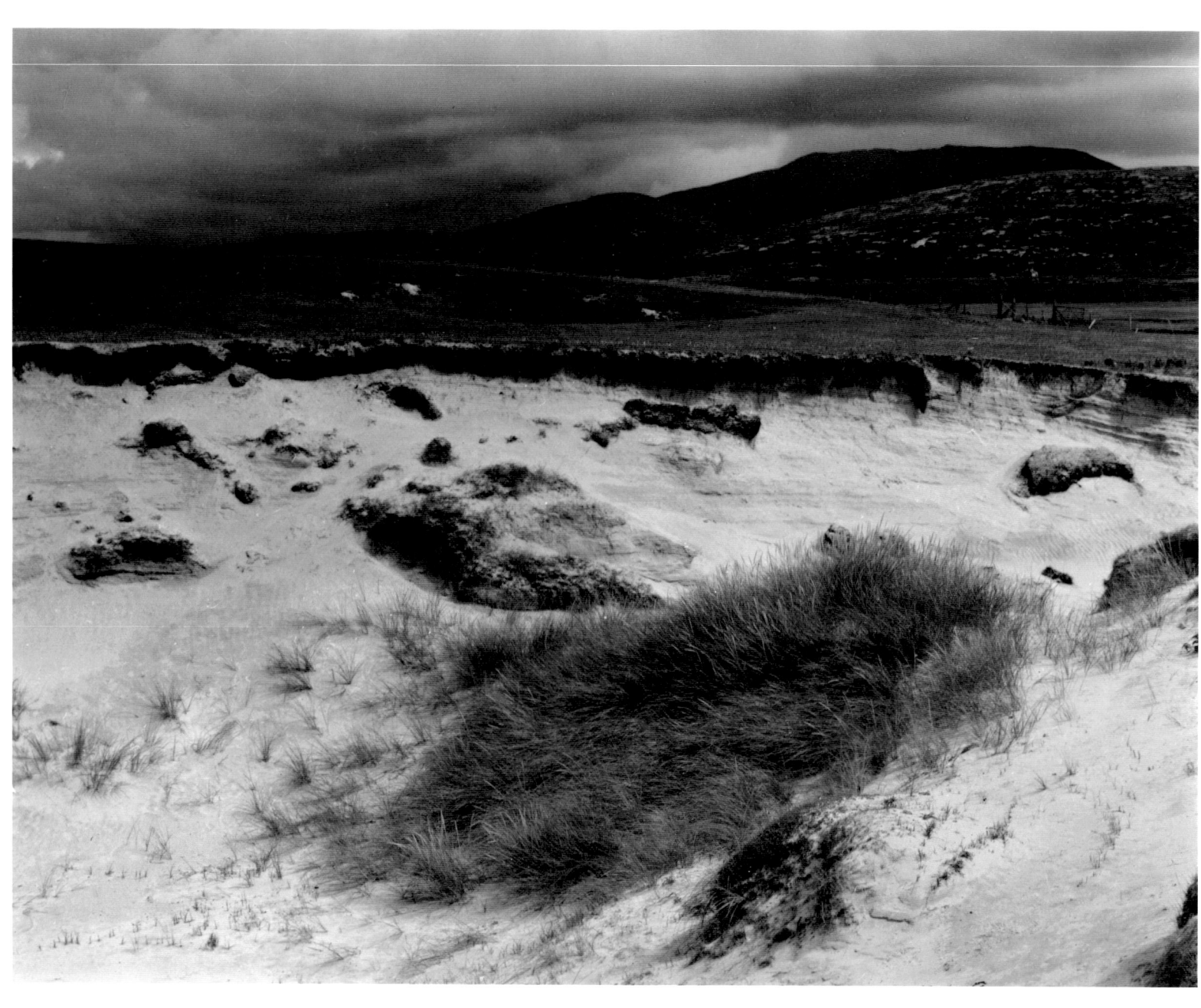

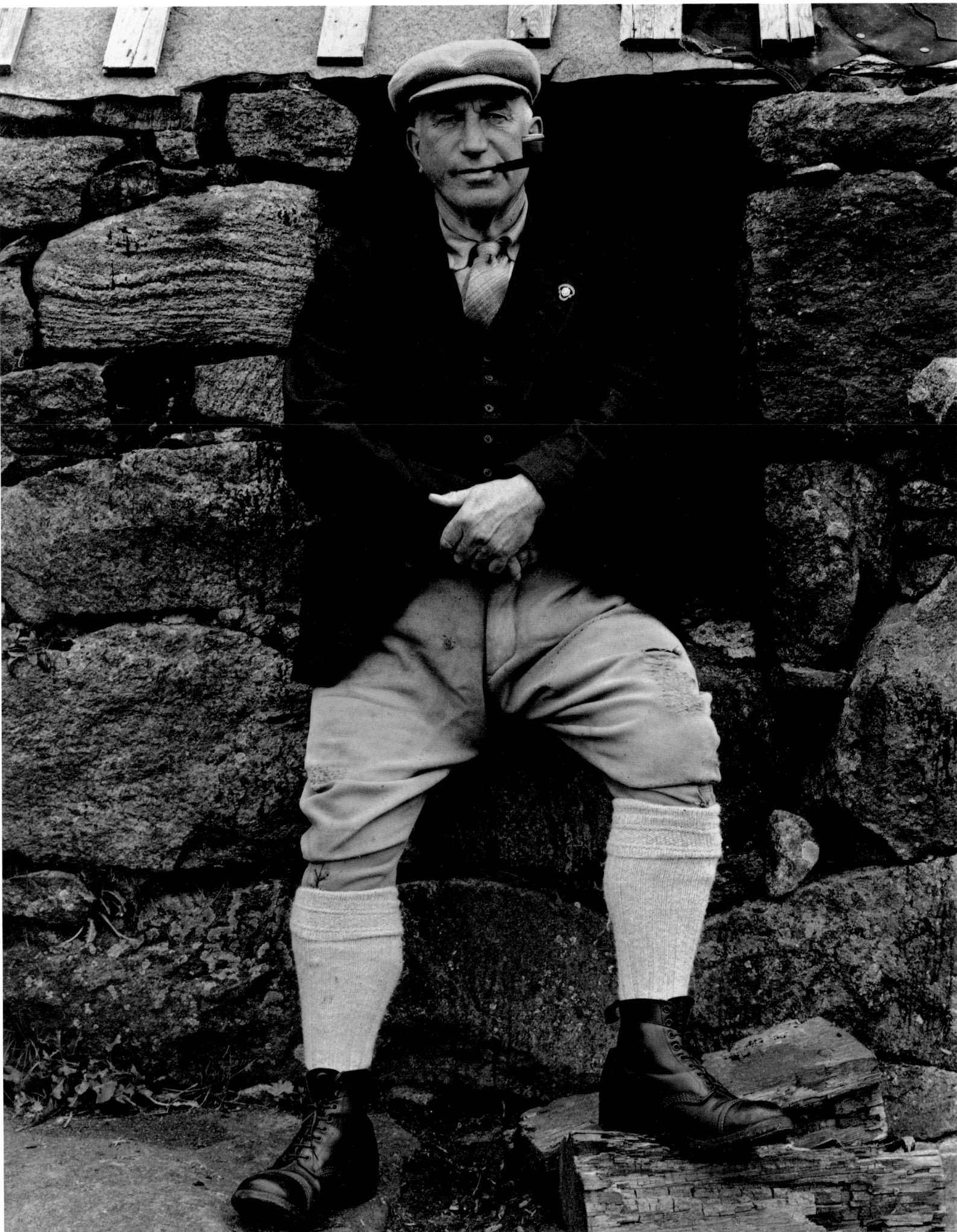

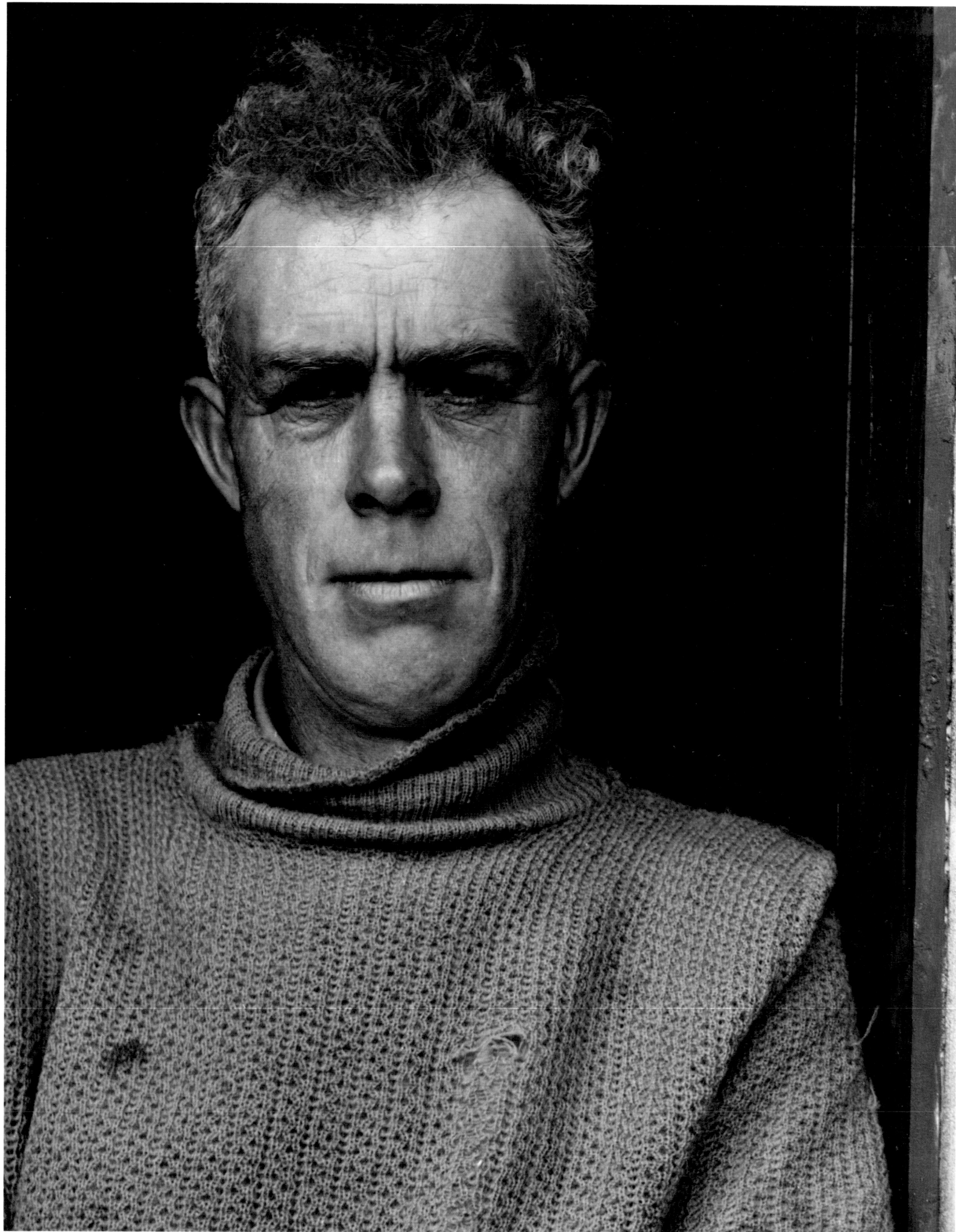

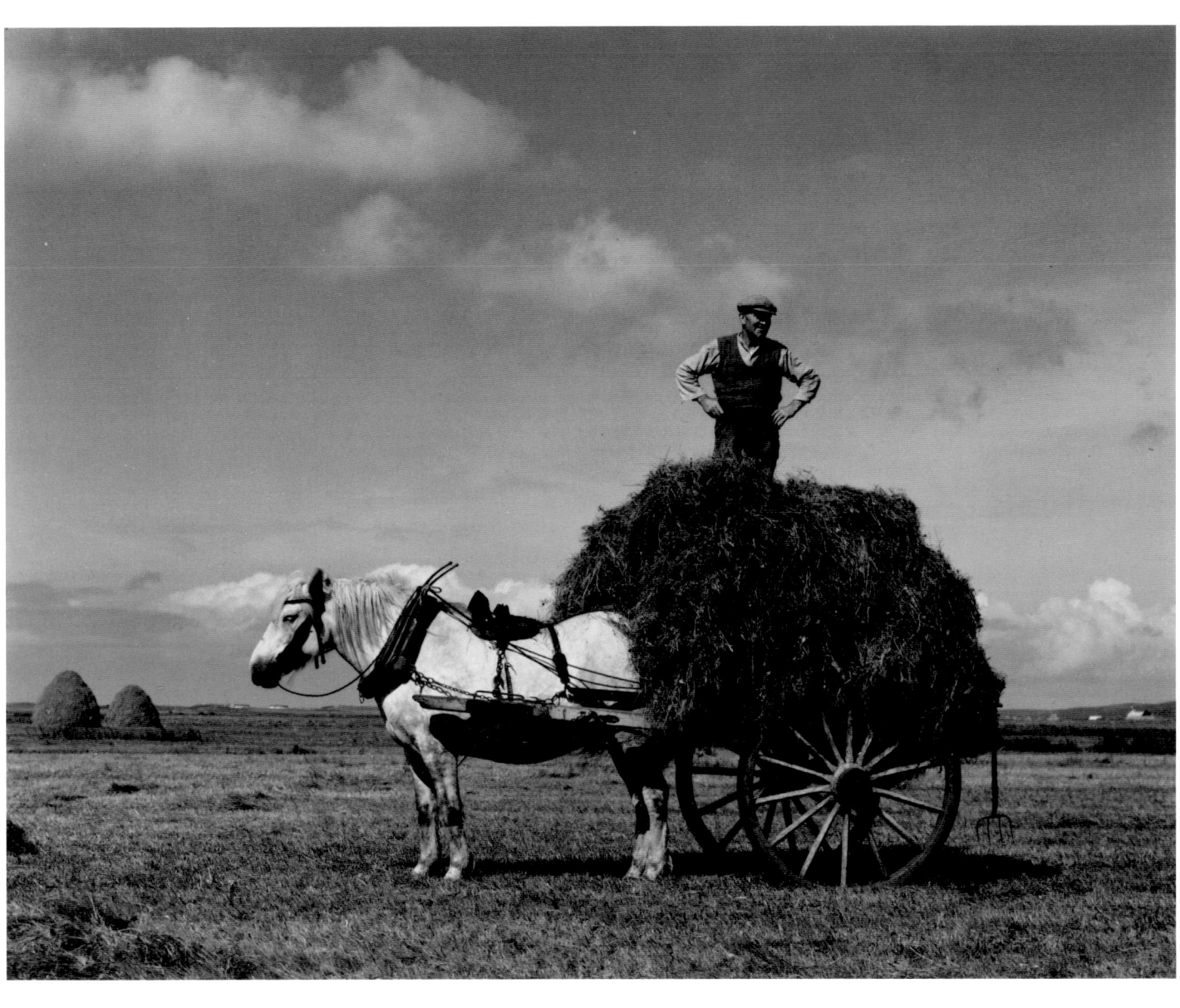

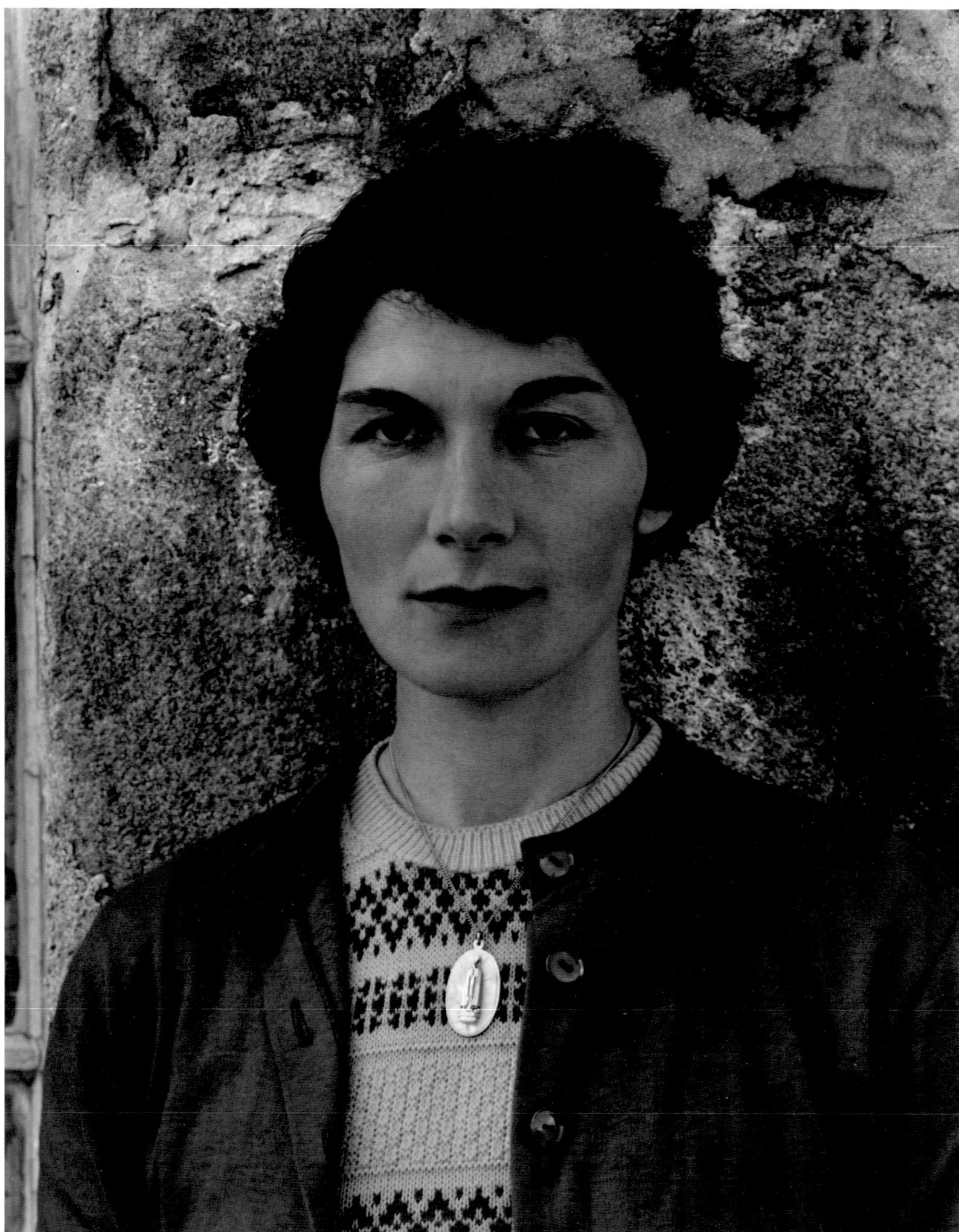

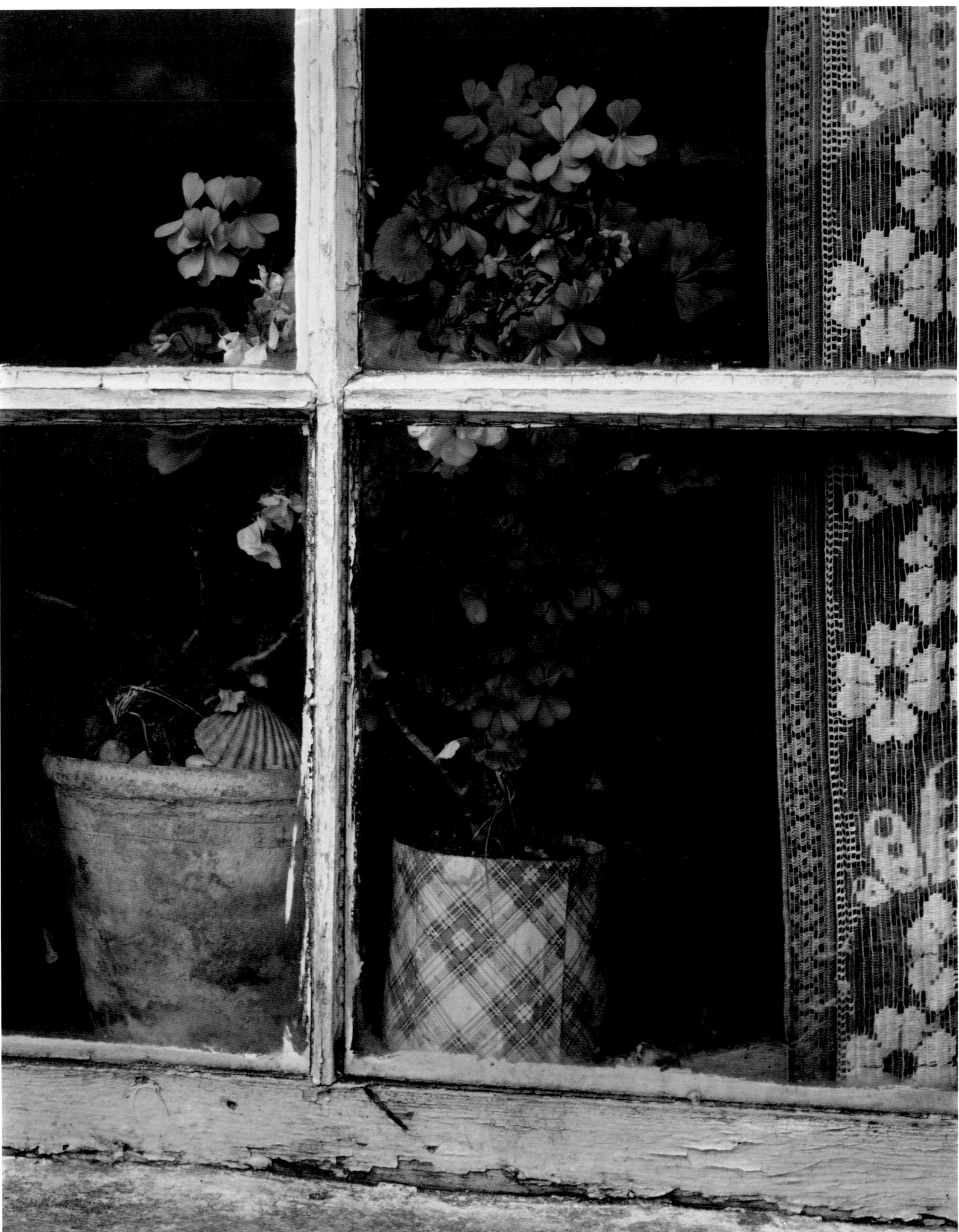

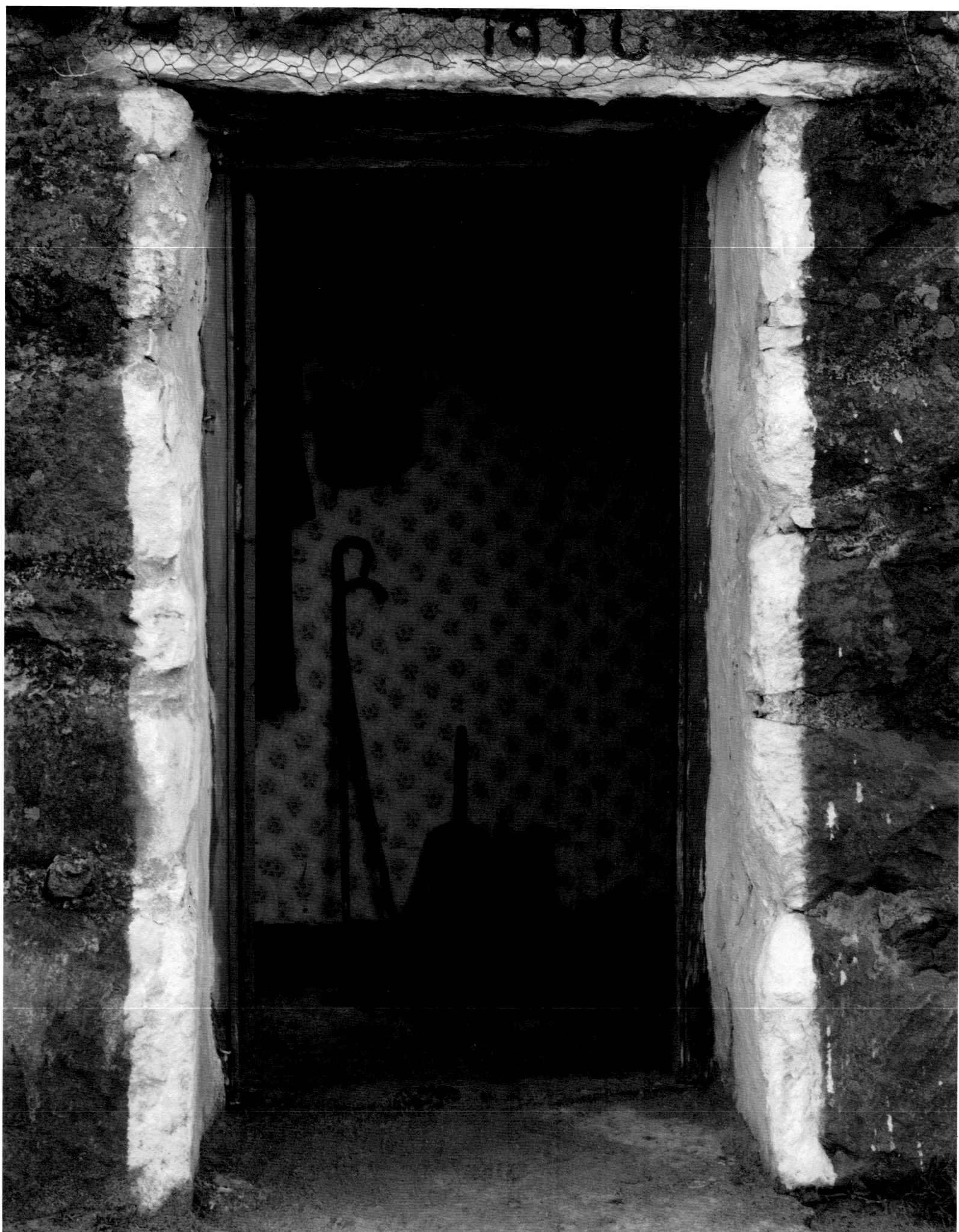

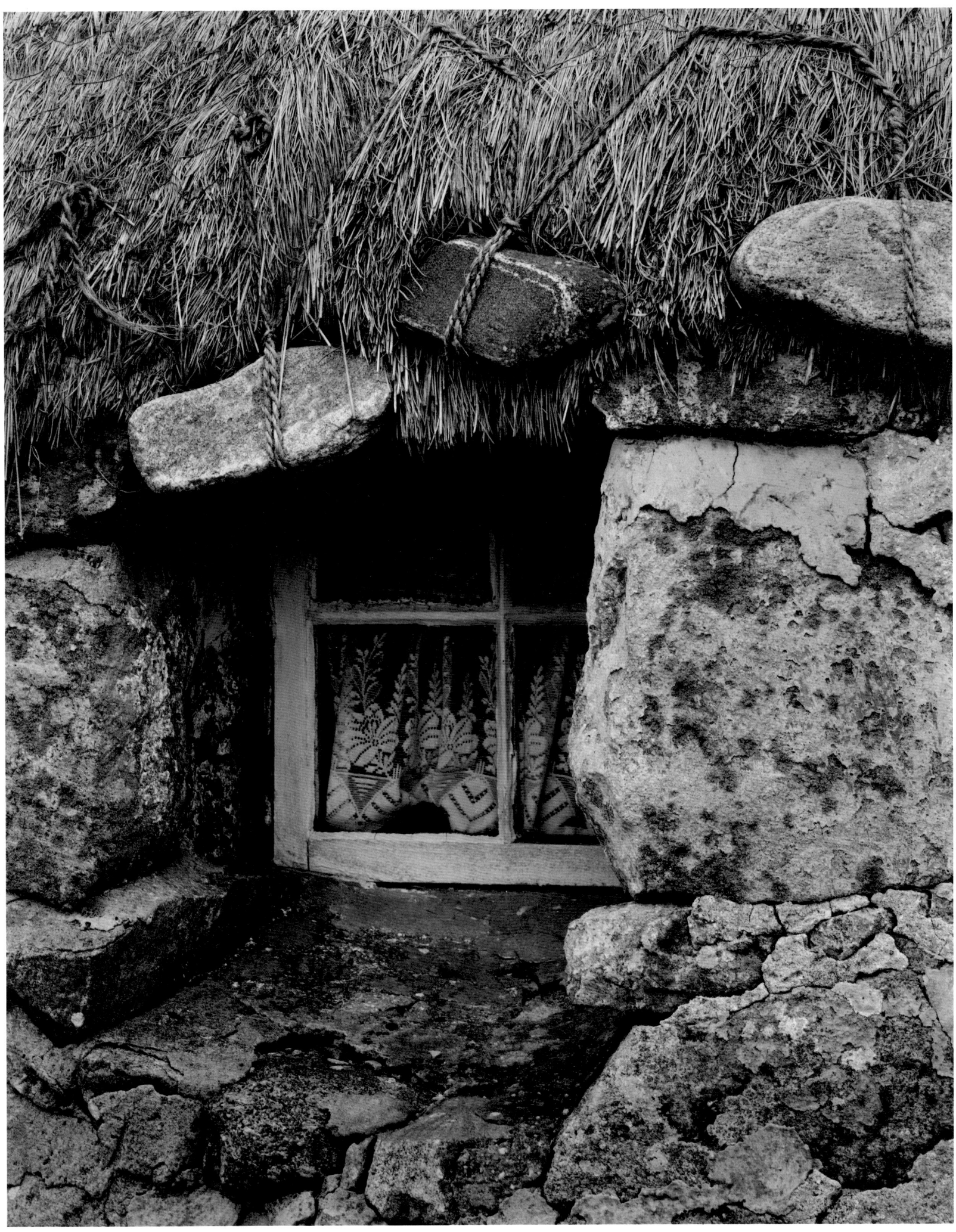

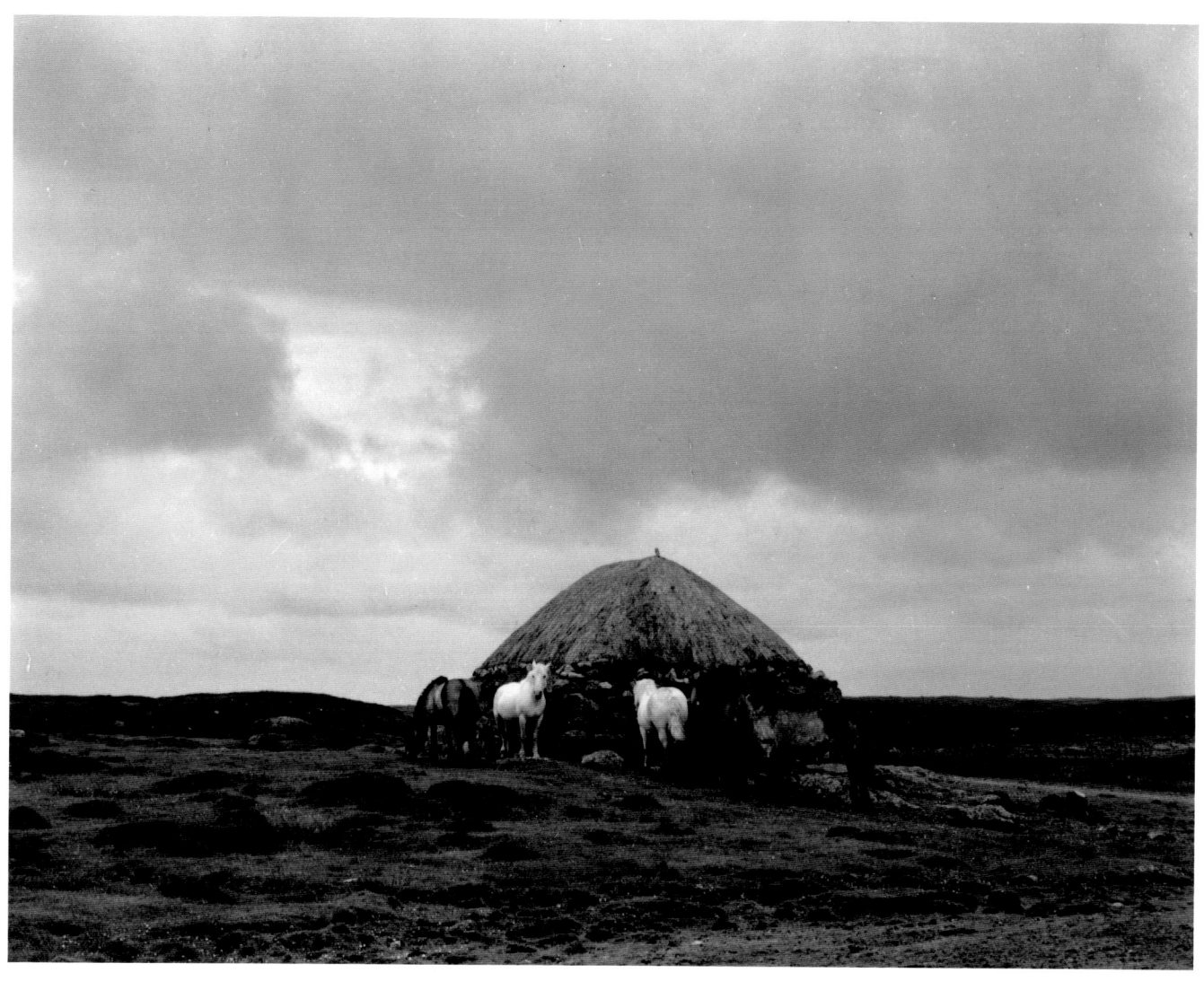

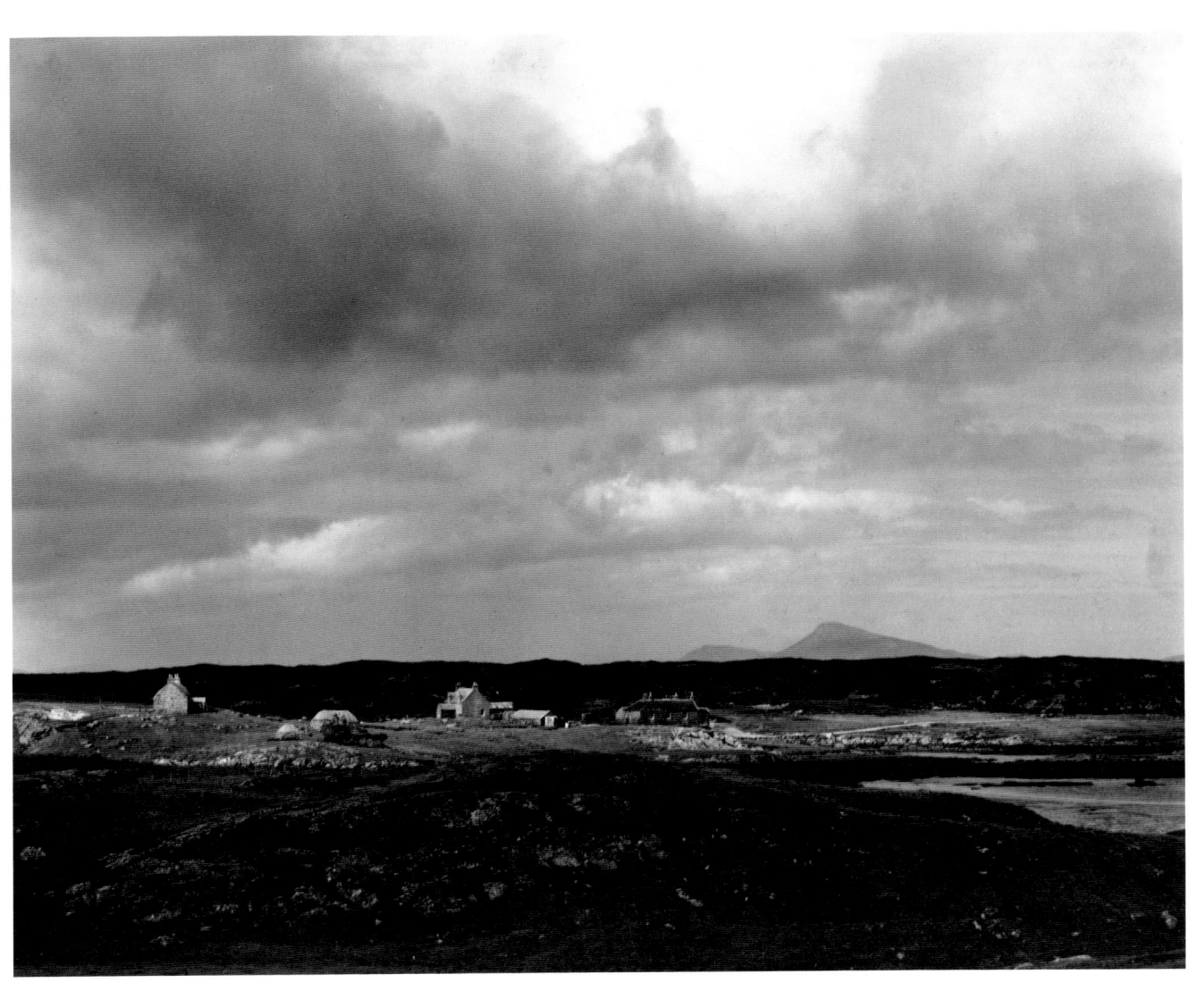

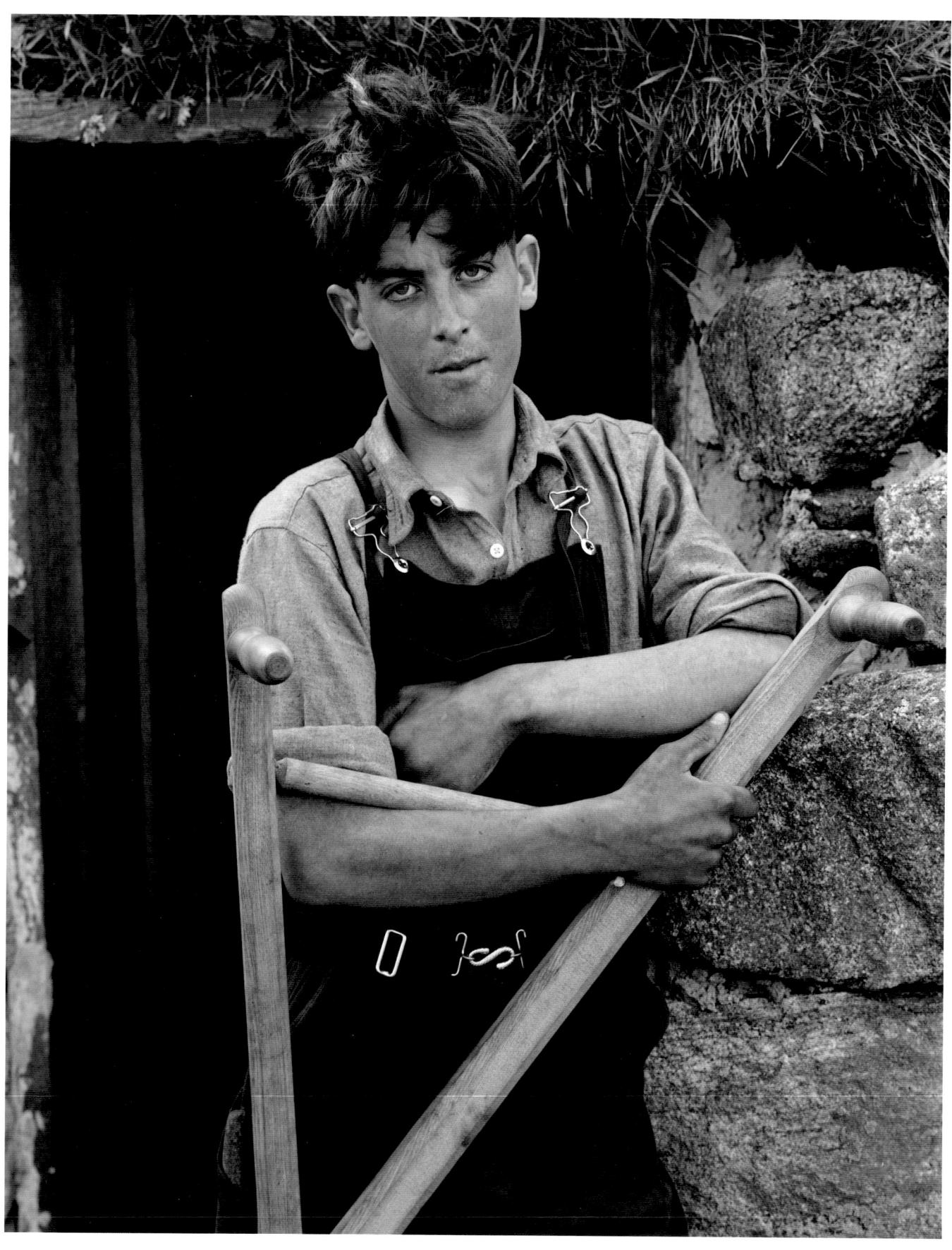

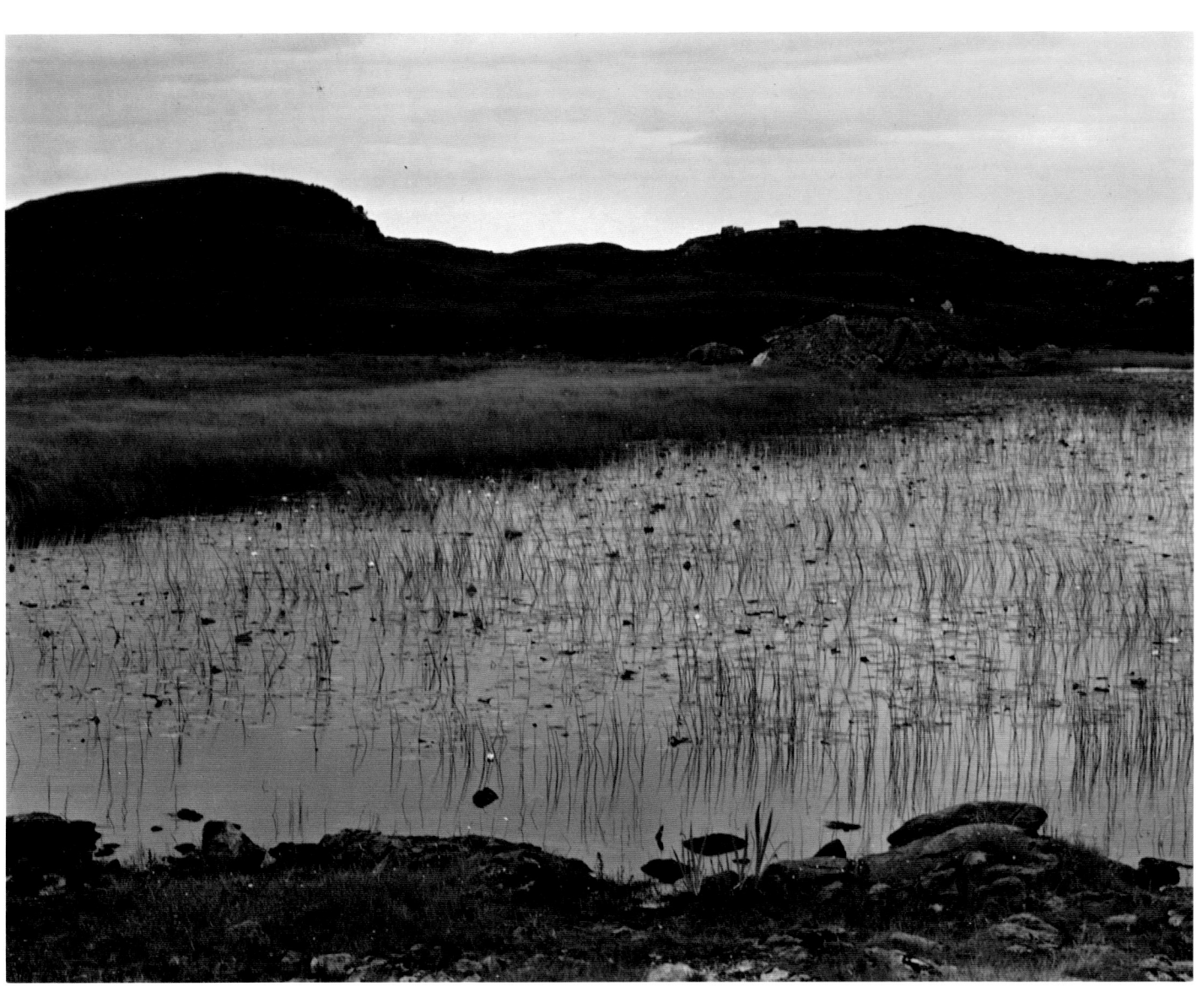

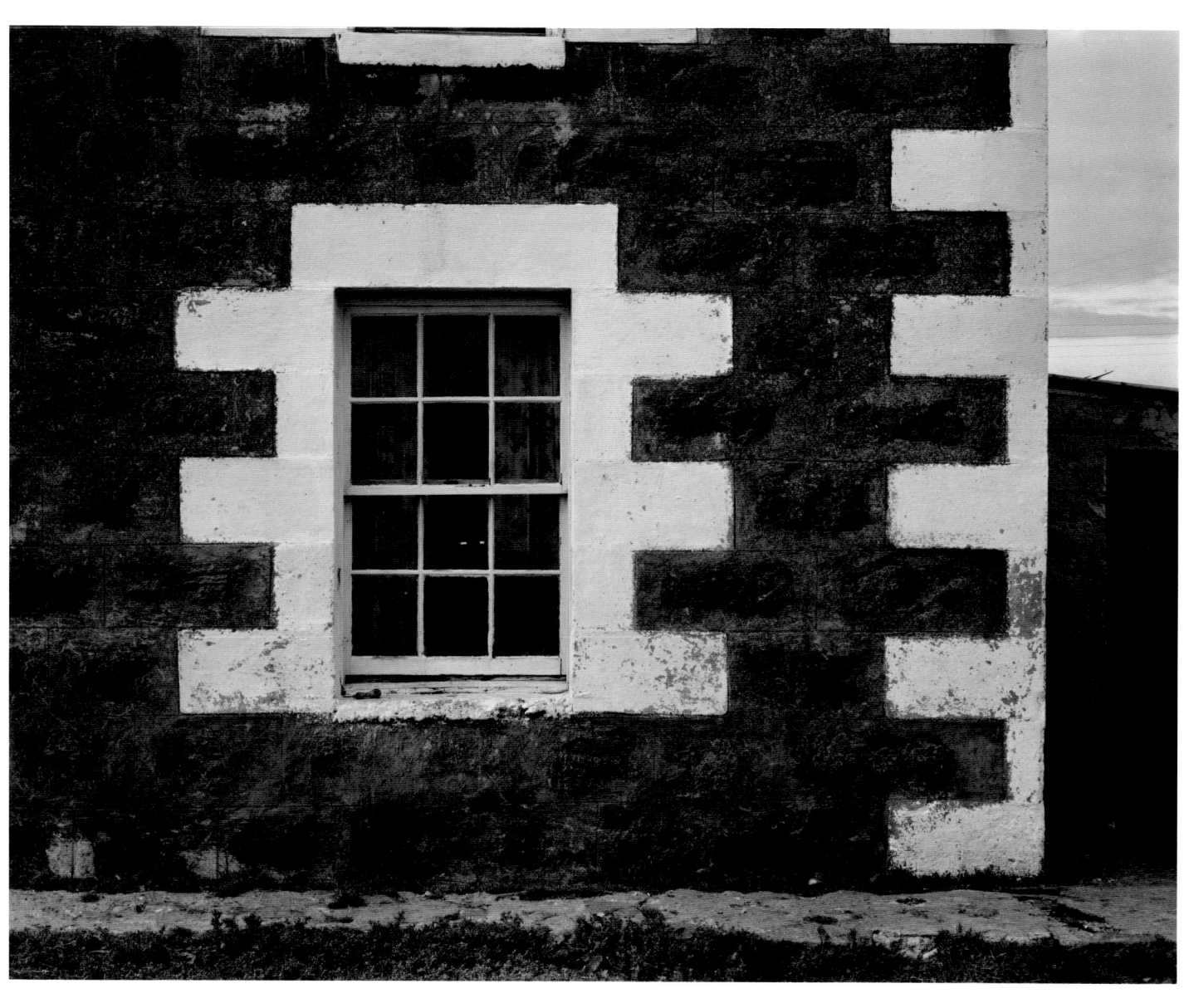

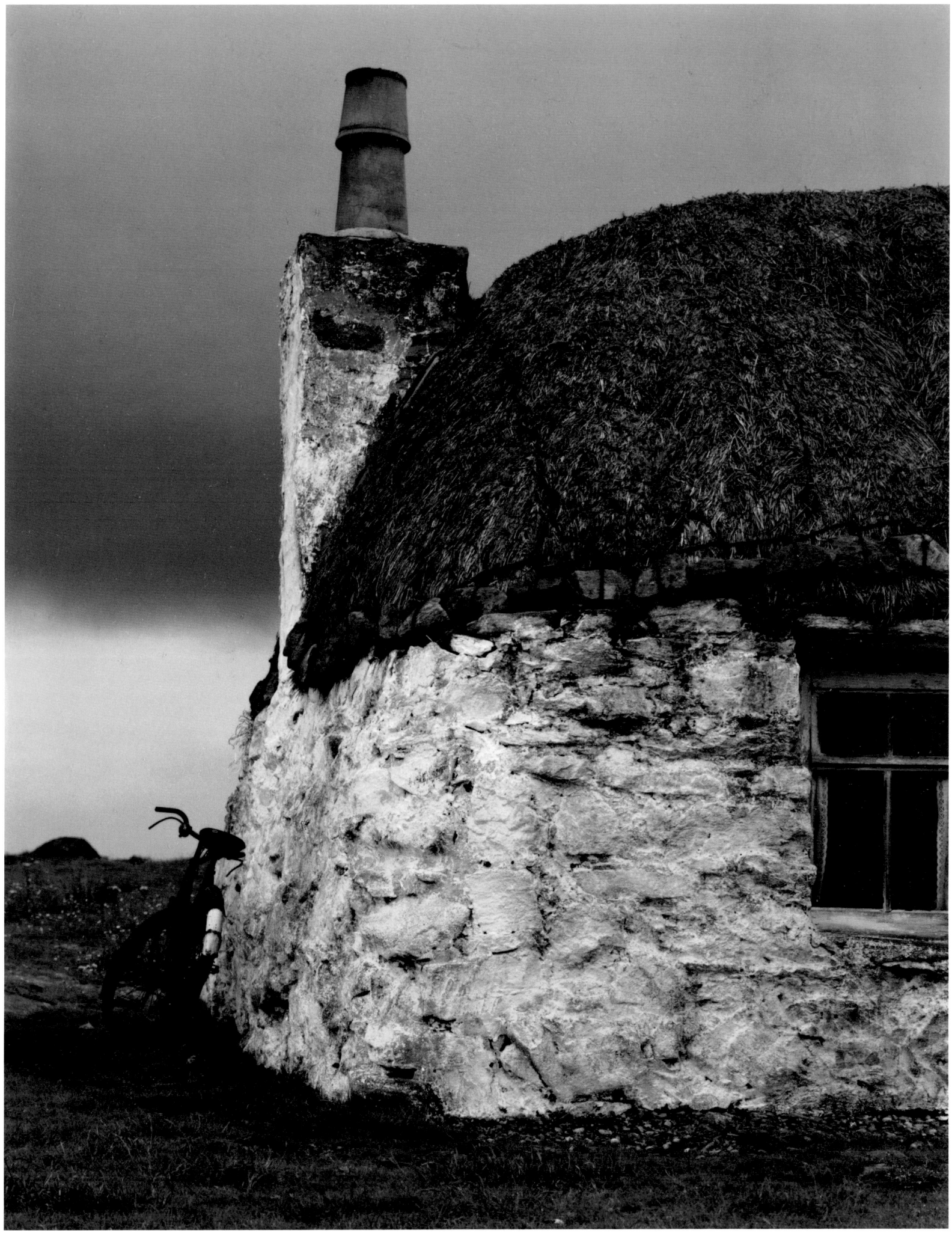

# EGYPT

The task we set ourselves was to try to lay the foundations for understanding Egypt and its people. Egypt's history has always evolved out of its rich land and its poor people. The photographs and the text of "Living Egypt" begin there and develop, on this basis, the idea that modern Egypt is emerging from her past and her poverty, and is trying to overcome the heritage of more than two thousand years of continuous occupation. Egypt is quite incomprehensible without this approach.

What emerges at the end of it all is the revolutionary Egypt which was born in 1952. In print we have to stop the revolution at a given moment and say: "That is where it is now." But what the text and the photographs have tried to show is that the problem of Egypt is not simply the development of day to day events. For Egypt it is still a matter of transforming, painfully and with great difficulty, what is already there. We did not want this obscured. We have therefore concentrated on the human material the Egyptian revolution is working with, and we have set out to show that in fact Egypt is still incredibly old, even at the moment when it is exhilaratingly young.

From the Foreword to *Living Egypt*,
by Paul Strand and James Aldridge, 1969

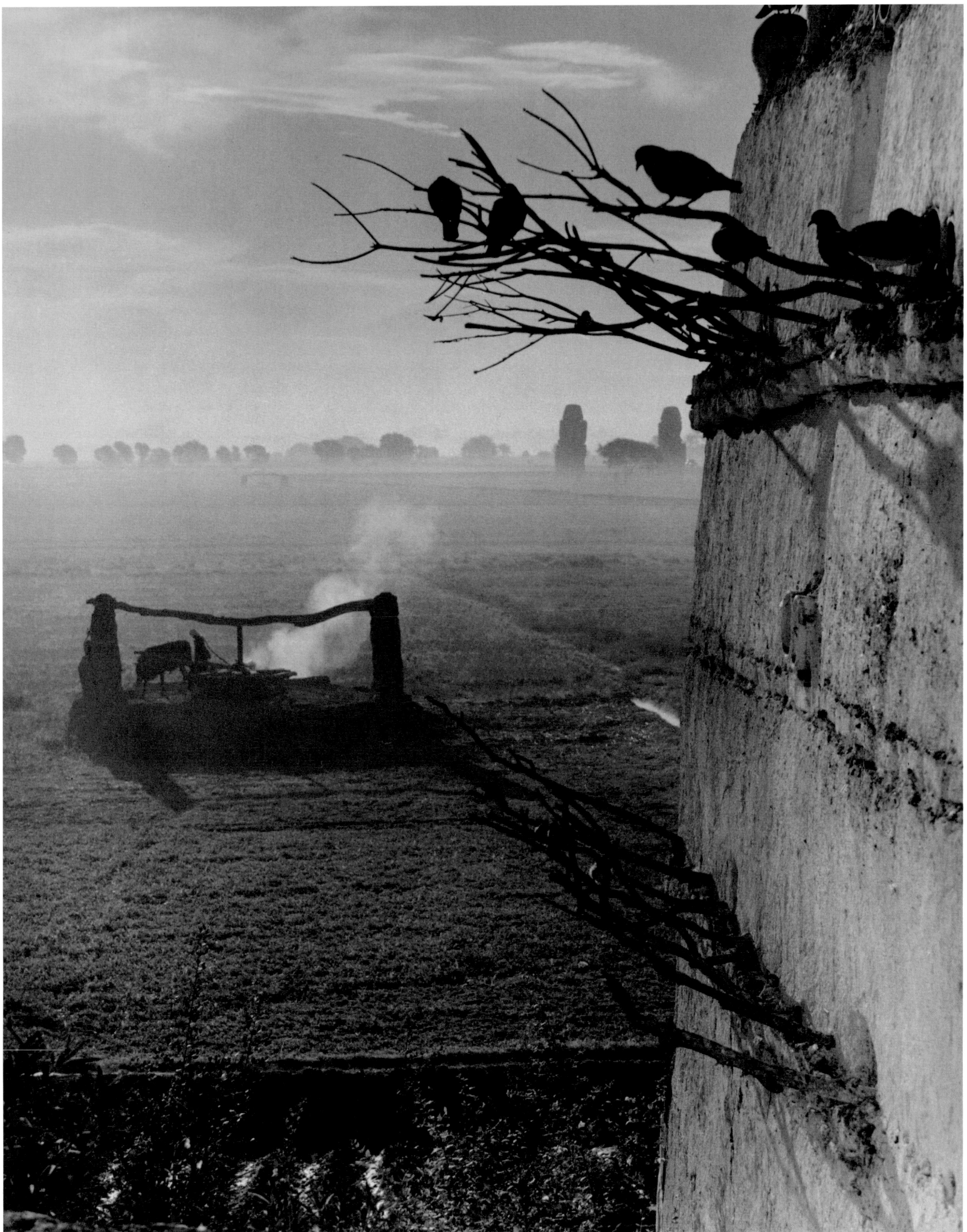

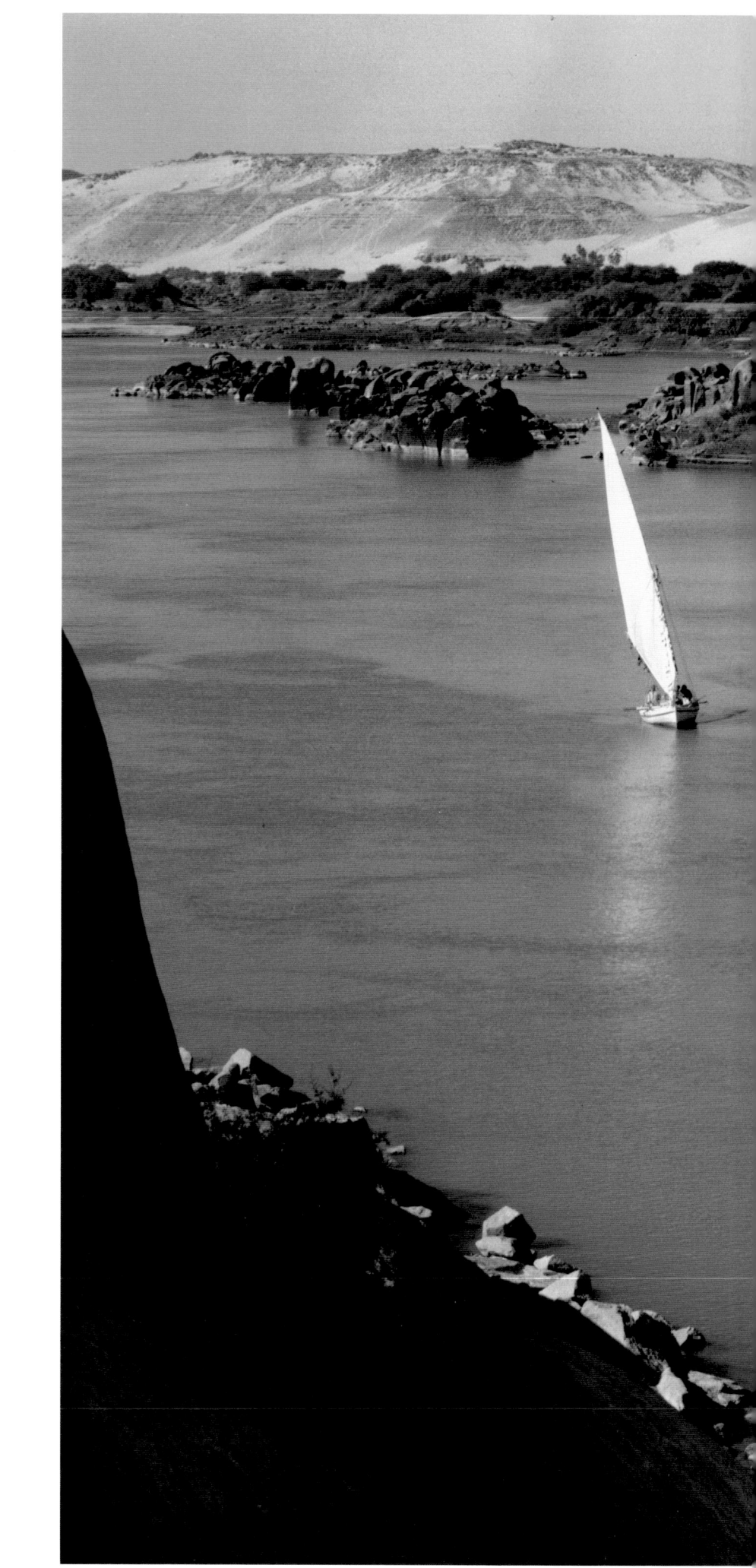

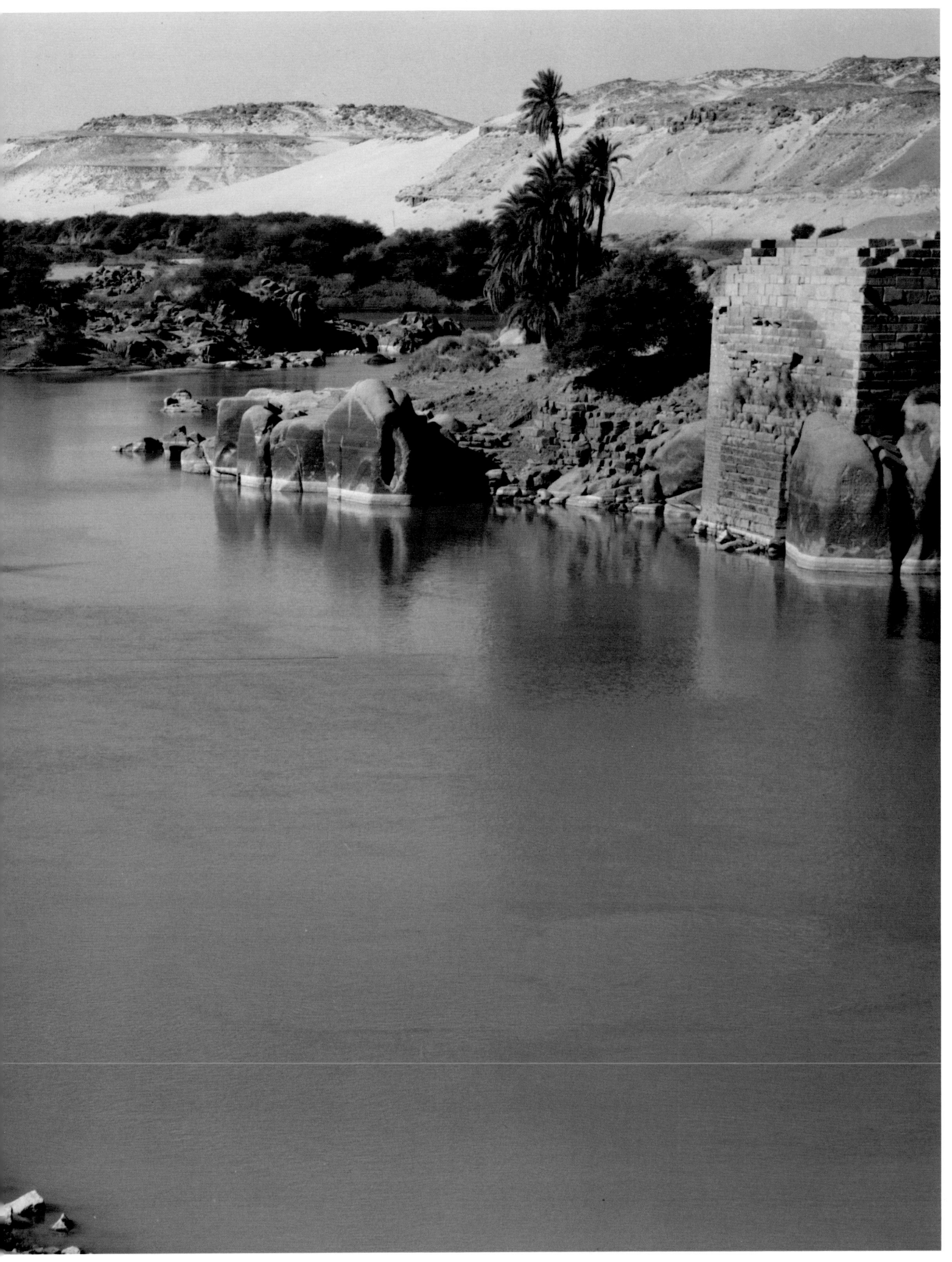

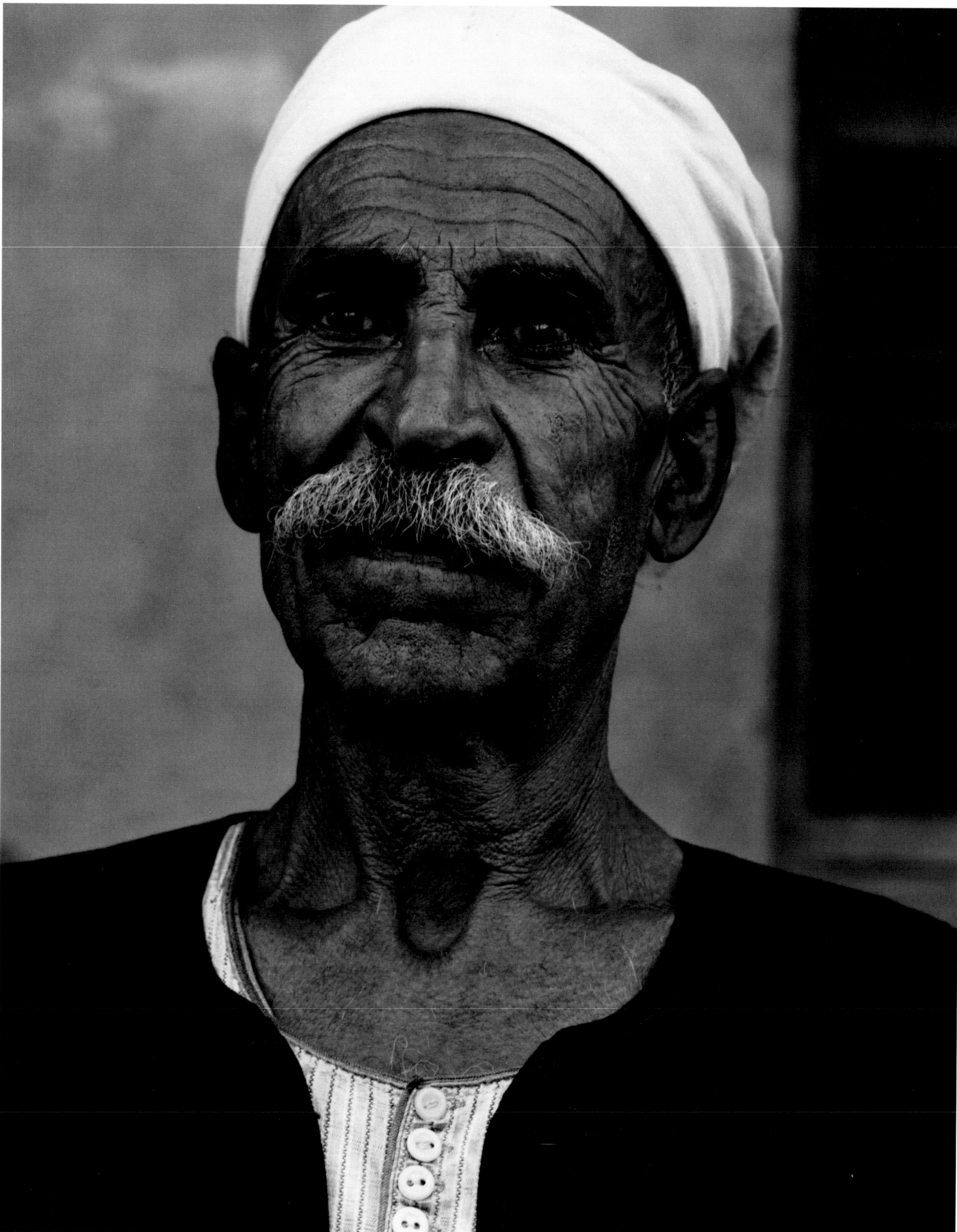

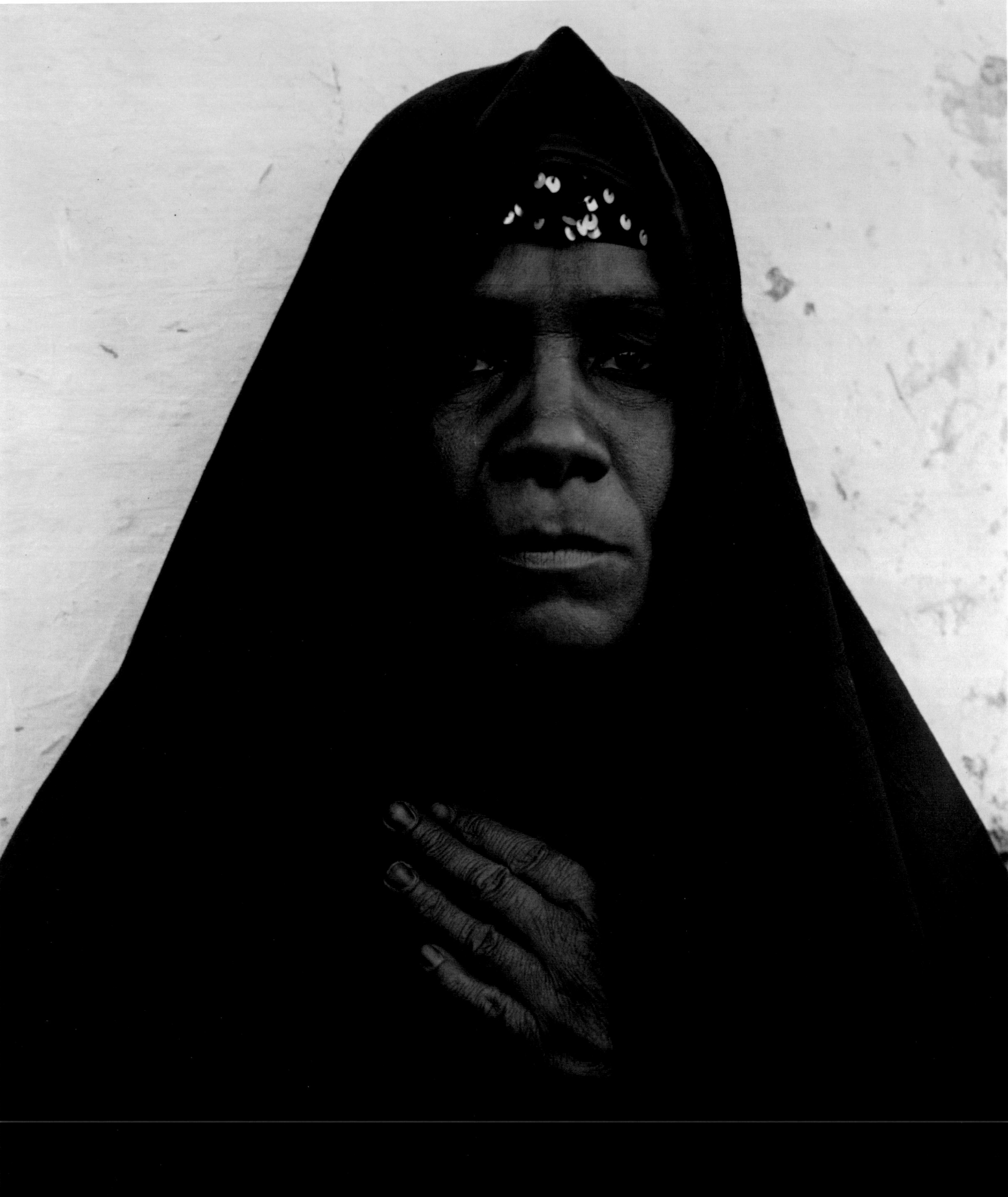

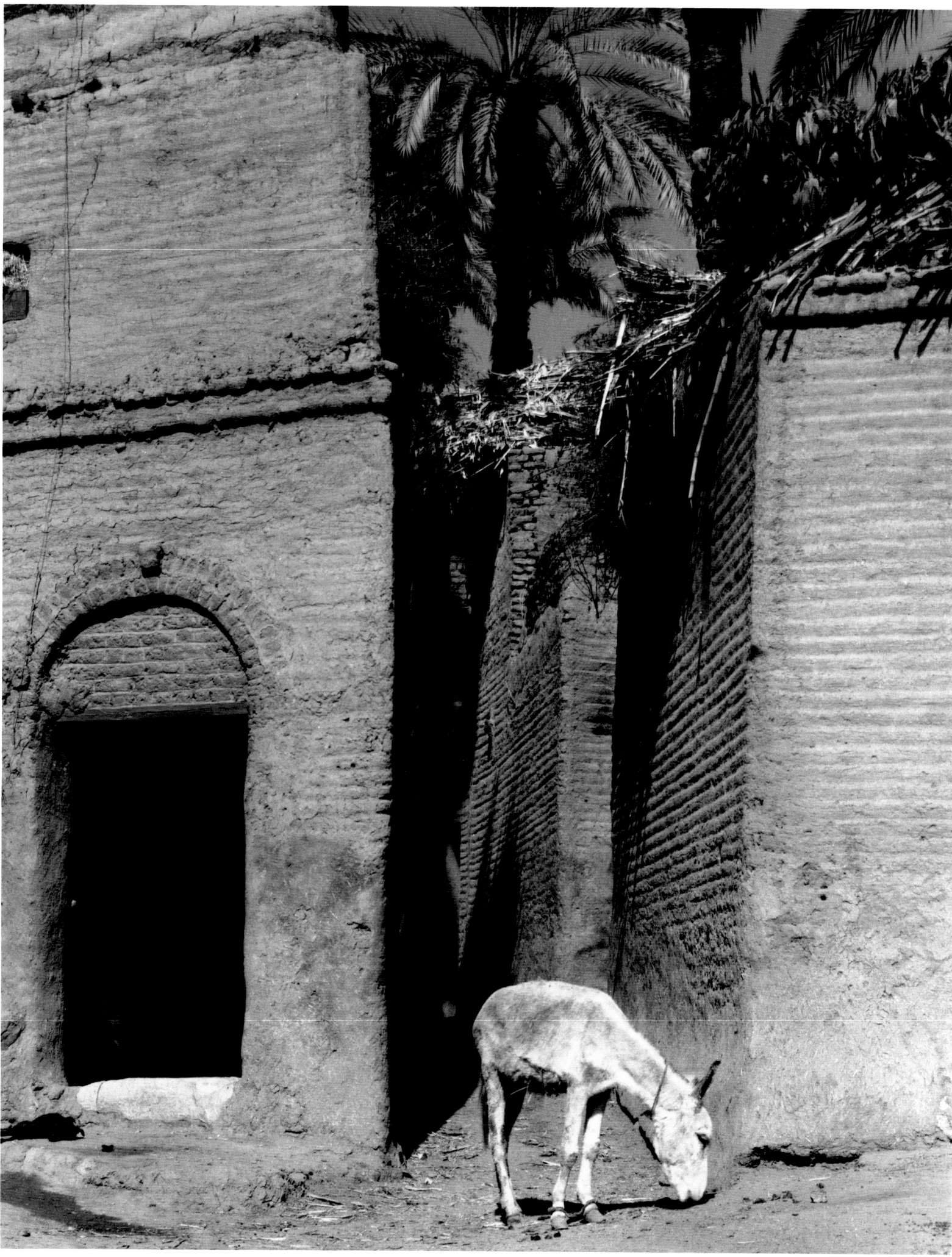

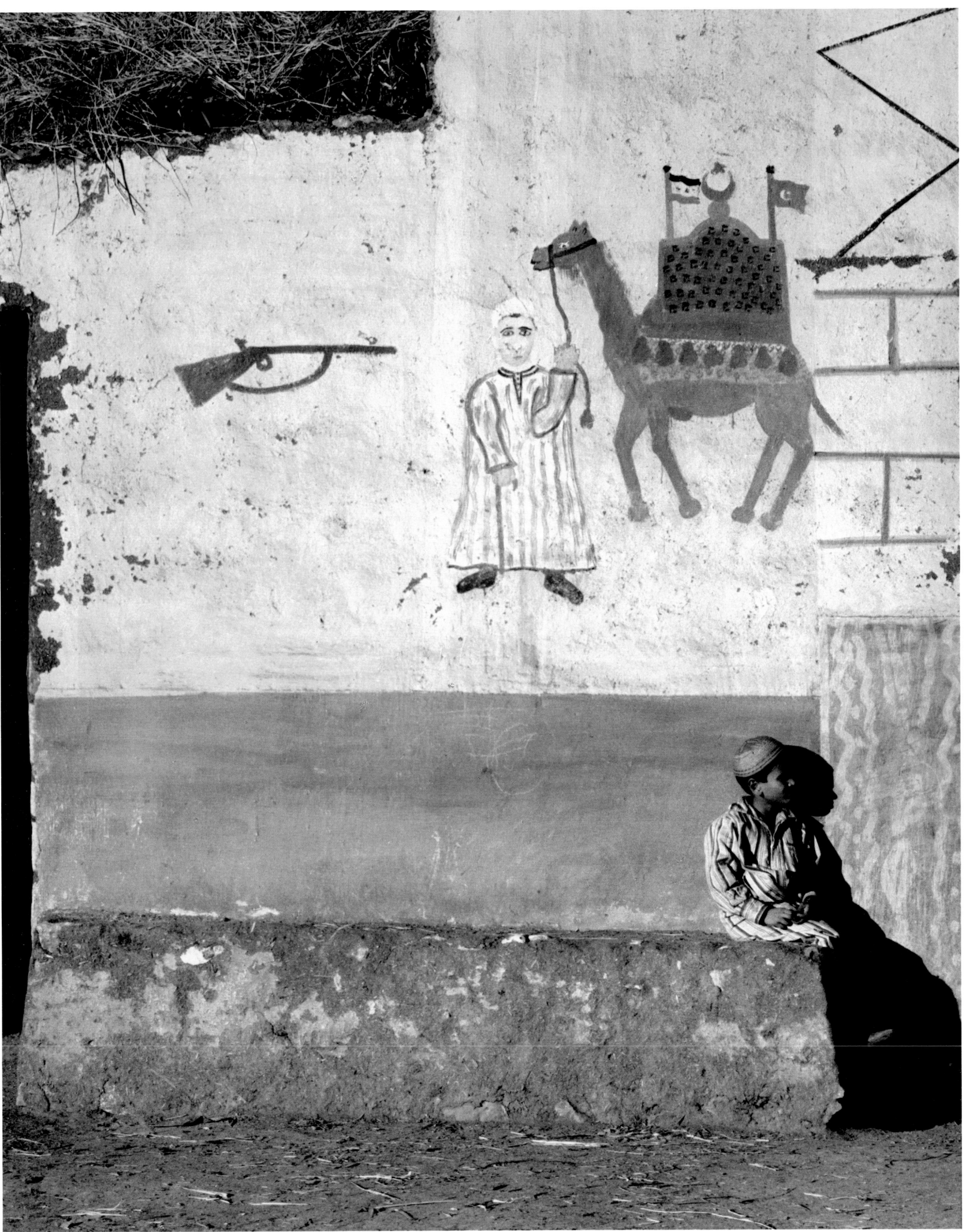

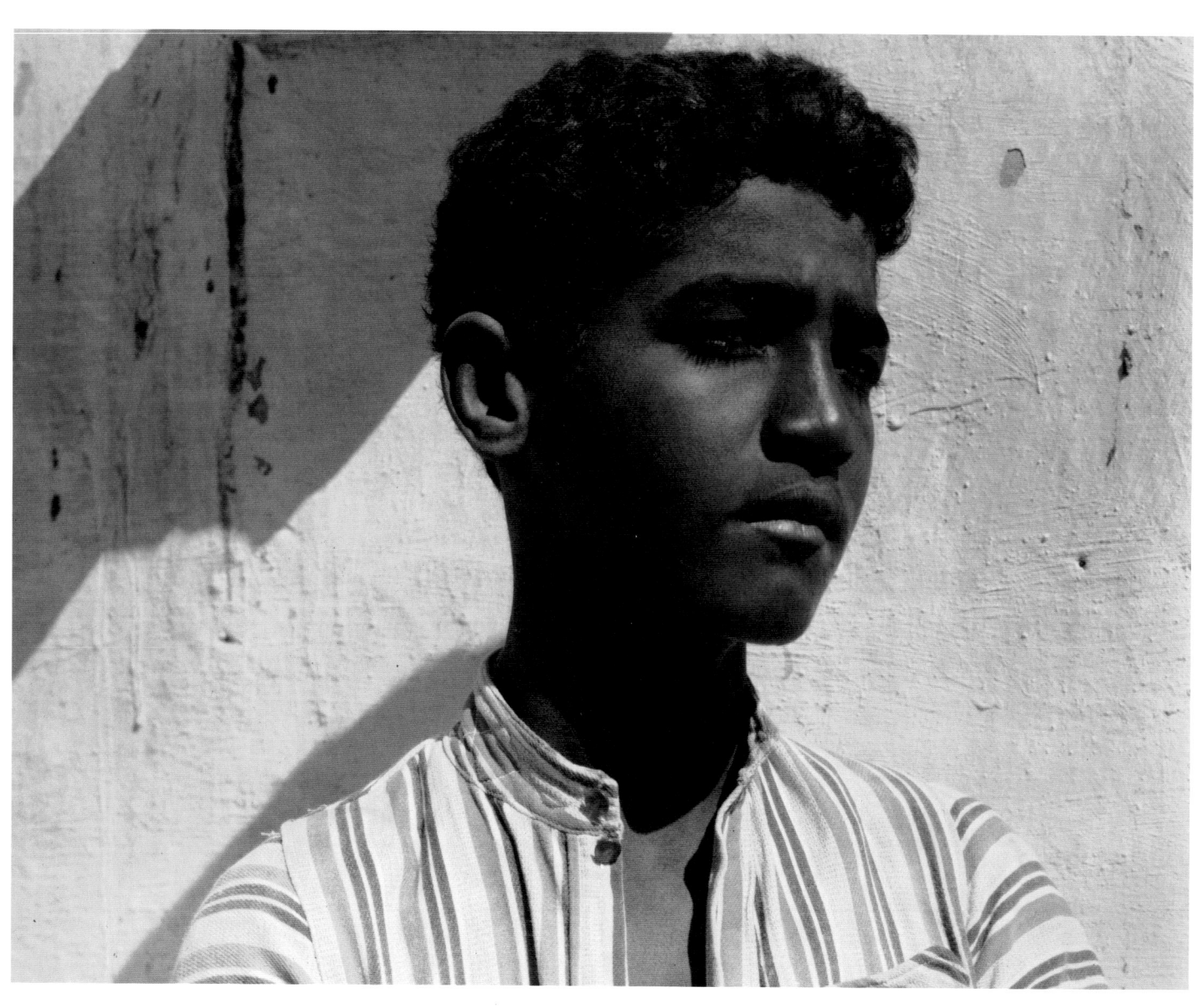

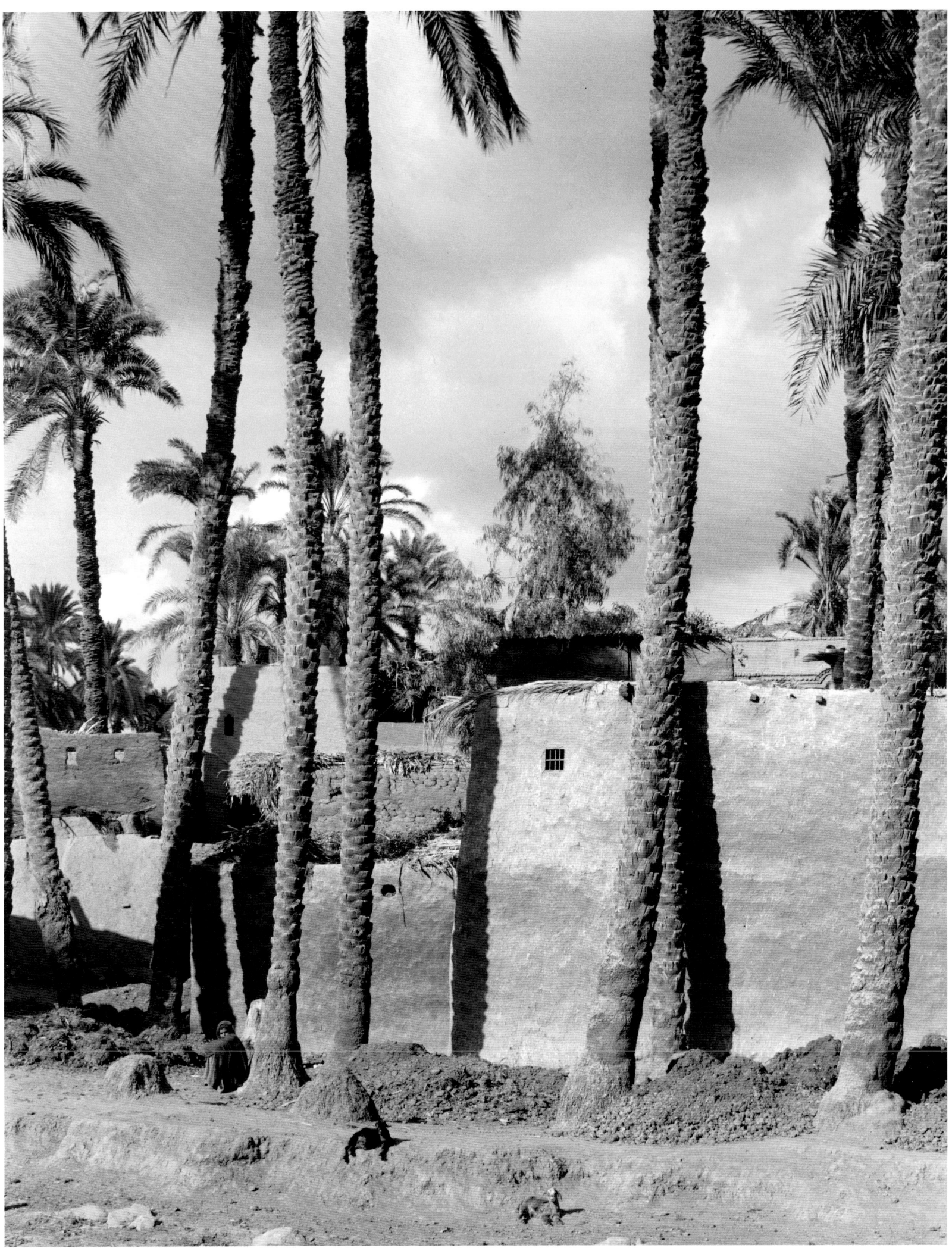

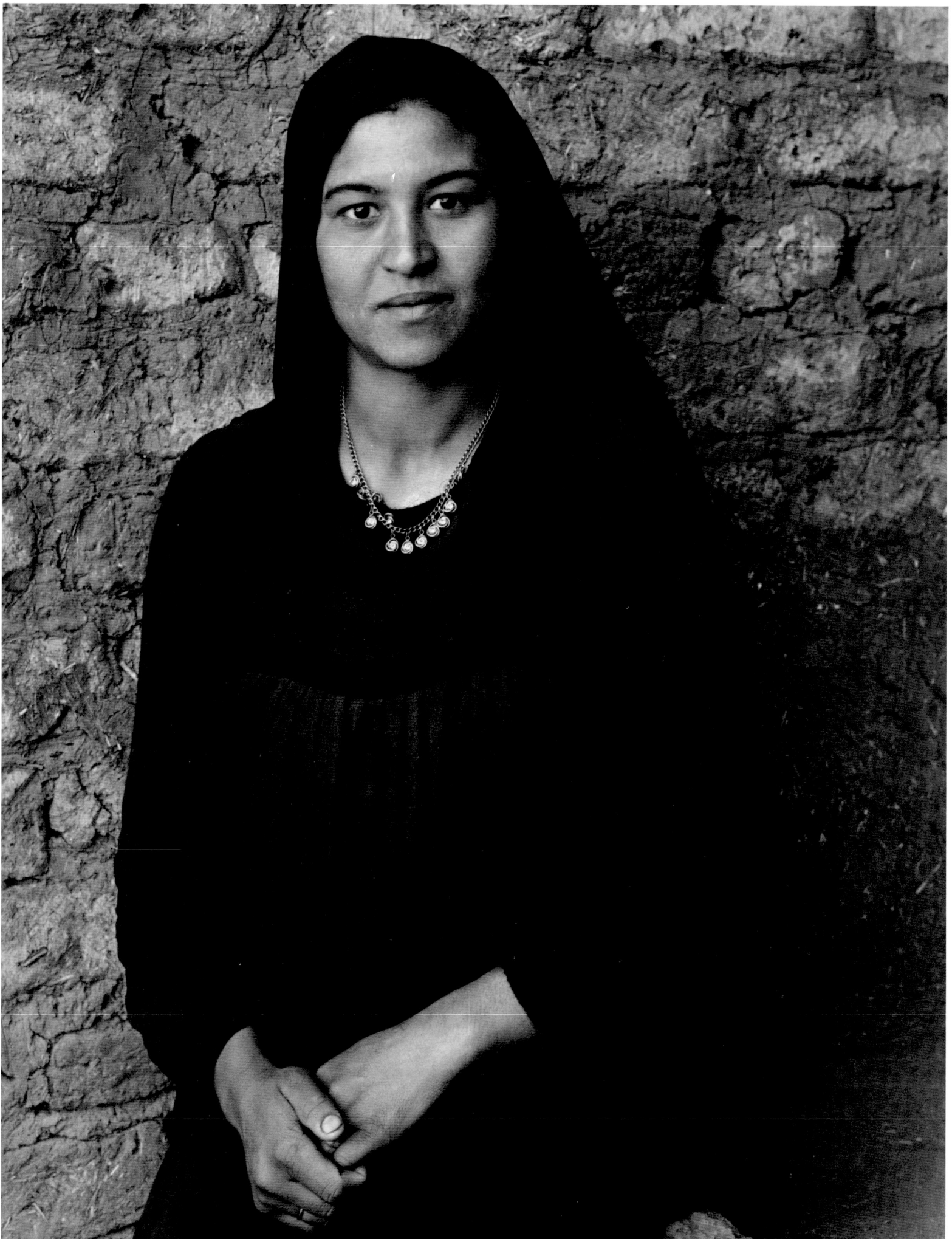

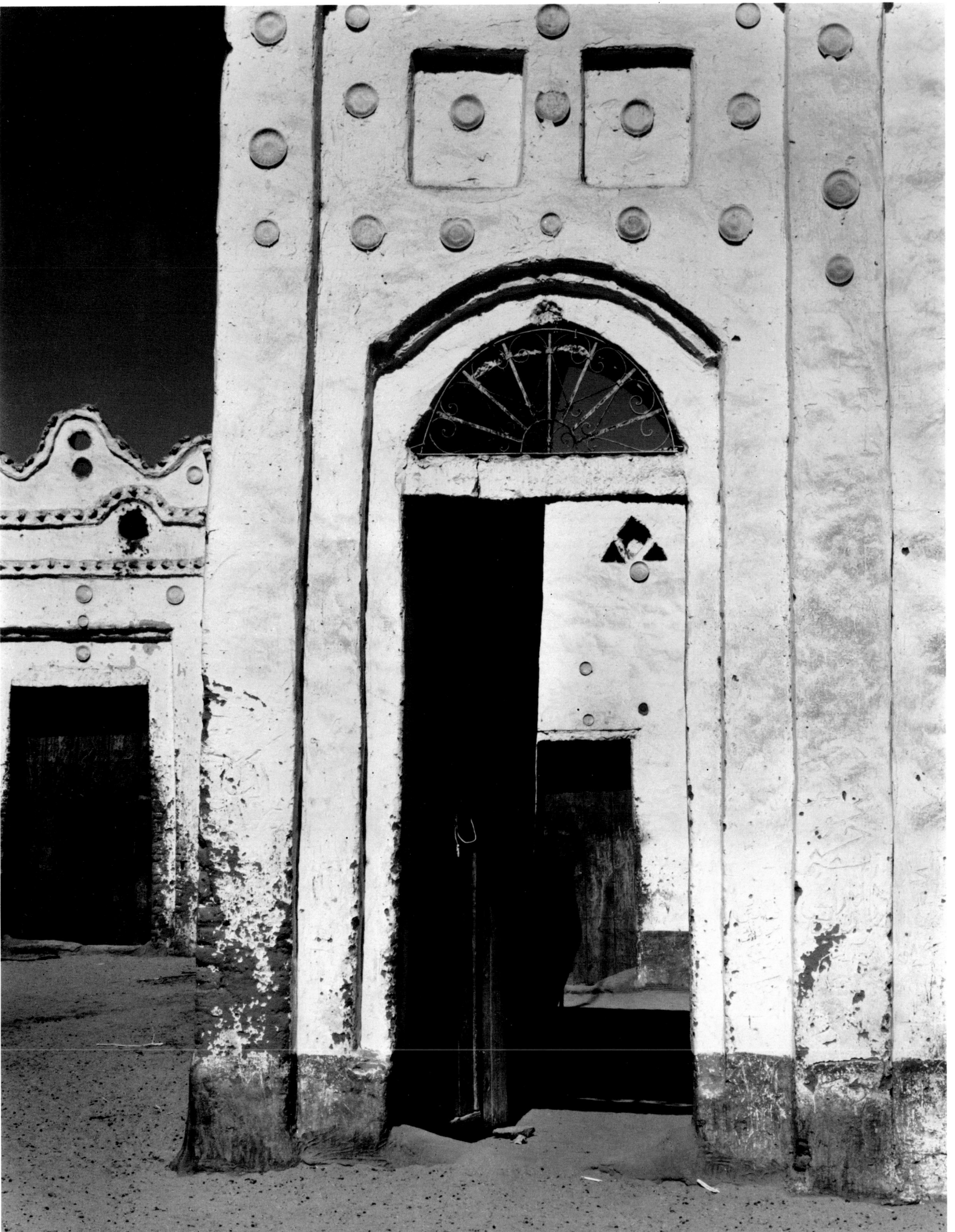

# MOROCCO

Wherever the painter, writer, or photographer may be working, he has, I think, a great responsibility for truthfulness. But if the place and the material chosen is a country which is not his own, that responsibility is heavier. Here he is relatively a stranger. He must come to know, to see, and to understand what he sees with a great deal of humility and respect. Otherwise what he does cannot be much more than an impertinence. In the past, European artists have come to America and tried to express the quality of life there before they really knew what it was all about. One may learn from such mistakes....

To know a land somewhat, its special character, the qualities which make its individuality, the temperament and life of its people is a process of gradual absorption, of sympathetic perception....

What happens, I think, is that the cultural treasures of the past lead one into the country itself, to the country and people who at one time or another produced them.... I arrive finally at the smaller, the less known, but I think not less expressive, aspects of life, in the landscape, the detail of a window, above all in the people themselves. It is my hope to find there what is explicit and implicit...that essential character which is compounded of both past and present. To find that, may be to arrive at the common denominator which makes us all kin.

Paul Strand in *U.S. Camera*, 1955

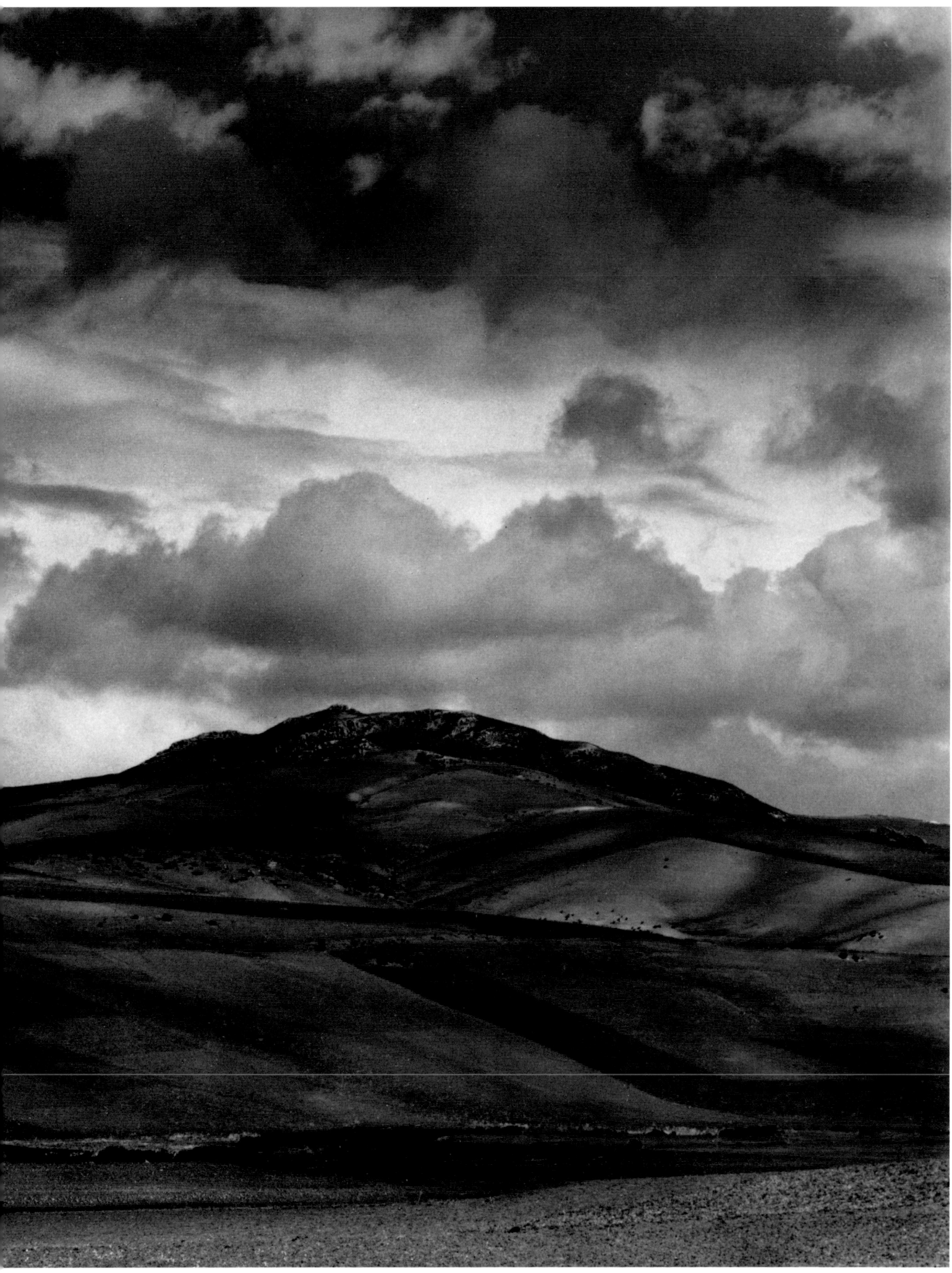

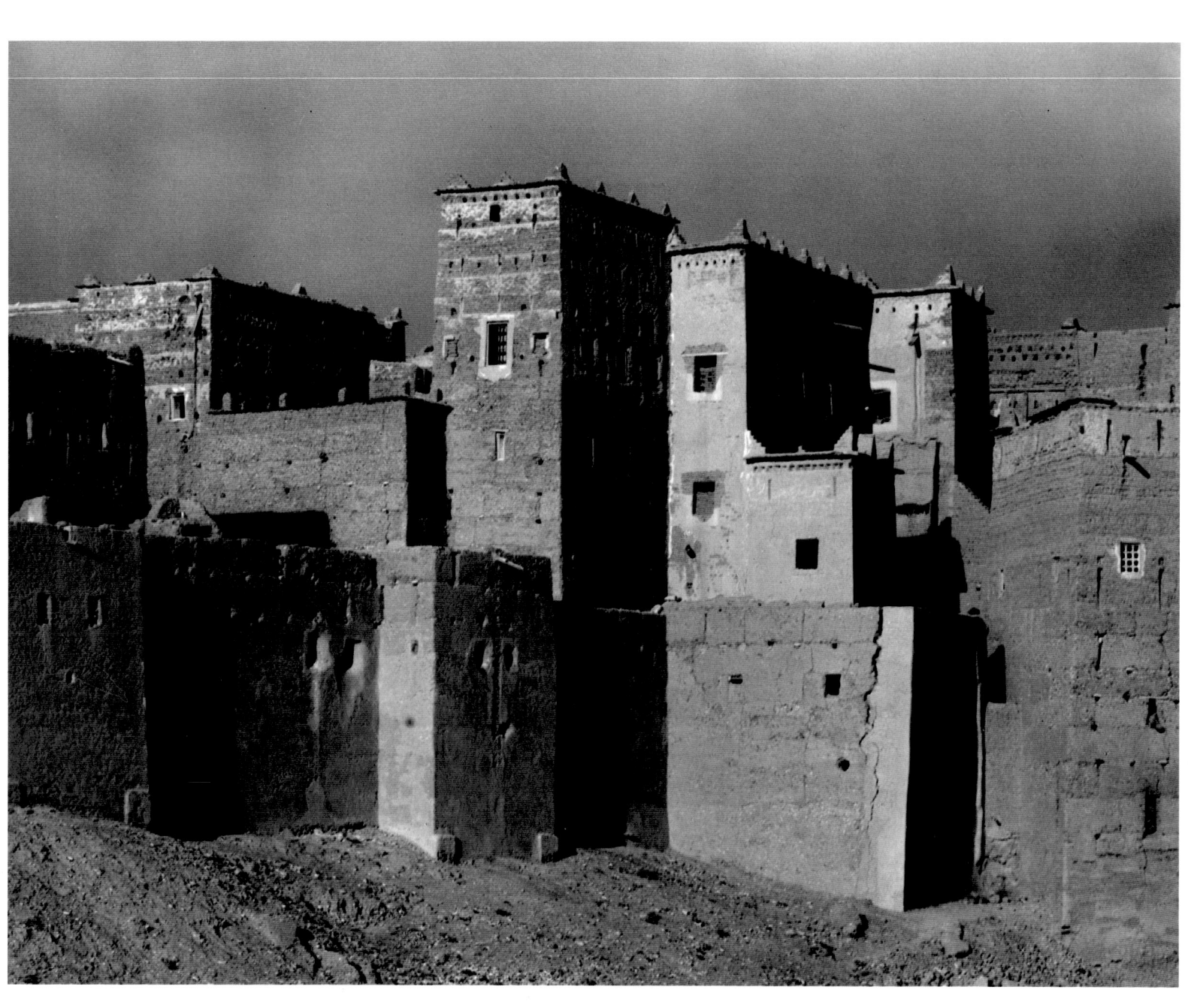

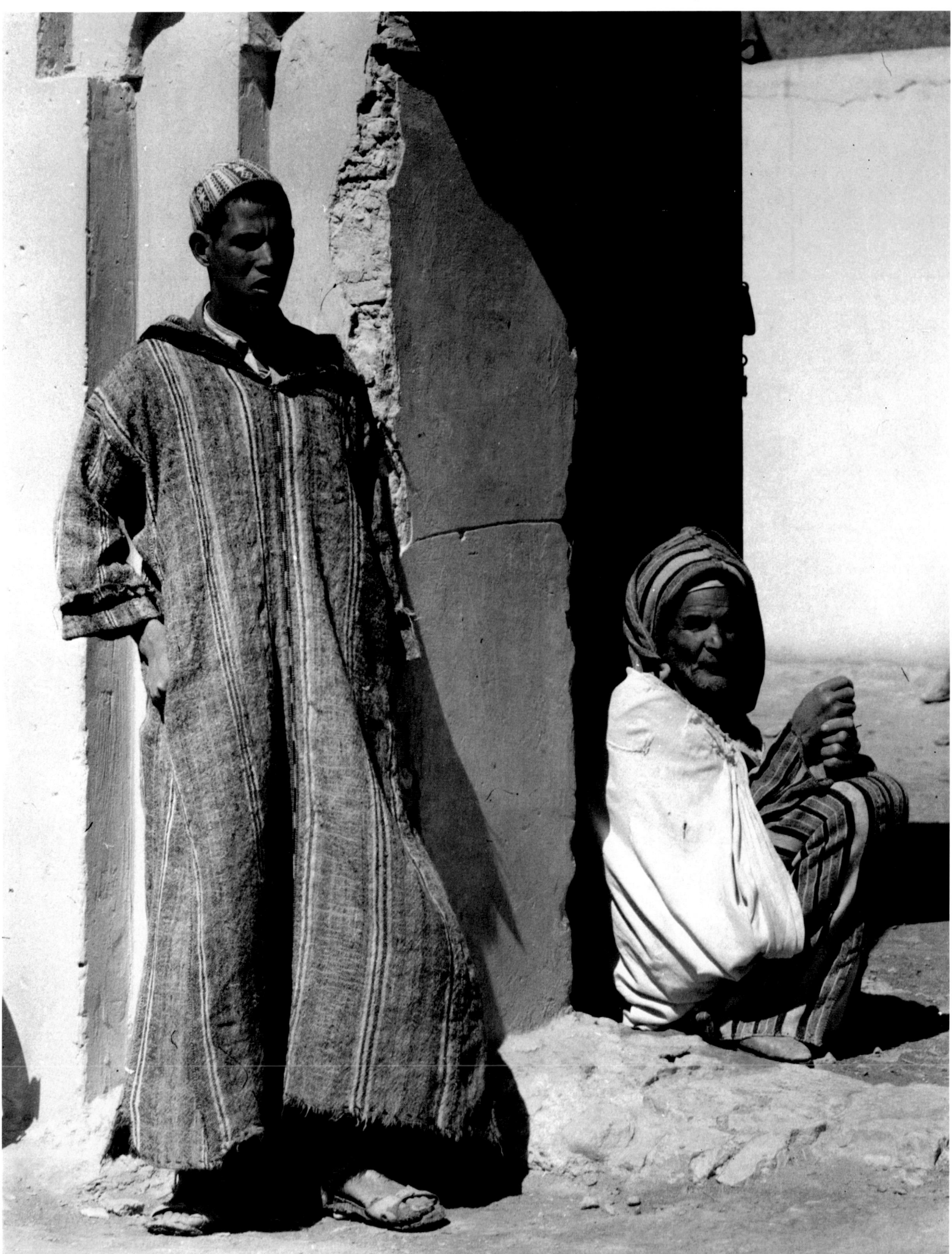

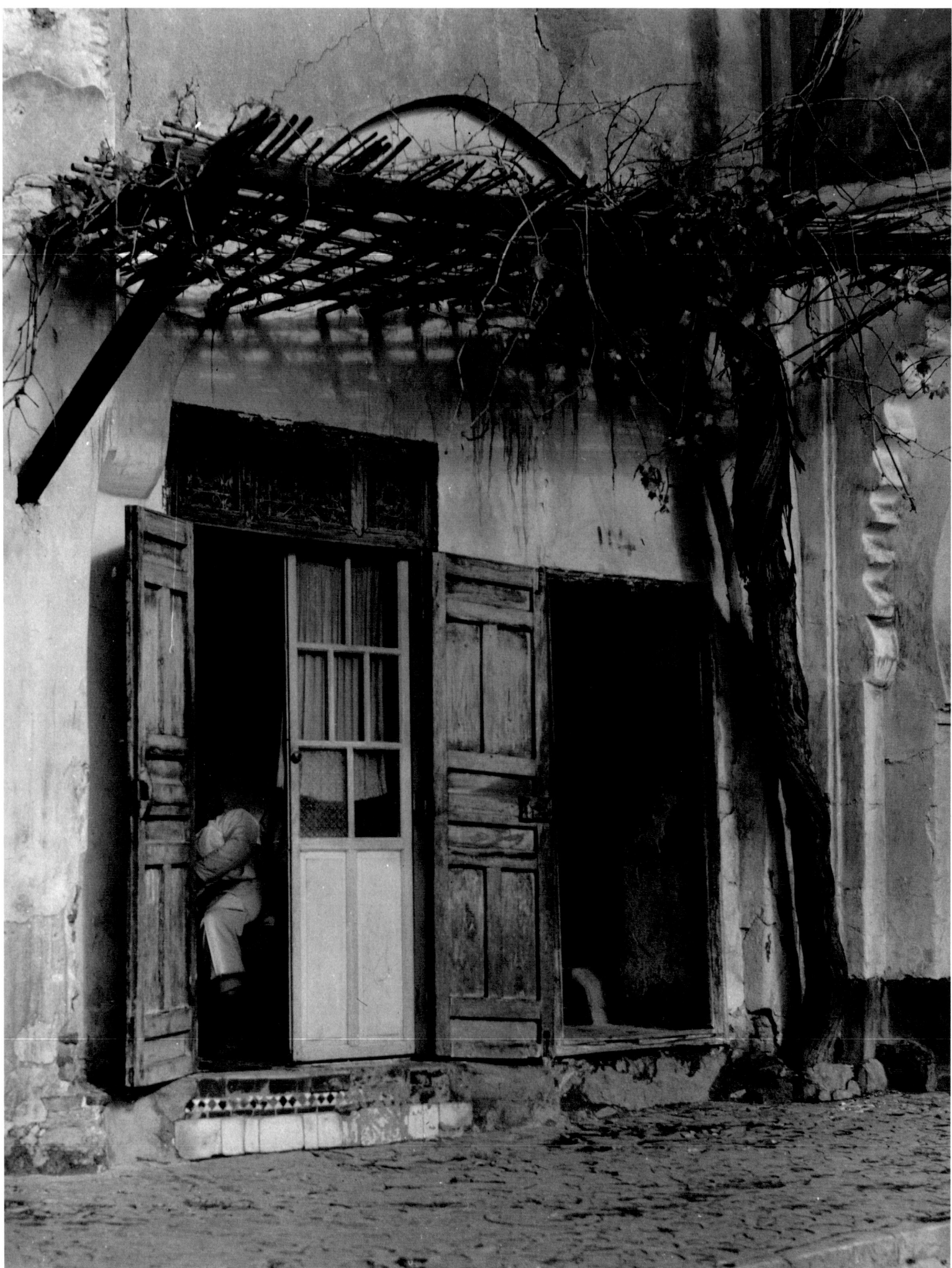

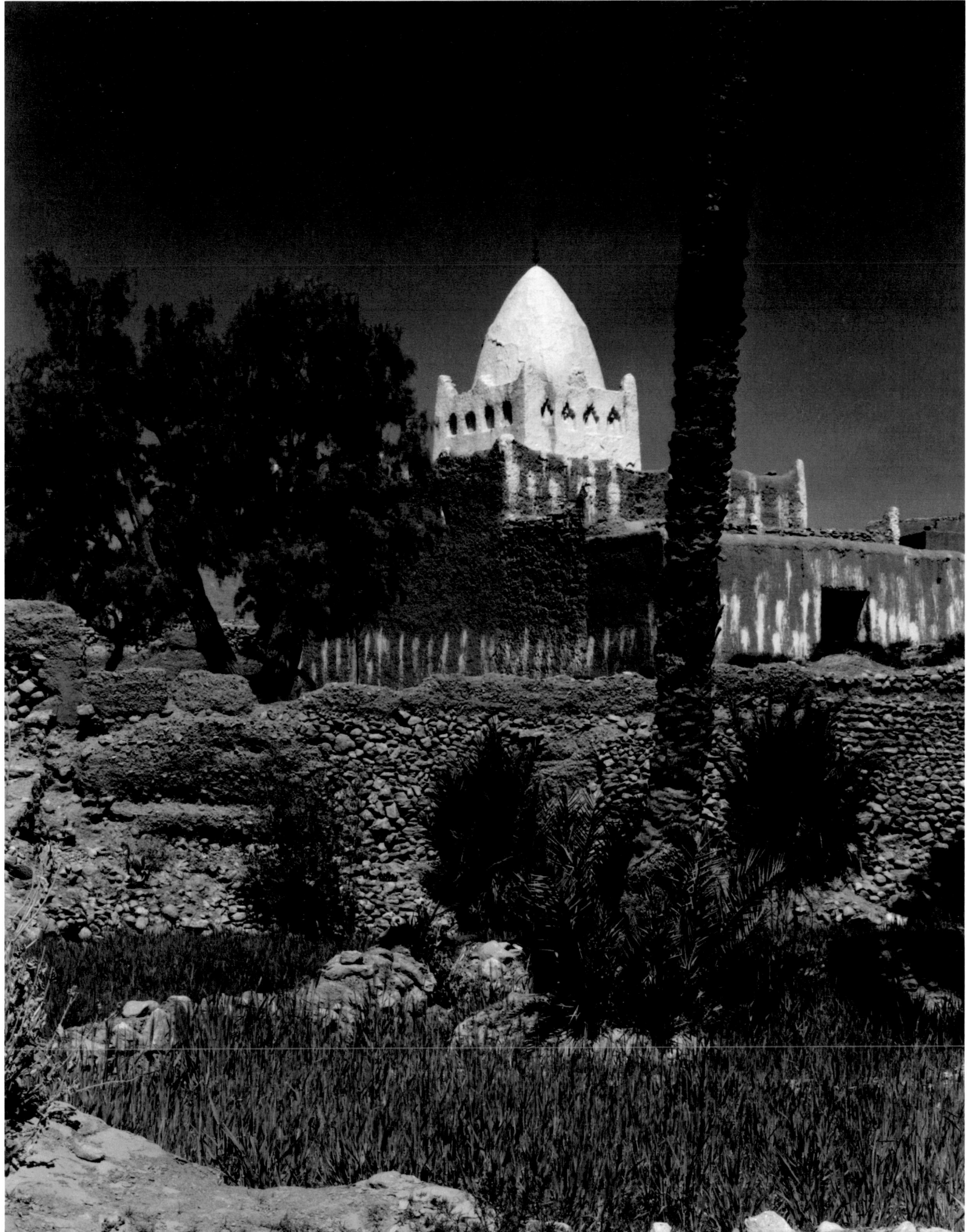

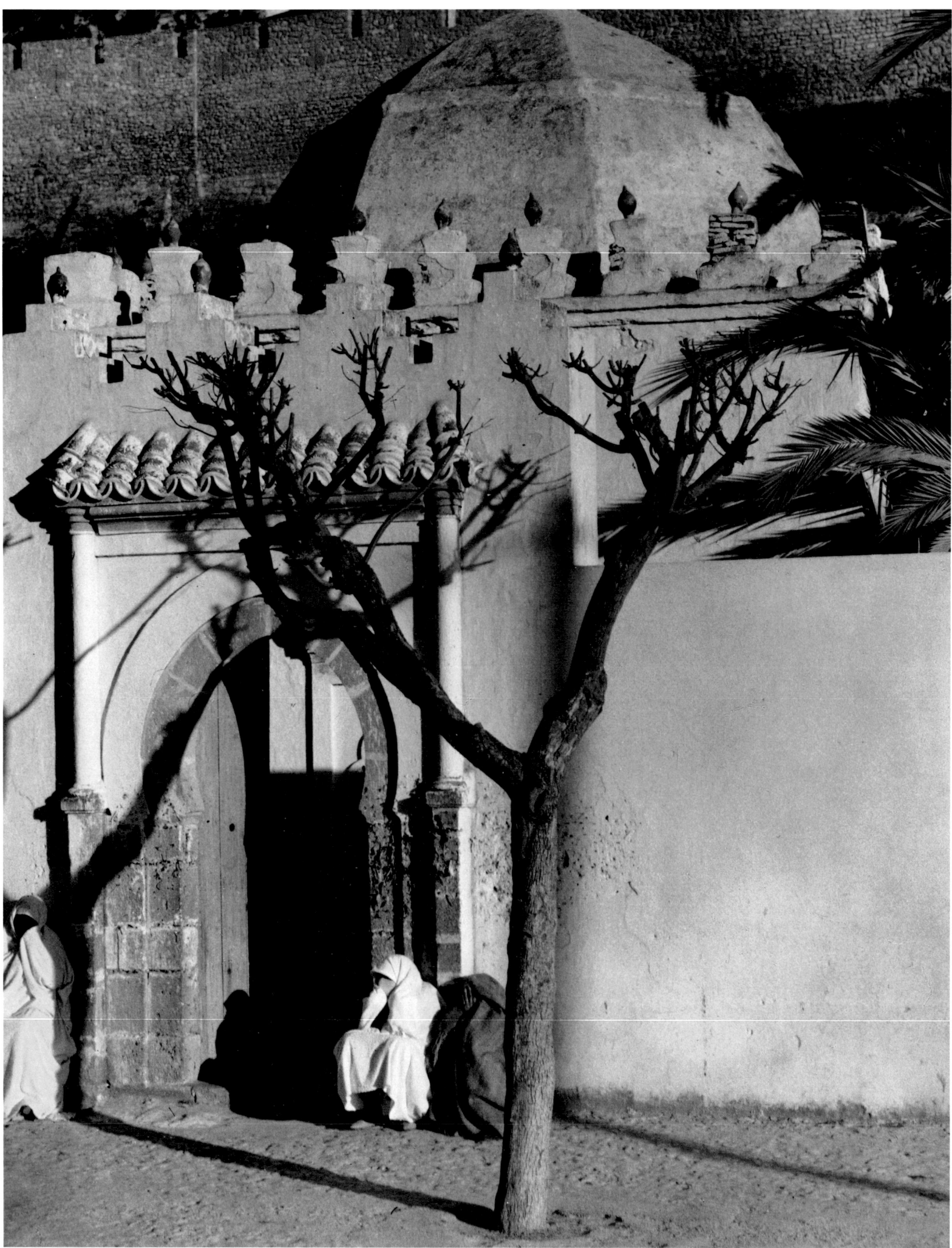

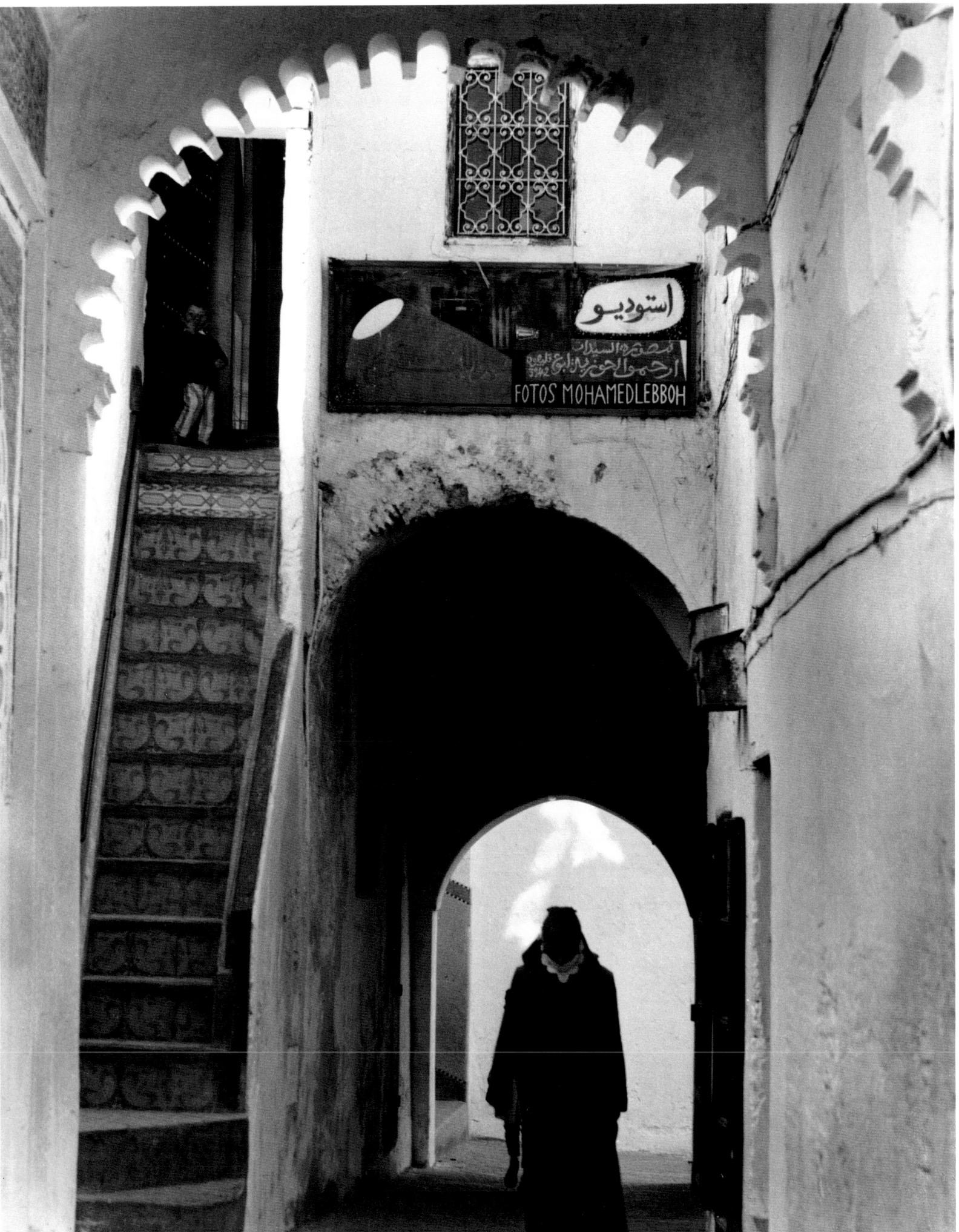

# GHANA

Some time ago, Paul Strand began to think about making a portrait of Africa and its people. Other peoples had already known his penetrating candor and received his stern, affectionate gaze—among them the Mexicans and New Englanders, and in Europe the Italians, the French and the islanders of Scotland's Celtic fringe. He had also worked in Egypt and Morocco.

Now he wanted to go beyond the Sahara and find, if possible, a group of subjects that would enable him to explore and celebrate the peoples who live there in great diversity but also within an underlying unity of culture. This would be a portrait of a specific group, yet a portrait whose specificity might characterize the sub-Saharan world as a whole.

But could it be done? In setting himself this problem, Strand was being true to his lifelong humanism. He has remained among those who believe that what unites people is always more than what divides them, even if many fail to understand this, and that a future Africa, for example, will think it as reasonable and useful to recognize its own organic unity as that of any other major but united portion of the globe.

From the Introduction to *Ghana: An African Portrait*,
by Basil Davidson

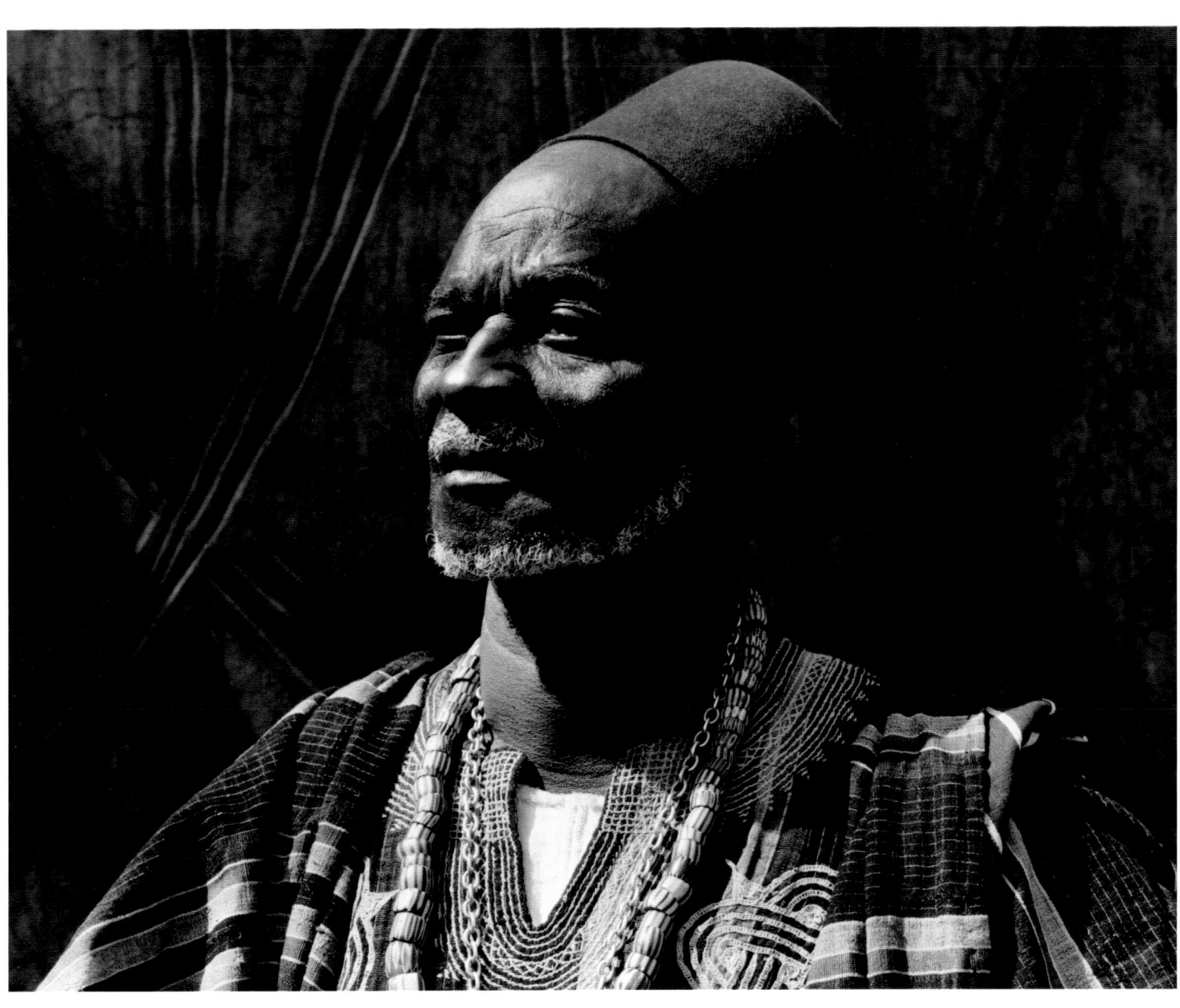

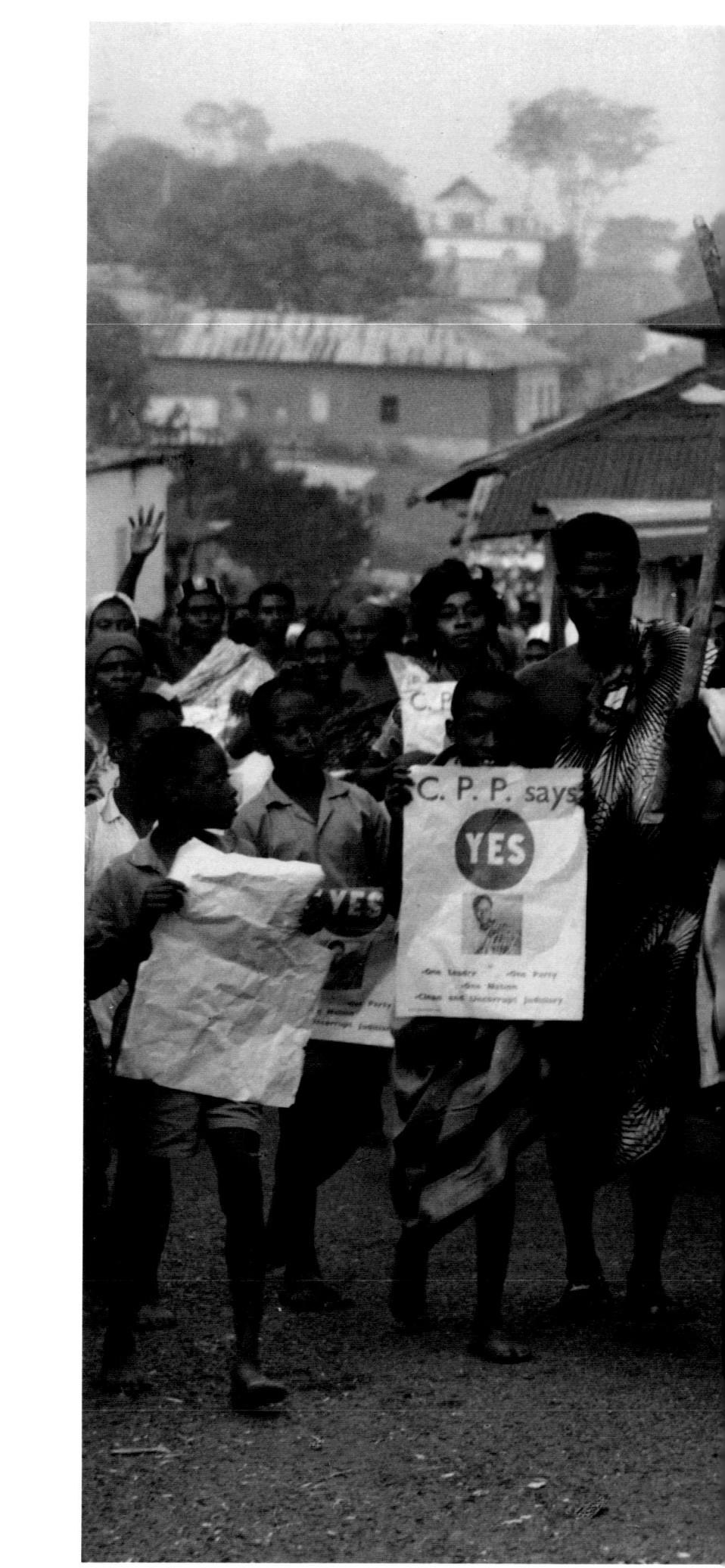

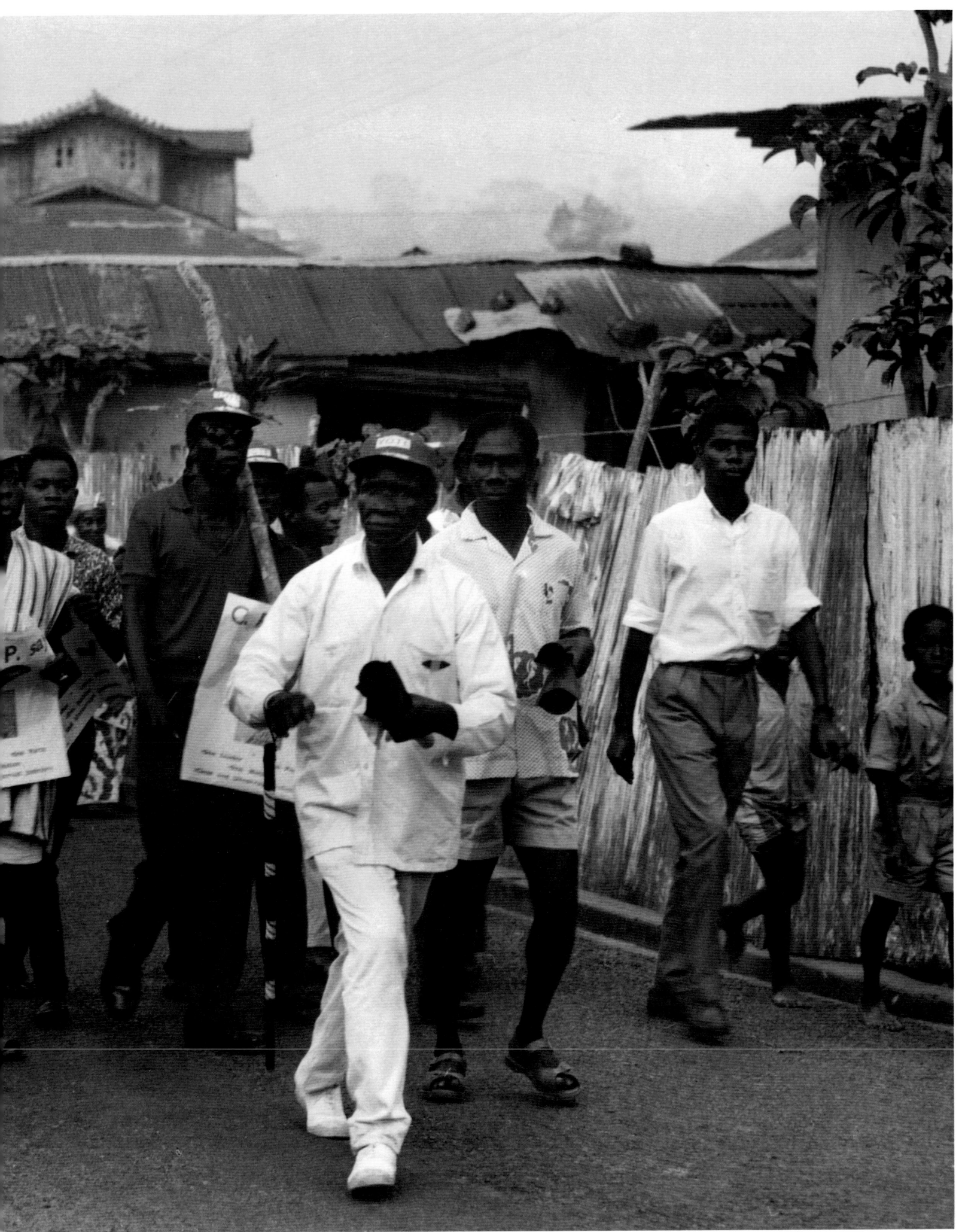

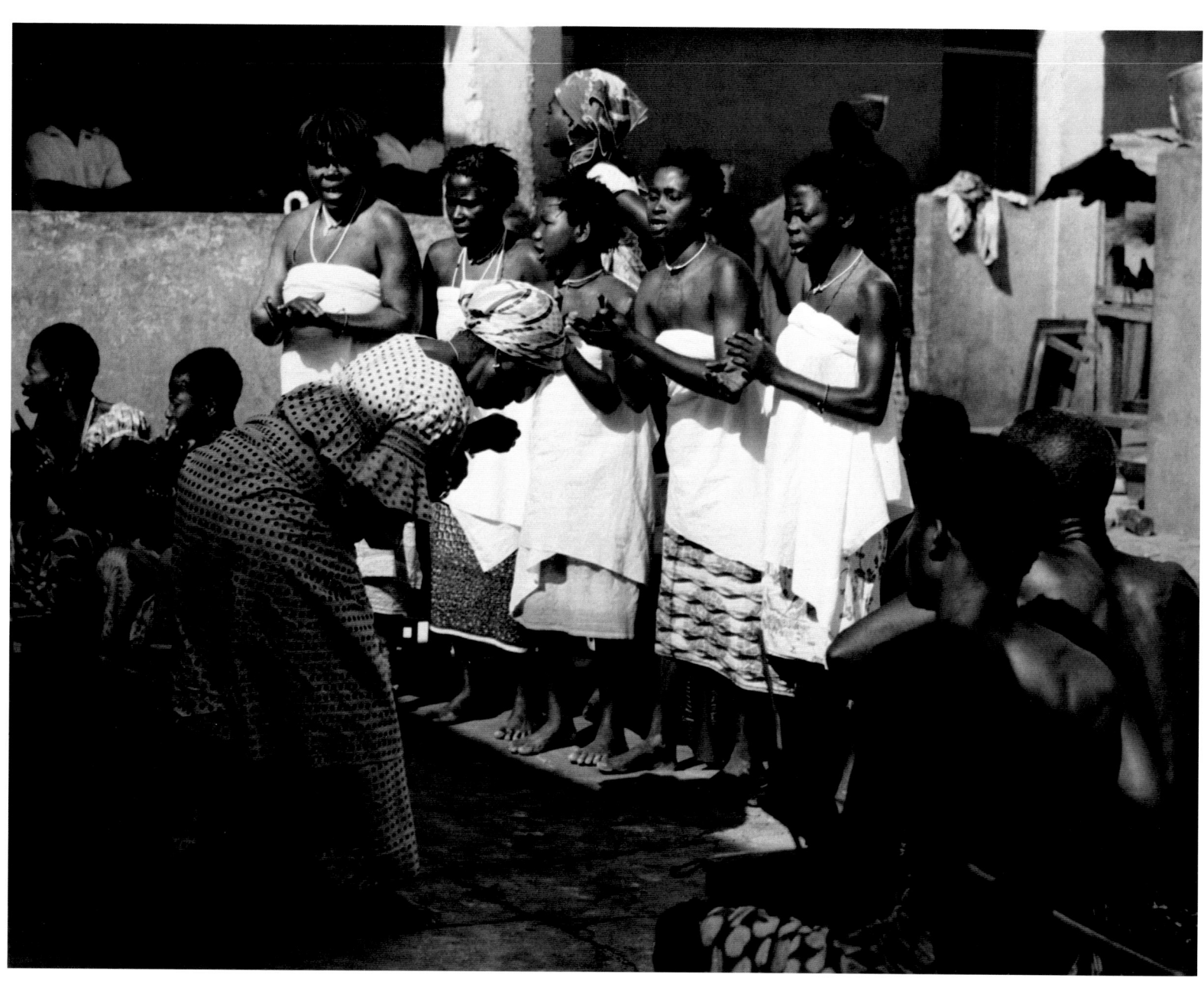

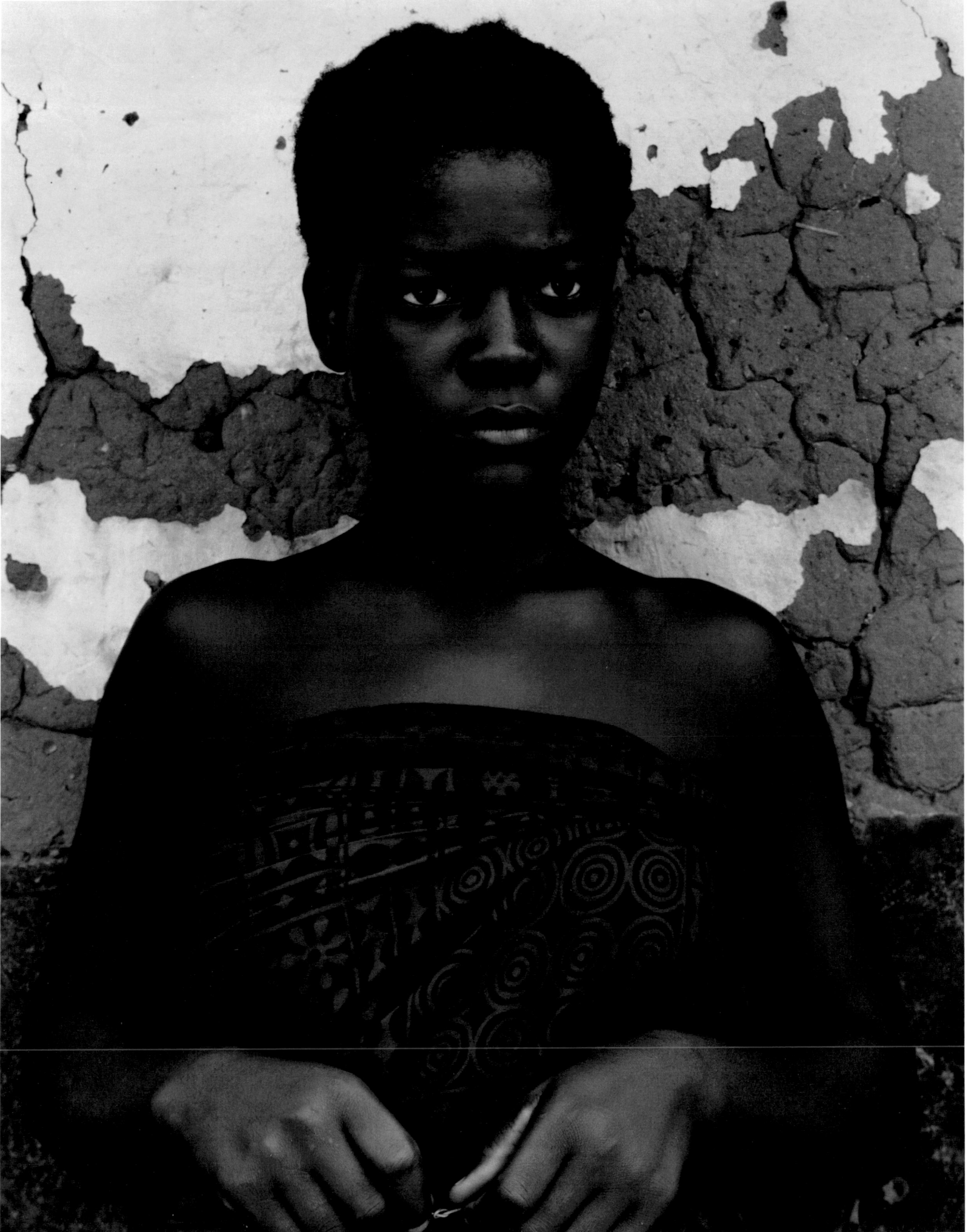

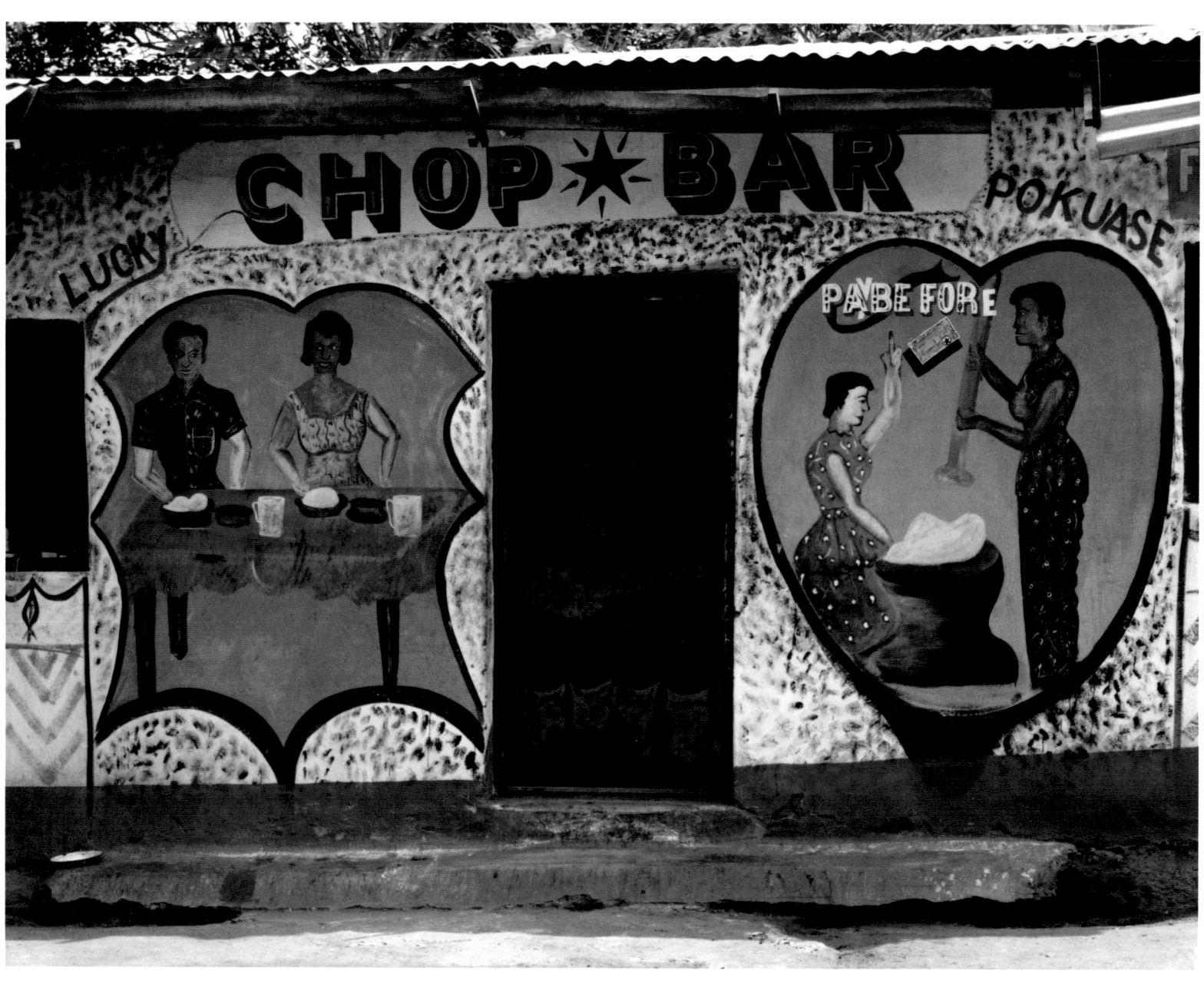

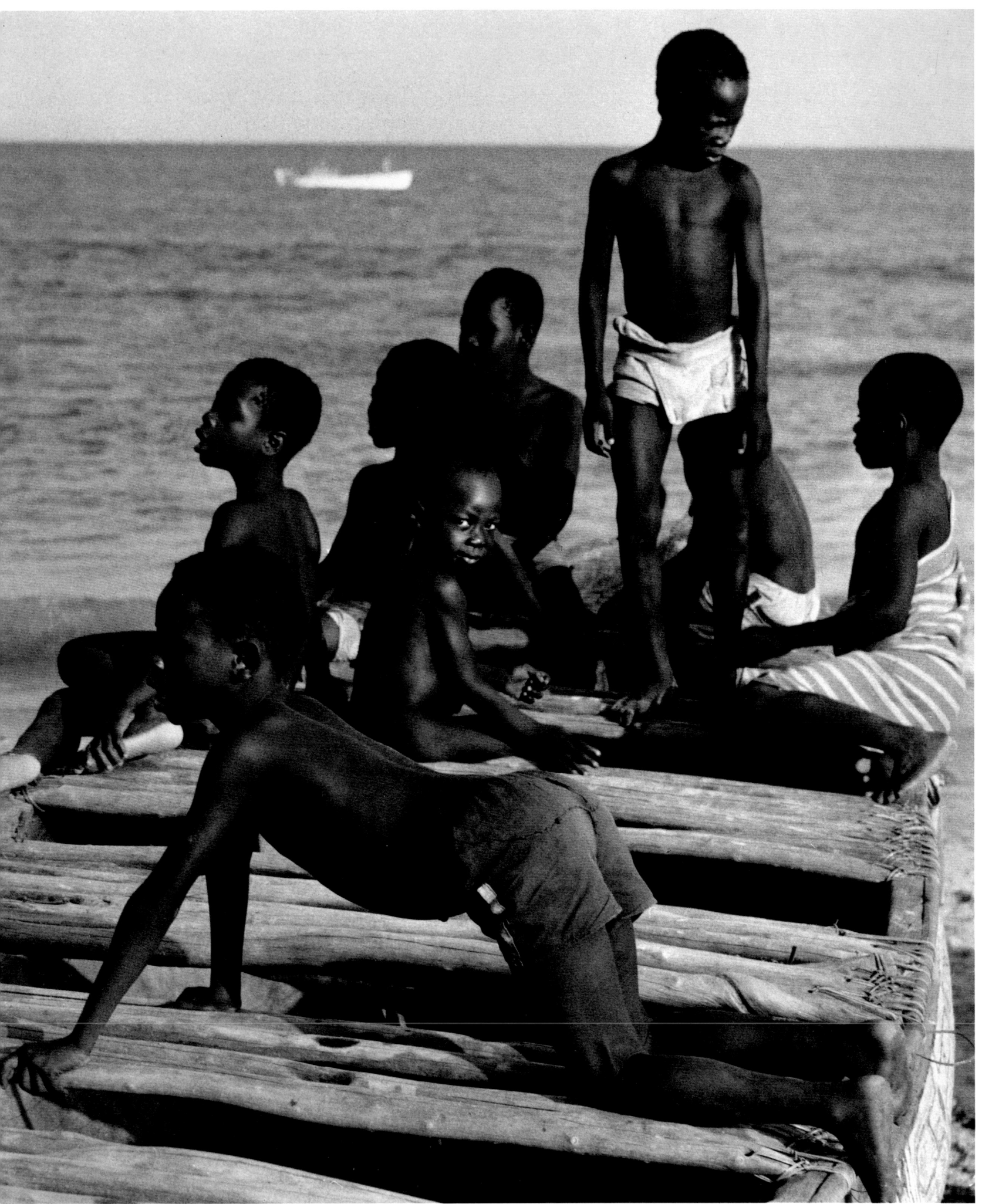

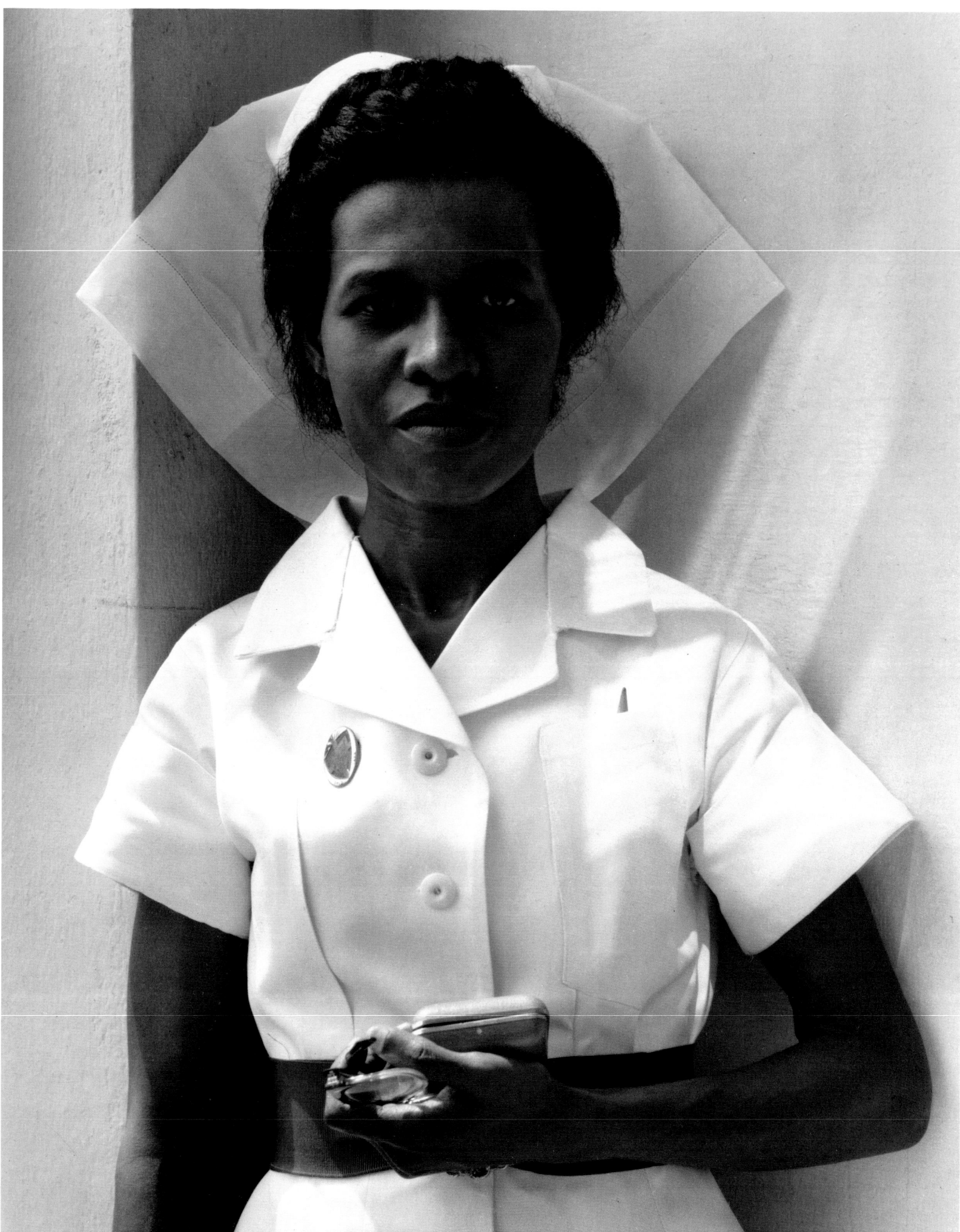

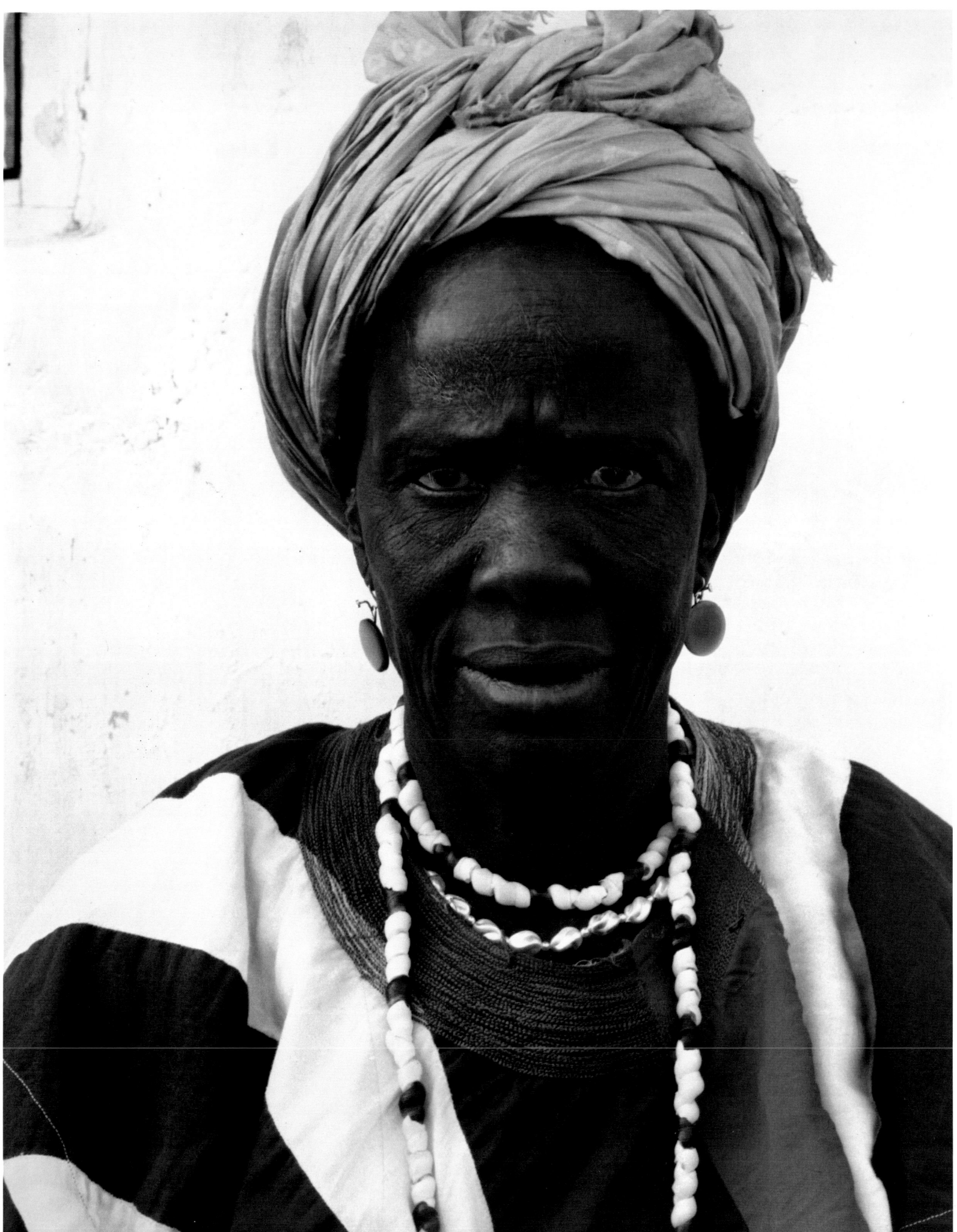

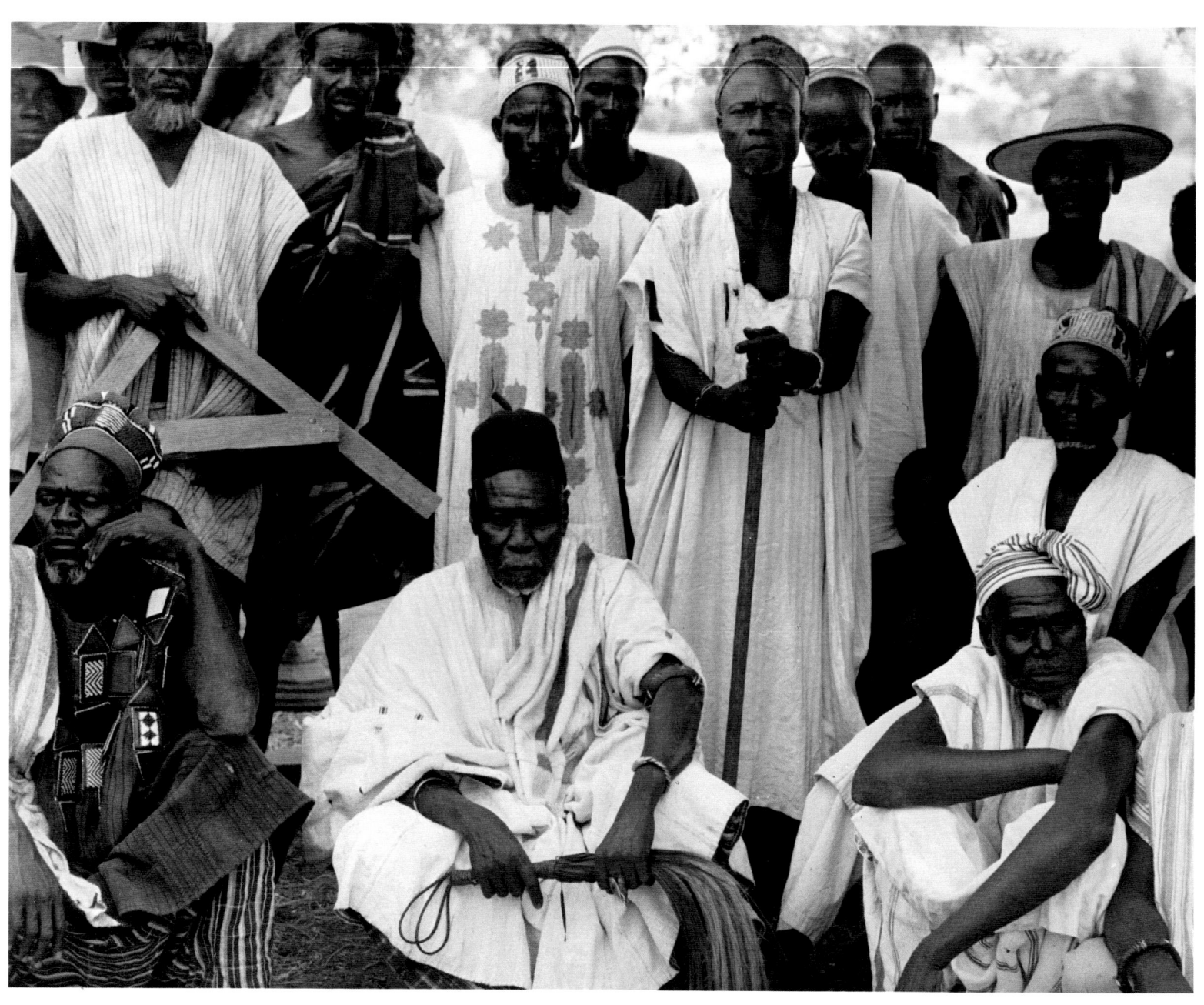

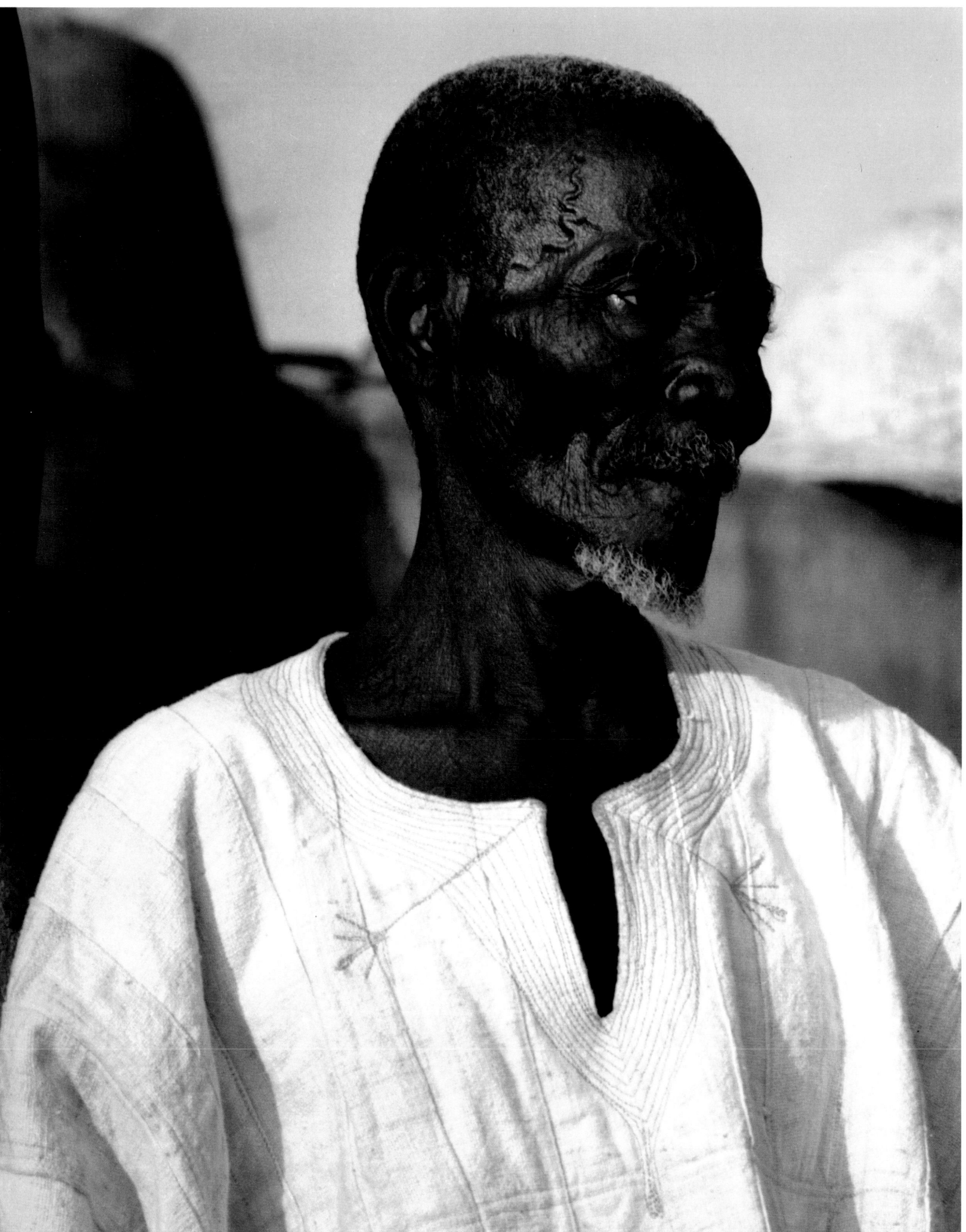

# ROMANIA

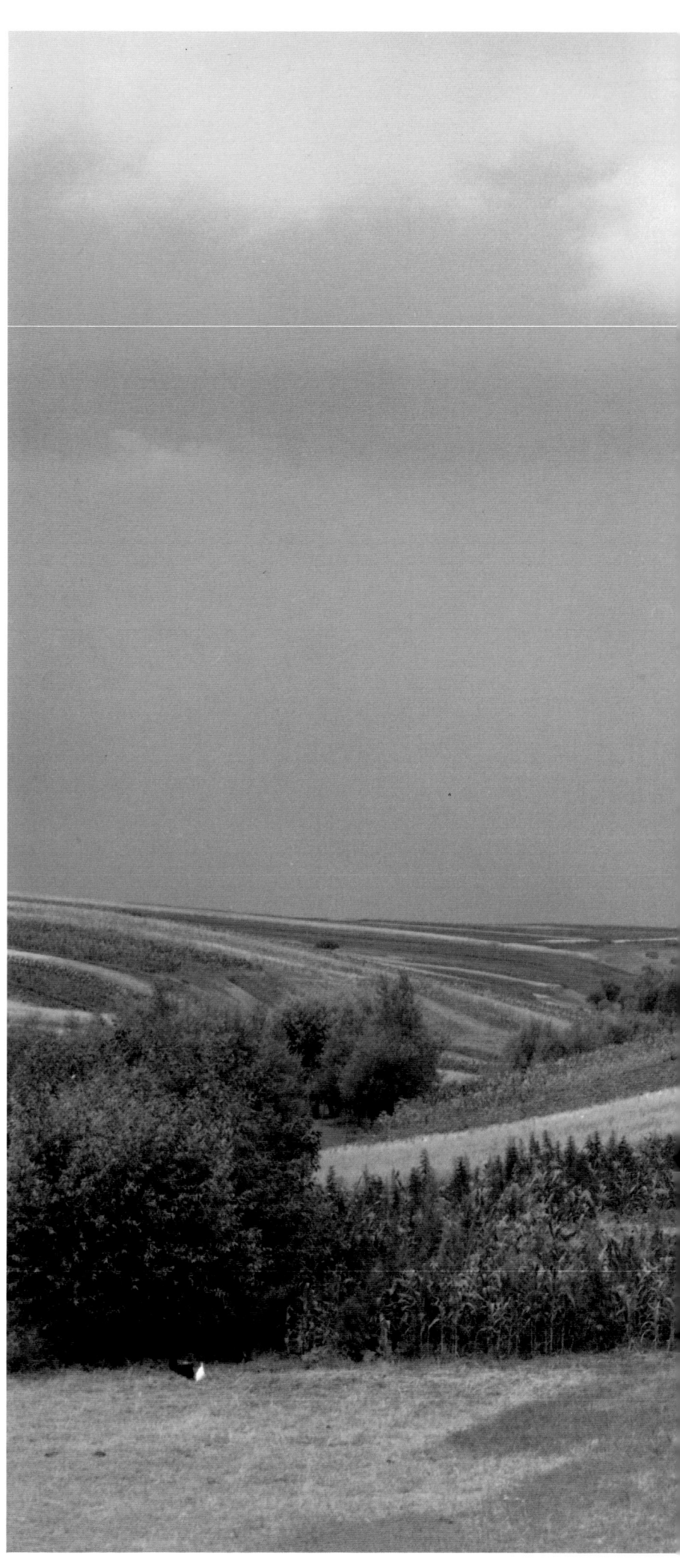

**I**t was a fine experience. For many years I wanted to expand the early work with machinery to large machines; I made up my mind that I wanted to photograph as much industry as possible....

I made a list of all the places I wanted to go... a petrochemical plant, a steel mill, a ship building site, a glass factory. I did a lot of things in Romania that I was *never* able to do anywhere else. There may never be a book [of the photographs], but I was able to work out these problems which had concerned me from the beginning....

I found all the things I discovered early in life useful, either as method or idea. I never discarded them; they always were valuable to me.

From "Completing the Circle,"
an interview with Paul Strand
by Naomi Rosenblum

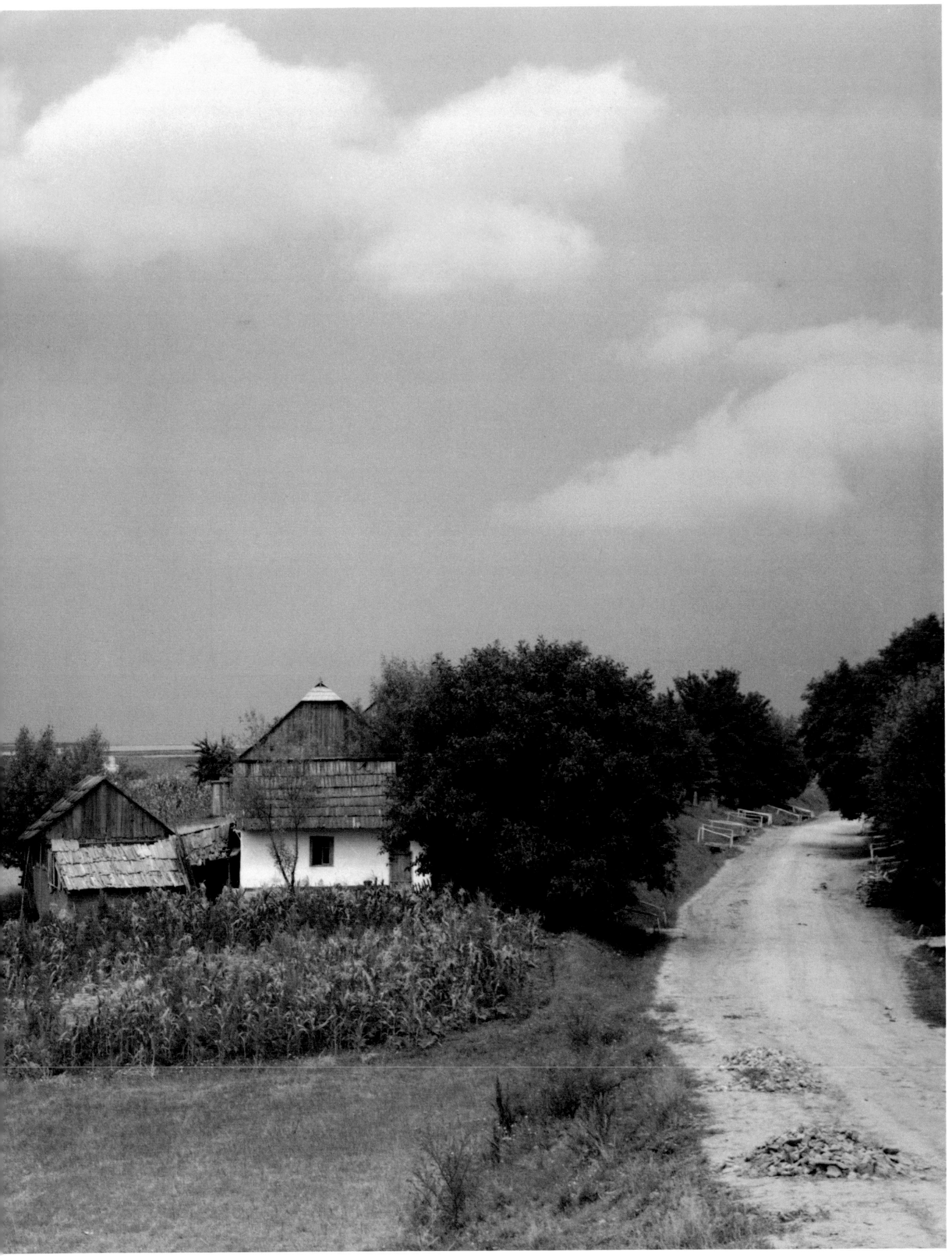

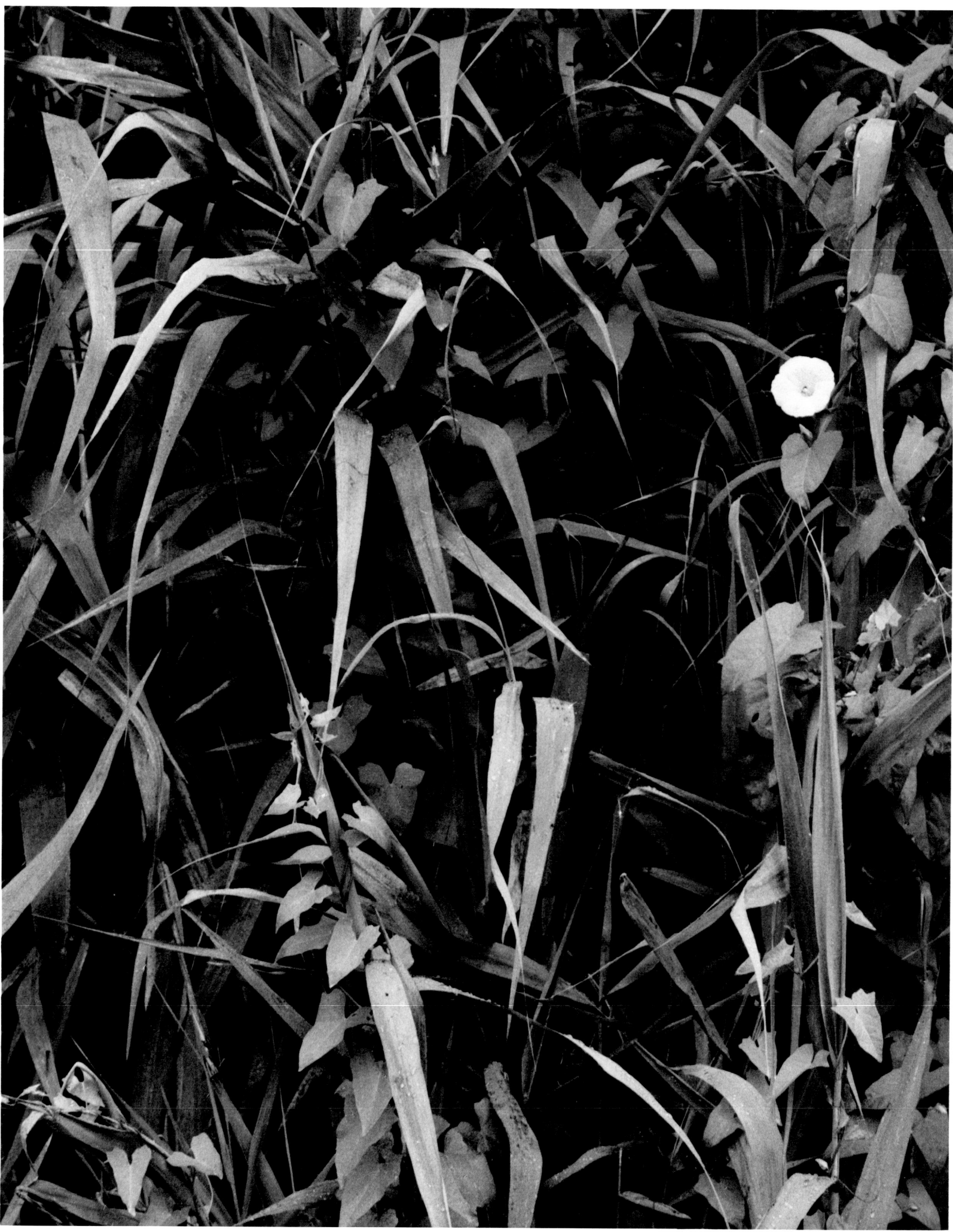

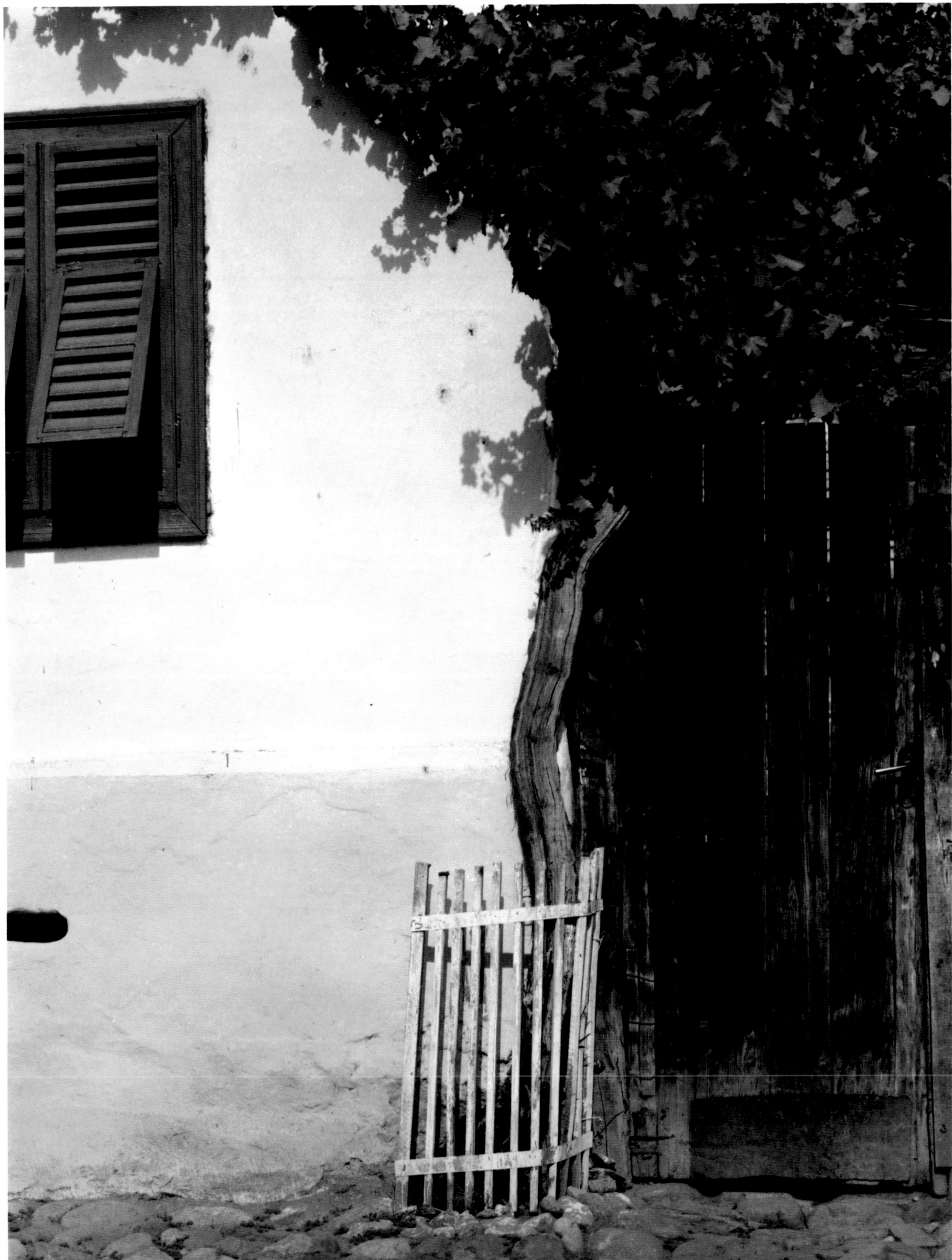

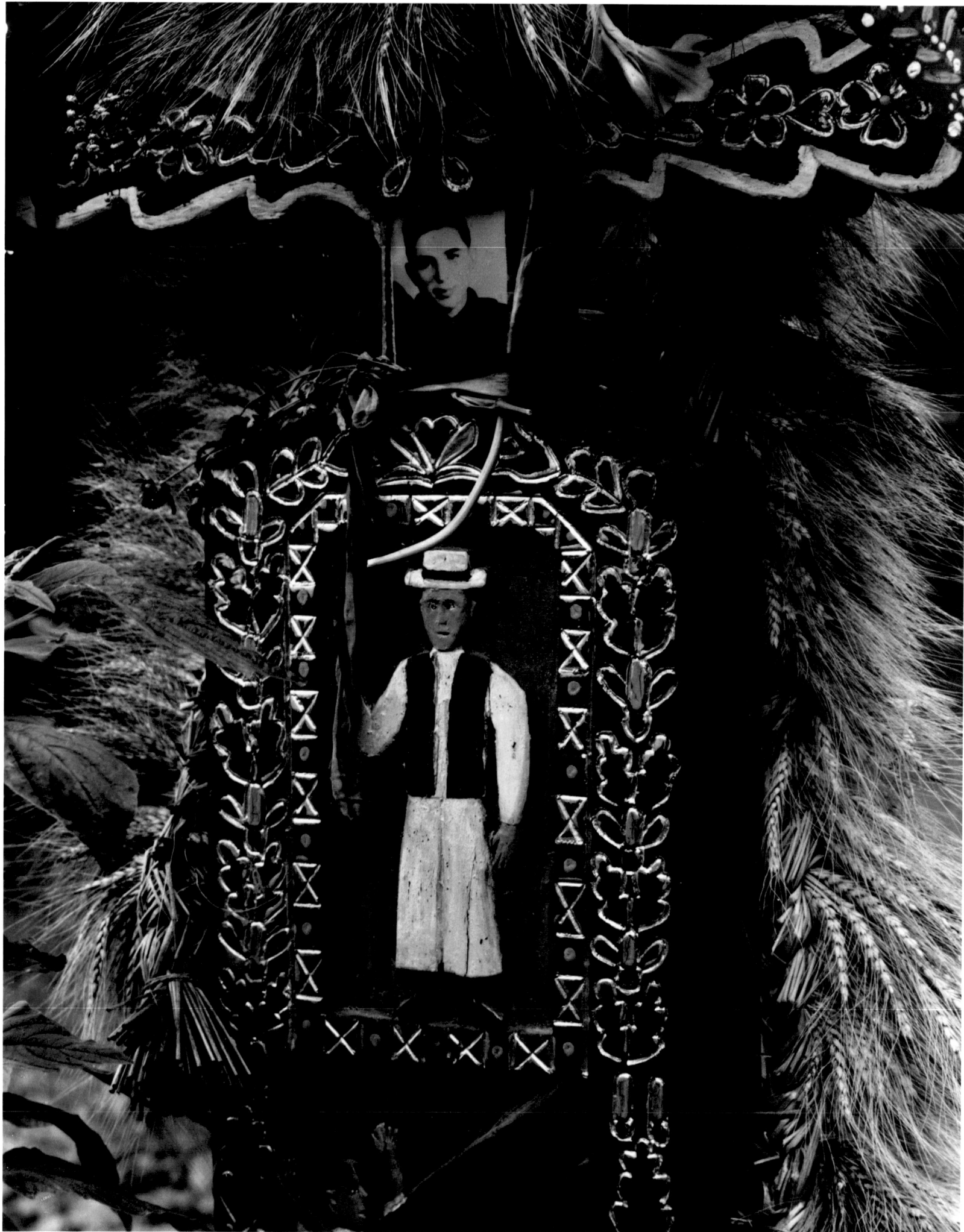

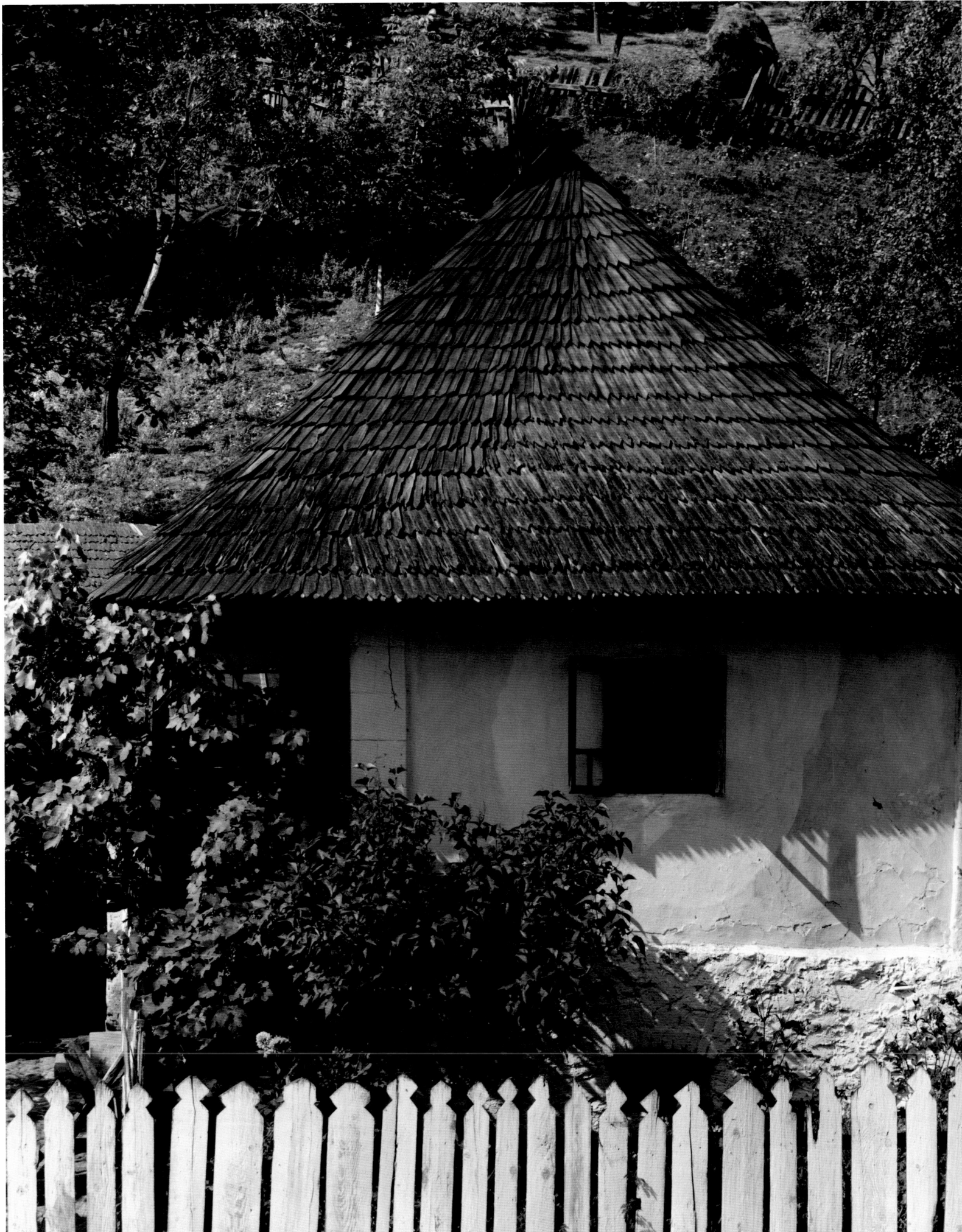

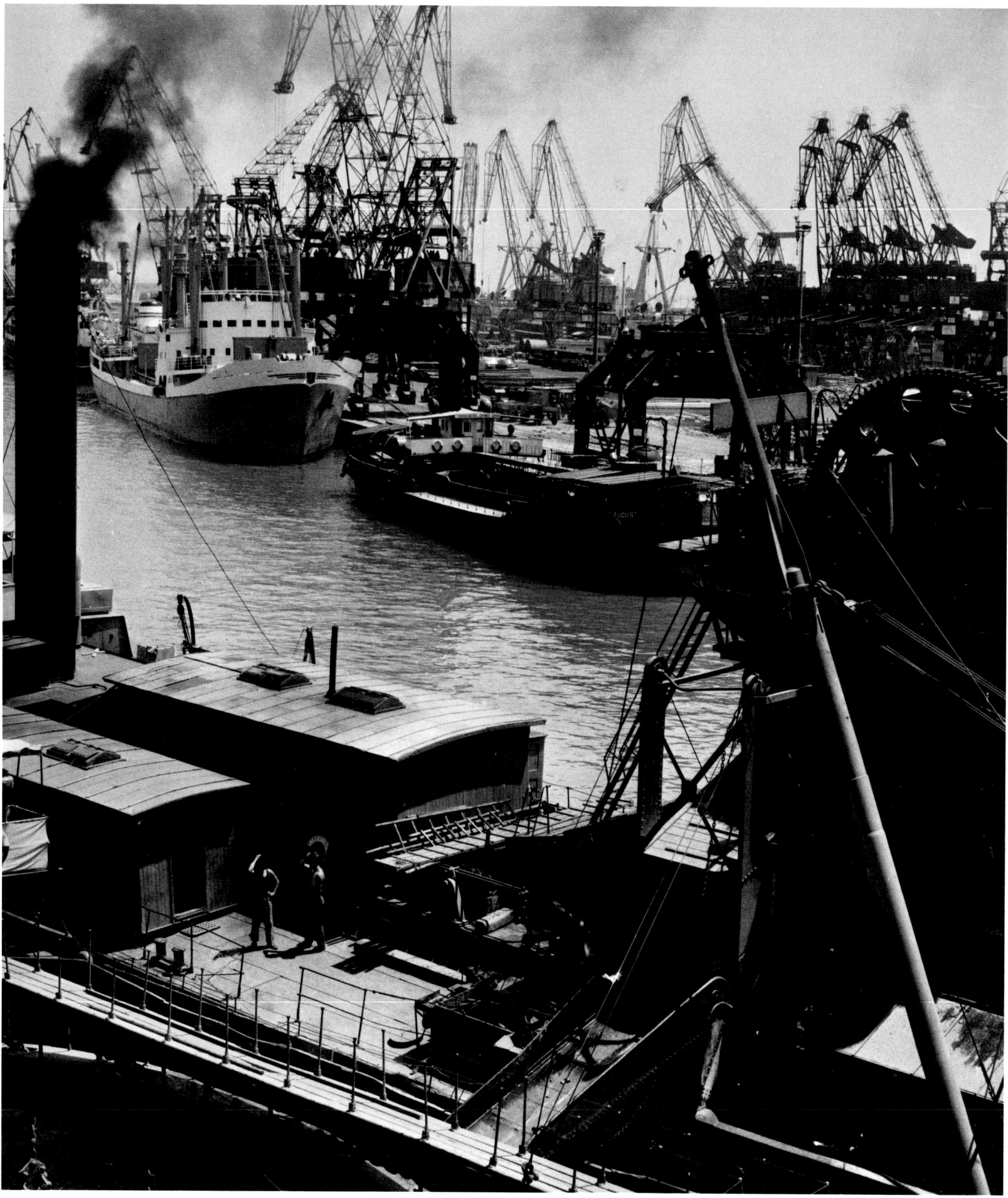

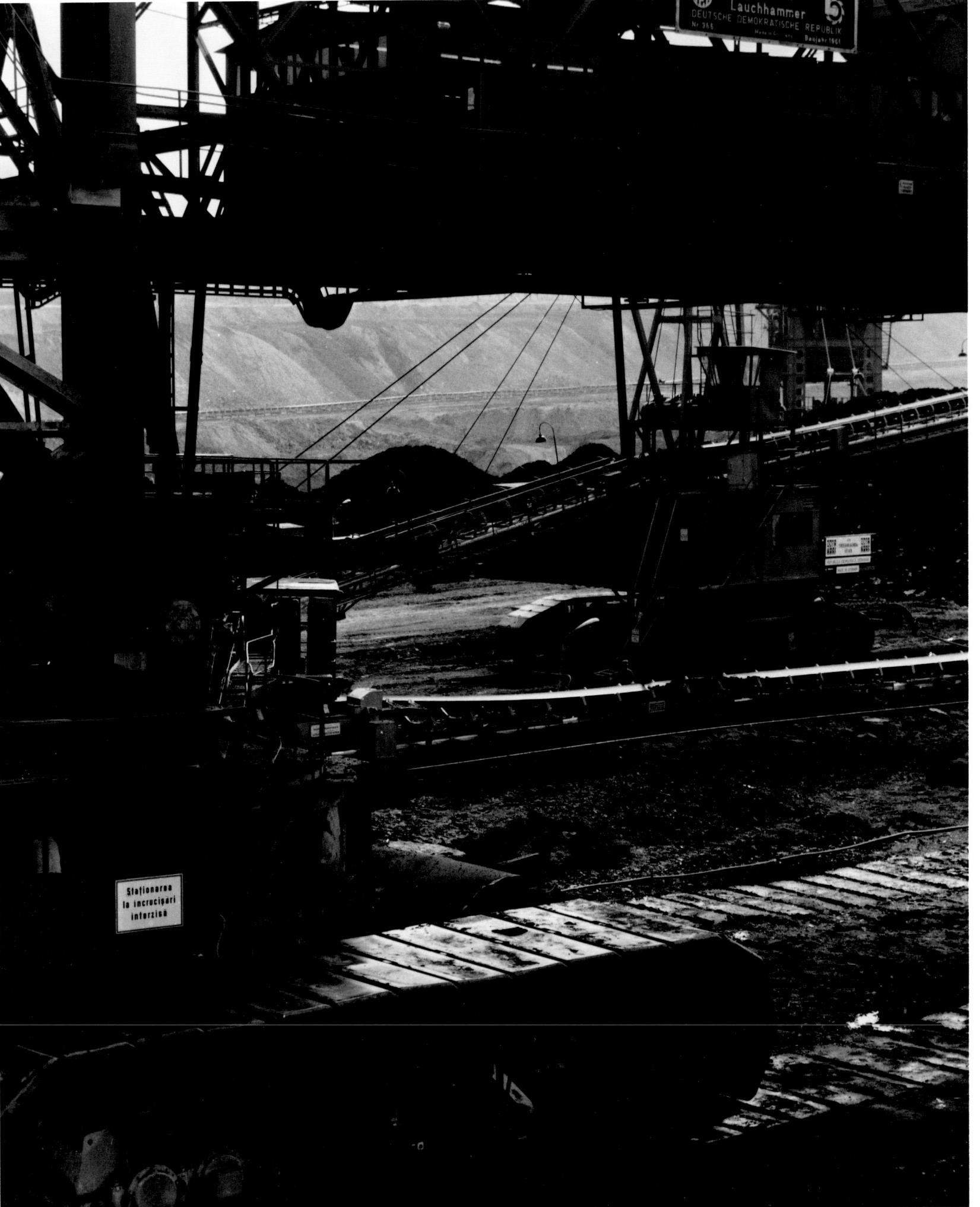

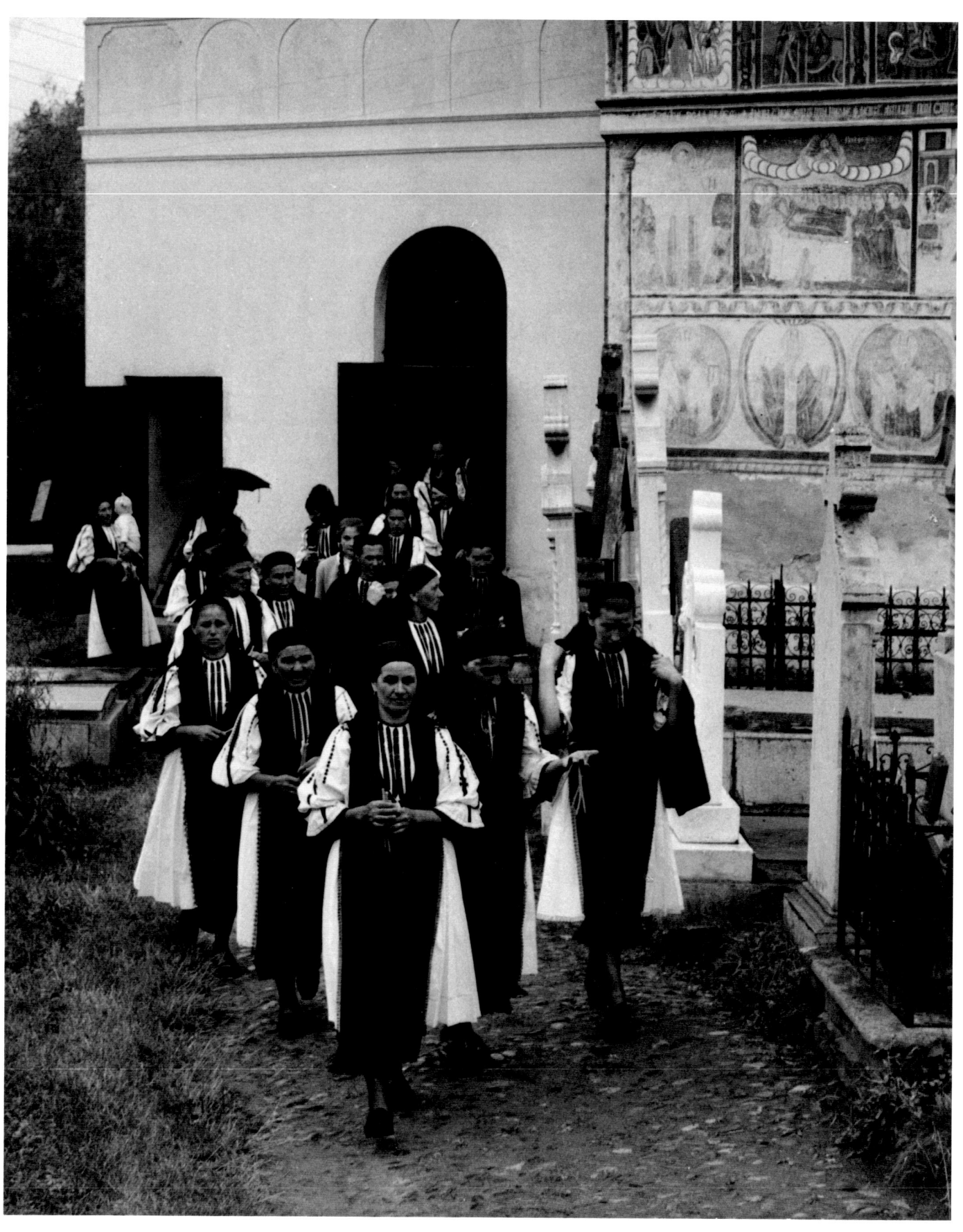

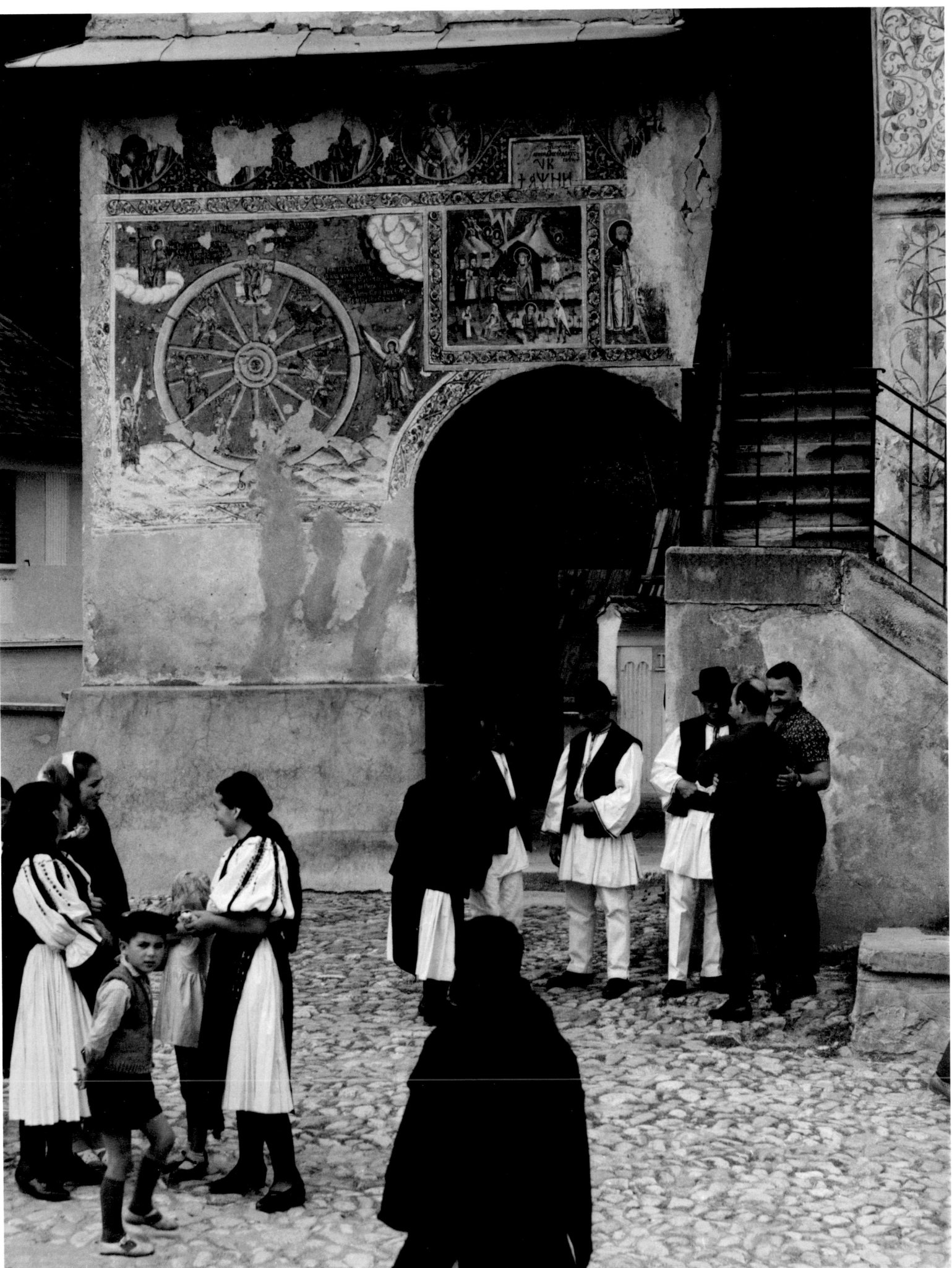

# CAPTIONS

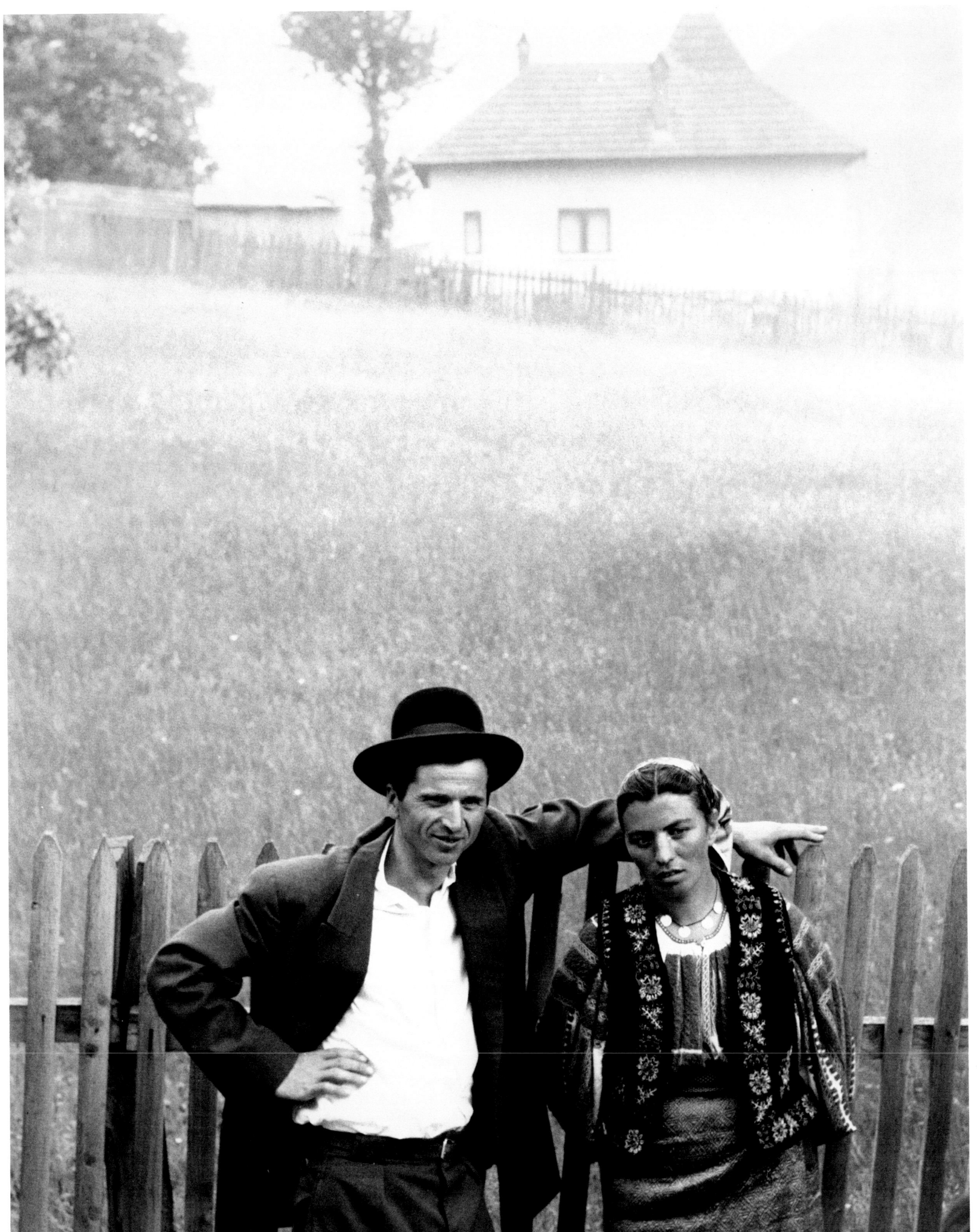

# CHRONOLOGY

**1890** Born October 16, in New York City, of Bohemian descent.

**1907** At the Ethical Culture School, studied under Lewis Hine, who took his class to Alfred Stieglitz's Little Galleries of the Photo-Secession at 291 Fifth Avenue.

**1909** Graduated from Ethical Culture School. Continued photographing in spare time and joined the New York Camera Club.

**1909–11** Worked in family enamelware business. Brief journey to Europe. First published photograph.

**1911–18** Set up as a commercial photographer. Experimented with soft-focus lenses, gum prints, and enlarged negatives.

**1913–14** Occasional visits to "291" to see exhibitions and to show photographs to Stieglitz for criticism. Influenced by Picasso, Braque, Brancusi, and others seen at "291" and the Armory Show.

**1915** Brought folio of new works to "291" to show Stieglitz.

**1916** First publication in *Camera Work*, no. 48. Close working relationship with Stieglitz. First one-person show at "291," March 13–28.

**1917** Last issue of *Camera Work*, nos. 49-50, devoted to Strand's new works. Began close-ups of machine forms.

**1918–19** Worked as an X-ray technician in the Army Medical Corps at Fort Snelling, Minnesota. Upon release from army began photographing landscapes and close-ups of rock formations.

**1920–21** Made film, *Manhatta*, with Charles Sheeler, which was later shown under title *New York the Magnificent*.

**1922** Began work as free-lance Akeley motion-picture camera specialist, continued as a free-lance movie cameraman until 1932. Made still photographs of machines. Married Rebecca Salsbury.

**1923** At invitation of Clarence White, delivered lecture at the Clarence H. White School of Photography in New York, subsequently printed in *British Journal of Photography*.

**1925** Part of "Seven Americans" exhibition at the Anderson Galleries, New York, March 9-28, with Charles Demuth, John Marin, Marsden Hartley, Georgia O'Keeffe, Alfred Stieglitz, and Arthur Dove.

**1926** Traveled to Colorado and New Mexico in summer. Photographed tree-root forms and Mesa Verde cliff dwellings.

**1927–28** Summered at Georgetown Island, Maine, near sculptor Gaston Lachaise and Madame Lachaise. Took close-ups of plants, rocks, and driftwood.

**1929** Solo exhibition at The Intimate Gallery, New York.

Traveled to the Gaspé peninsula in the summer. Strand's first interpretation of a locality, and his first attempt to integrate a landscape, to find the relationship of land and sky.

**1930–32** Summered in New Mexico. Landscape interest continued in clouds, adobe architecture, ghost towns.

**1932** Exhibited with Rebecca Strand in April at An American Place, New York. Further work in New Mexico. Strand's marriage dissolves.

**1932–34** Traveled to Mexico to photograph. One-person show at Sala de Arte, Mexico City, February 1933. Appointed chief of photography and cinematography, Department of Fine Arts, Secretariat of Education of Mexico. Photographed and supervised production for the Mexican government of film *Redes*, released in the United States in 1936 as *The Wave*.

**1935** Joined Group Theater directors Harold Clurman, Lee Strasberg, and Cheryl Crawford on a brief trip to Moscow. On return to the United States, photographed with Ralph Steiner and Leo Hurwitz *The Plow That Broke the Plains*, produced for the Resettlement Administration and directed by Pare Lorentz.

**1936** Returned to the Gaspé in summer, made new Gaspé series. Married Virginia Stevens.

**1937–42** Became president of Frontier Films, a nonprofit educational film production group with which Hurwitz, Lionel Berman, Steiner, Sidney Meyers, Willard Van Dyke, David Wolf, and others were originally associated.

**1937** Edited the first Frontier Films release, *Heart of Spain,* with Hurwitz.

**1940** Completed portfolio of twenty hand-pulled gravures of Mexico, published in New York by Virginia Stevens as "Photographs of Mexico."

**1942** *Native Land* released, a Frontier Film photographed by Strand and co-directed by Strand and Hurwitz.

**1943** Camera work on films for government agencies. As chairman of the Committee of Photography of the Independent Voter's Committee of the Arts and Sciences for President Roosevelt, edited exhibition with Hurwitz and Robert Riley at Vanderbilt Gallery, New York City.

**1943–44** Traveled to Vermont, returned to still photography after ten years in film work.

**1945** Solo exhibition, The Museum of Modern Art, New York.

**1945–47** Traveled in New England, worked on book with Nancy Newhall, subsequently published as *Time in New England.*

**1949** Invited to Czechoslovakia Film Festival in July, at which *Native Land* was awarded a prize.

**1950** Traveled to Paris, began work on a book subsequently published as *La France de Profil,* with text by Claude Roy.

**1951** Married Hazel Kingsbury. France became home and center for work.

**1952–53** Made photographs of Italy that were later used in *Un Paese,* text by Cesare Zavattini.

**1954** On the island of South Uist, in the Outer Hebrides, made photographs for *Tir a'Mhurain, Outer Hebrides,* text by Basil Davidson.

**1955** Bought house in Orgeval, France.

**1955–58** Worked on series of portraits of prominent French intellectuals, and close-ups of the Orgeval garden.

**1956** Exhibited with Walker Evans, Manuel Alvarez Bravo, and August Sander in the exhibition "Diogenes with a Camera III," directed by Edward Steichen at The Museum of Modern Art, New York.

**1959** In Egypt, photographed for the book *Living Egypt,* text by James Aldridge.

**1960** Brief photographic trip to Romania.

**1962** In Morocco, began work on series of photographs and researched Arab life.

**1963** Placed on Honor Roll of the American Society of Magazine Photographers, New York.

**1963–64** Traveled to Ghana at the invitation of President Nkrumah to make a book with text by Basil Davidson.

**1965** Nancy Newhall introduced Michael Hoffman, publisher of Aperture, to Strand.

**1967** Awarded David Octavius Hill Medal by the Gesellschaft Deutscher Lichtbildner in Mannheim, Germany. Returned to Romania to complete photographs begun in 1960. Supervised second printing of *The Mexican Portfolio,* produced by Aperture for Da Capo Press.

**1969** Exhibitions at Kreis Museum, Haus der Heimat, Freital, East Germany, and Museum of Fine Arts, St. Petersburg, Florida.

**1969–70** One-person exhibition organized by Gilbert de Keyser and Yves Auquéir for the Administration Générale des Affaires Culturelles Françaises of Belgium, shown throughout Belgium and the Netherlands.

**1970** Held an exhibition of gravures, Stockholm, Sweden, as guest of the Swedish Photographers Association, received Swedish Film Archives Award, film series showed *Heart of Spain, The Wave,* and *Native Land.* Worked with Hoffman on selecting and printing photographs for the monograph and Philadelphia Museum retrospective.

**1971–72** Retrospective exhibition, Philadelphia Museum, November 24, 1971, to January 30, 1972. Exhibition traveled to the Museum of Fine Arts, Boston; the City Art Museum, St. Louis; The Metropolitan Museum of Art, New York; and the Los Angeles County Museum of Art. *Paul Strand: A Retrospective* monograph published by Aperture in two volumes.

**1973** Strands return to the U.S. for two years. Attended the opening of the retrospective exhibition at the Metropolitan Museum of Art in New York City and the Los Angeles County Museum. Strand operated on for cataracts.

**1974** Calvin Tomkins's profile of Strand published in the *New Yorker,* September 16.

**1975** Photographed in the backyard of the Fifth Street apartment in New York during the summer. Returned to Orgeval to work on the text of a book on his garden with Catherine Duncan. Prepared and signed prints for two portfolios: *On My Doorstep* and *The Garden.*

**1976** *Ghana: An African Portrait* published by Aperture. Strand dies in Orgeval, France. Two portfolios, *On My Doorstep* and *The Garden,* published.

# QUIET.

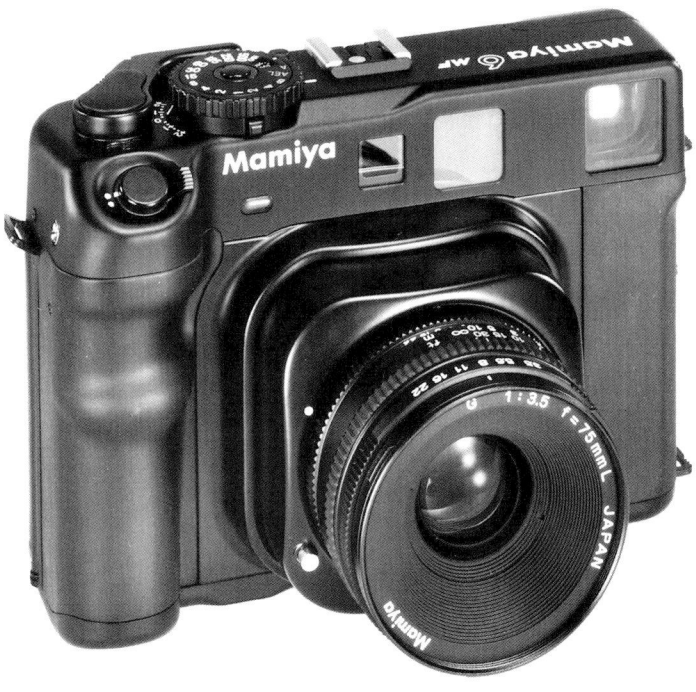

Let the new
Mamiya 6MF
capture your
imagination.

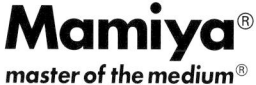
**Mamiya**®
*master of the medium*®

The new Mamiya 6MF gives you the elegant **Simplicity** simplicity, speed, accuracy, and super-quietness of a classic 35mm rangefinder camera, with the immense benefit of a big, beautiful 2¼" square image. All in a professional 2¼" camera that weighs less than many of today's top 35mm SLRs.

A camera for purists, the new Mamiya 6MF offers fully manual operation, or **Creativity** completely accurate ⅙ step auto exposure built-in metering. For ultimate precision with today's critical films.

The new Mamiya 6MF is a portable, compact system offering three interchangeable lenses of world renown — crafted in limited quantities by Mamiya's own optical **Versatility** designers and engineers. Each lens has a built-in, fully flash synched, electromagnetic leaf shutter with dead accurate speeds from 4 seconds to 1/500 sec.– 50mm f/4 Wide Angle, 75mm f/3.5 Standard Lens, 150mm f/4.5 Telephoto.

And to top it off, the new Mamiya 6MF's unique, multi-format (MF) capability lets you choose from traditional 2¼" square; to ideal format 6 x 4.5cm for full frame 8 x 10 enlargements; to true panoramic 24 x 54mm format, using 35mm film. Unparalleled creative freedom.

Experience the new Mamiya 6MF at the Mamiya Professional Dealer near you. Or request a full color brochure from Dept. 5A at the address below.

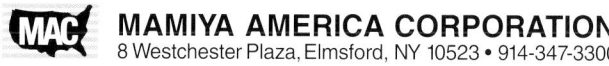
**MAMIYA AMERICA CORPORATION**
8 Westchester Plaza, Elmsford, NY 10523 • 914-347-3300

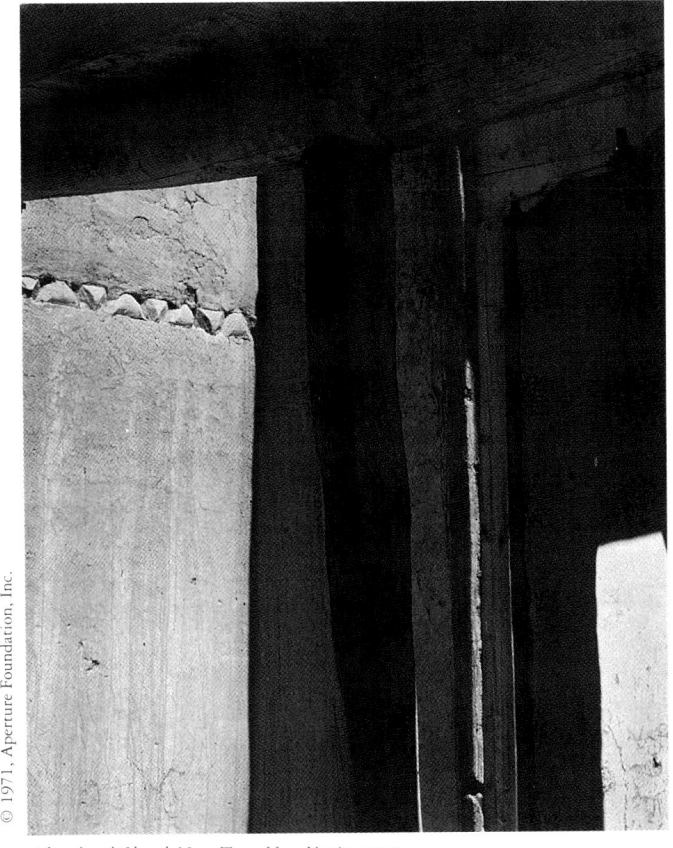

*Abandoned Church Near Taos, New Mexico*, 1932
vintage platinum print, 10 by 8 inches

# Paul Strand

an exhibition of selected works
May 1 - 31, 1994

*exhibition catalogue available*

# GERALD GP PETERS GALLERY

439 CAMINO DEL MONTE SOL, P.O. BOX 908   SANTA FE, NM   87504-0908
TELEPHONE 505 988-8961   FAX 505 983-2481

SANTA FE · NEW YORK · DALLAS

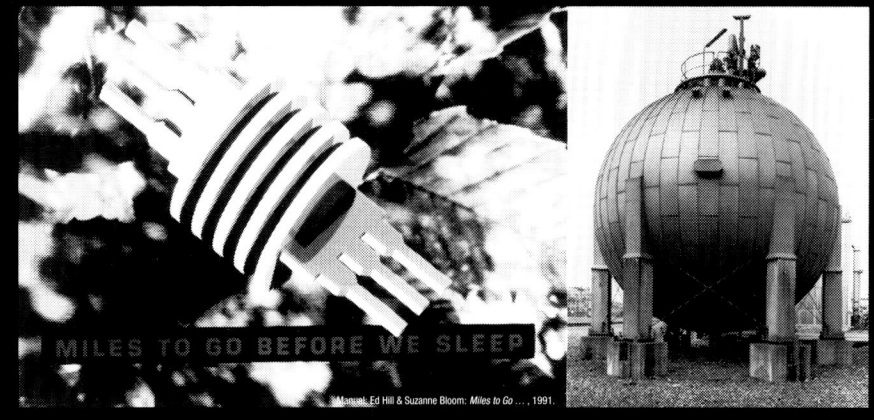
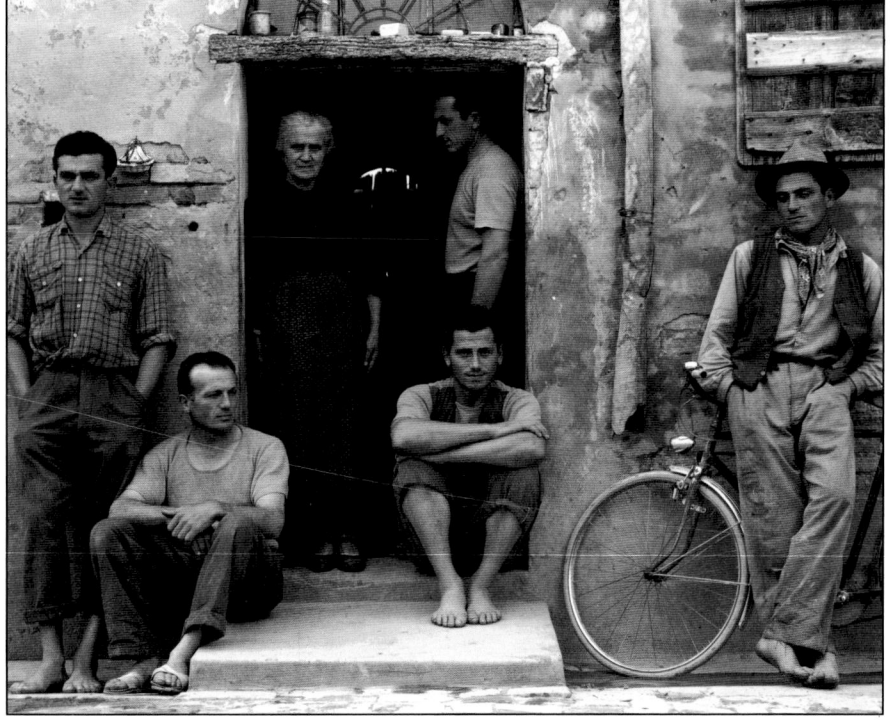

Printed from the original negative, this edition is limited to 100 numbered copies and ten artist's proofs. Each print is numbered and the text folio bears the authorized seal of the Paul Strand Archive.

Platinum palladium, 9 13/16 x 12 11/16 inches.
Matted to 22 x 18 inches.
$3,500.
**Special subscriber price $3,150.**

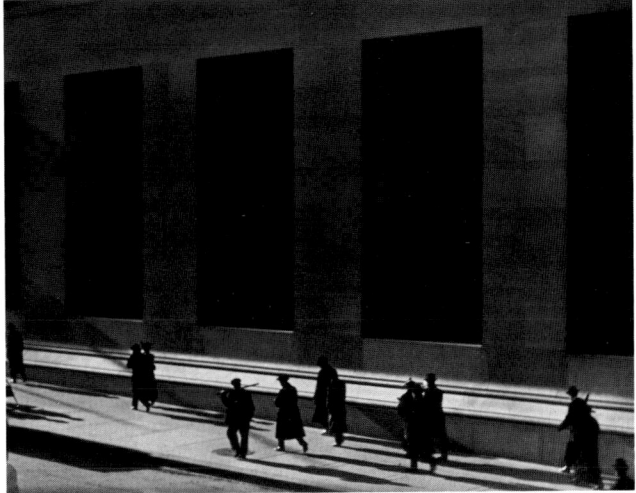

*Wall Street*, New York, 1915

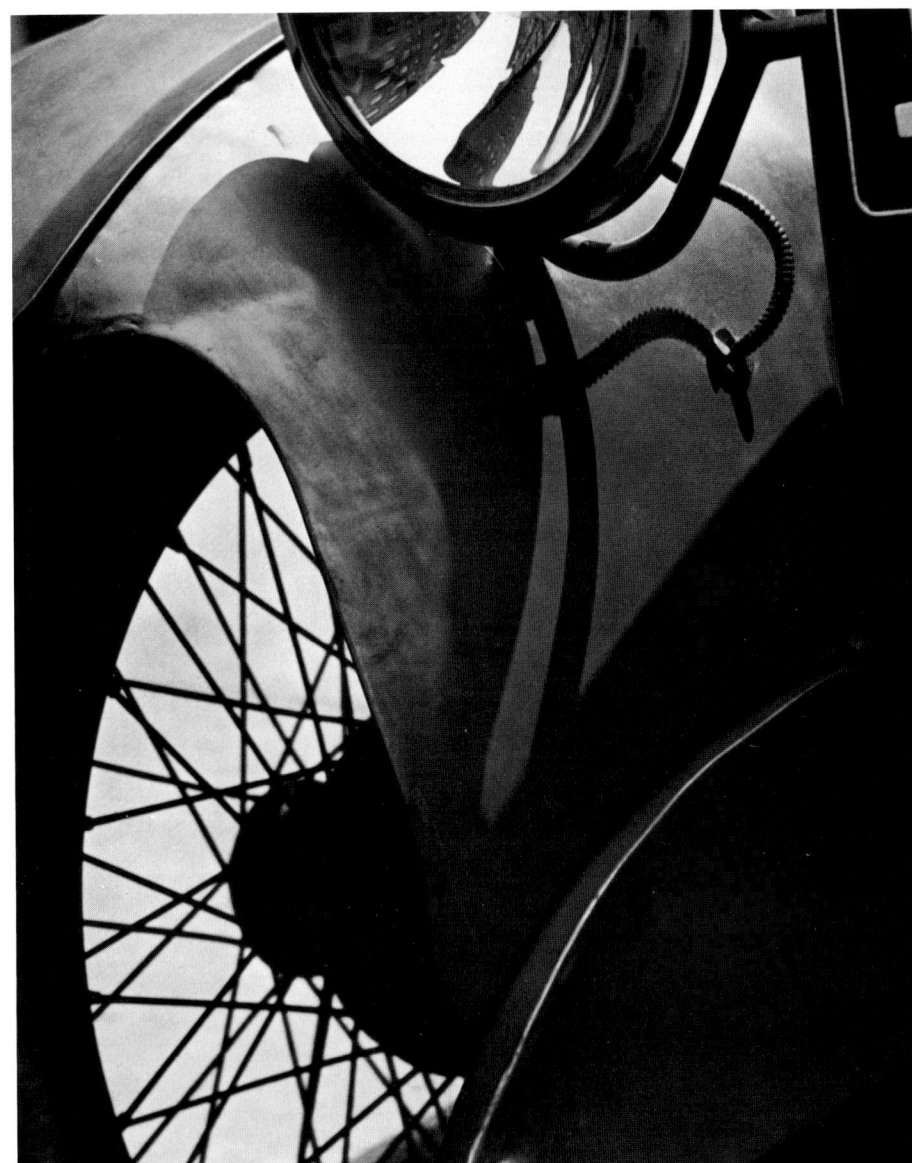

Printed from the original negative, this edition is limited to 100 numbered copies and ten artist's proofs. Each print is numbered and the text folio bears the authorized seal of the Paul Strand Archive.

Platinum palladium, 12 1/2 x 9 7/8 inches.
Matted to 22 x 18 inches.
$3,500.
**Special subscriber price $3,150.**

*Wire Wheel*, New York, 1917

# PORTFOLIO 1

On My Doorstep
A portfolio of eleven photographs,
1914 – 1973

Made under the direction of and approved
by Paul Strand in his darkroom at Orgeval,
these prints are on the gelatin-silver
photographic papers he regularly used. In
accordance with his practice, each print is
archivally processed, gold-toned, and
varnished. Limited to an edition of 50
numbered copies and eight unnumbered
artist's proofs, each portfolio is signed by
Paul Strand and each print bears his seal.

Eleven silver prints mounted and matted to
16 x 20 inches.
Introduction by Paul Strand.
$30,000. **Only 1 copy remains.**

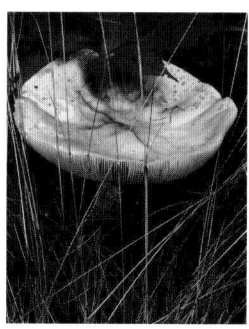 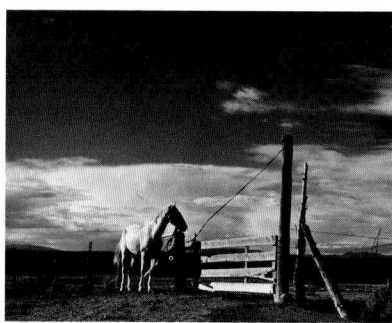 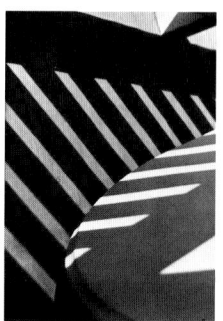

**Selected images from this portfolio:**
*Toadstool and Grasses*, Georgetown, Maine, 1928 (image 9 9/16 x 7 9/16), *White Horse*,
Ranchos de Taos, New Mexico, 1932 (image 9 1/16 x 11 9/16), *Abstraction, Porch Shadows*,
Connecticut, 1916 (image 13 1/16 x 9 1/16)

Included but not illustrated: *Jug and Fruit*, Connecticut, 1916 (image 11 1/4 x 7 3/8), *Torso*, Taos, New Mexico,
1930 (image 9 15/16 x 10 1/16), *Akeley Motion Picture Camera*, New York City, 1923 (image 9 1/2 x 7 5/8),
*Iris Facing the Winter*, Orgeval, 1973 (image 12 3/8 x 9 7/8), *Susan Thompson*, Cape Split, Maine, 1945
(image 9 15/16 x 7 5/16), *Side Porch*, Vermont, 1947 (image 9 5/8 x 7 5/8), *Snow, Backyards*, New York City,
1914 (image 9 11/16 x 12 1/2), *Rebecca*, New York City, 1922 (image 7 3/4 x 9 5/8)

# PORTFOLIO 2

The Garden
A portfolio of six photographs

These photographs were made under the
direction of and approved by Paul Strand in
his darkroom at Orgeval, printed on the
gelatin-silver photographic papers he regularly used. In accordance with his practice,
each print is archivally processed, gold-toned,
and varnished. Limited to an edition of 50
numbered copies and eight unnumbered
artist's proofs, each portfolio is signed by
Paul Strand and each print bears his seal.

Six silver prints mounted and matted to
16 x 20 inches.
Introduction by Paul Strand.
$7,500.
**Special subscriber price $6,750.**
**Only 17 remain available for sale.**

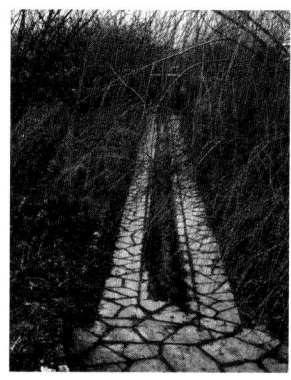 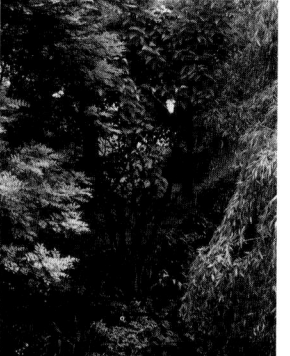 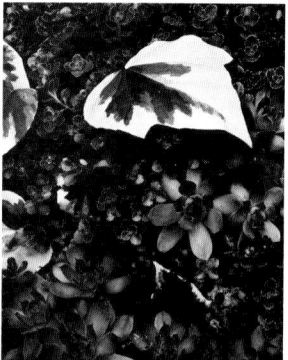

**Selected images from this portfolio:**
*Driveway*, Orgeval, 1957 (image 9 5/8 x 7 5/8), *The Garden*, Orgeval, 1964 (image 9 5/8 x 7 5/8),
*The Happy Family*, Orgeval, 1958 (image 9 5/8 x 7 5/8)

Included but not illustrated: *Crocus and Primroses*, Orgeval, 1957 (image 9 9/16 x 7 5/8), *Fungus*, Orgeval,
1967 (image 9 5/8 x 7 5/8), *Yellow Vine and Rock Plants*, Orgeval, 1960 (image 9 9/16 x 7 5/8)

# PORTFOLIO 3

### A portfolio of ten photographs

The master prints used to prepare these portfolios were approved and initialed by Paul Strand in 1975 and 1976 and printed by Richard Benson in 1976 and 1977. Limited to an edition of 100 numbered copies and ten artist's proofs, each portfolio is signed by Hazel Strand on her husband's behalf. Each print bears the authorized seal of the Paul Strand Foundation.

Ten silver prints mounted and matted to 16 x 20 inches.
Introduction by Mark Haworth-Booth,
Curator of Photography,
Victoria and Albert Museum.
$9,500.

**Special subscriber price of $8,550 through January 15, 1995.**

**After January 15, 1995, the price of any remaining portfolios will go up to $12,500.**

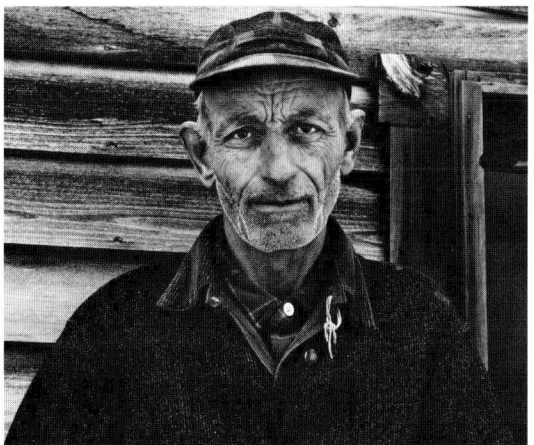
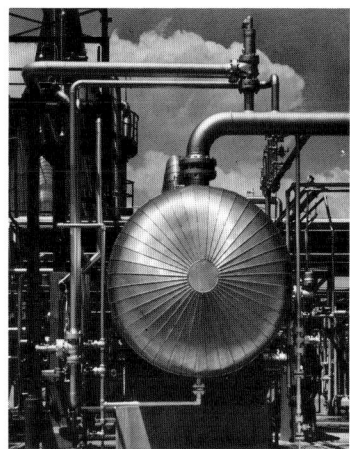
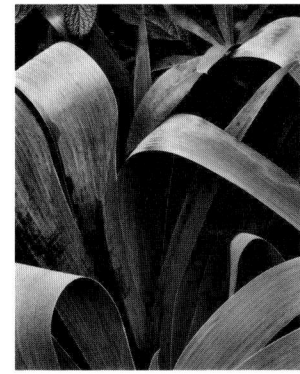
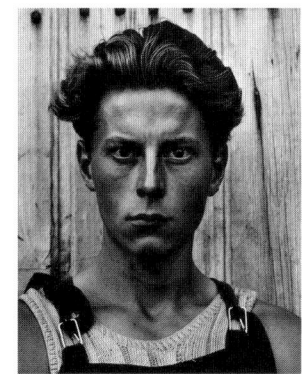
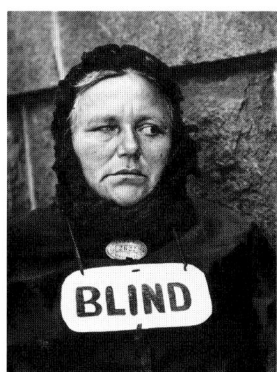
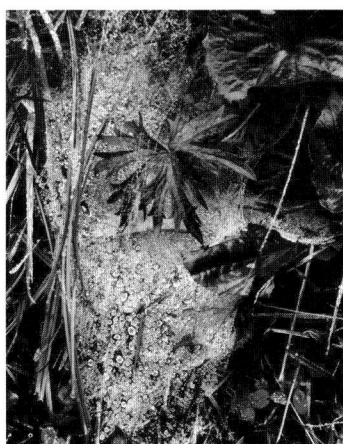
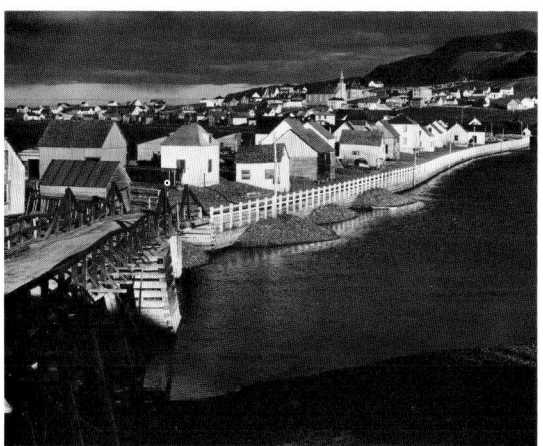

Selected images from this portfolio:
*Mr. Bennett*, Vermont, 1944 (image 7 5/16 x 8 13/16), *Oil Refinery*, Tema, Ghana, 1963 (image 9 1/4 x 7 1/2), *Iris*, Georgetown, Maine, 1928 (image 9 1/2 x 7 9/16), *Young Boy*, Gondeville, Charente, France, 1951 (image 11 x 8 3/4), *Blind Woman*, New York, 1916 (image 12 7/8 x 9 13/16), *Cobweb in Rain*, Georgetown, Maine, 1927 (image 9 9/16 x 7 9/16), *Fox River*, Gaspé, 1936 (image 8 7/8 x 11 3/16)

Included but not illustrated: *The Camargue*, France, 1951 (image 8 7/16 x 10 13/16), *Truckman's House*, New York, 1920 (image 9 1/2 x 7 9/16) *The White Fence*, Port Kent, New York, 1916 (image 9 11/16 x 12 13/16)

# PORTFOLIO 4

A portfolio of ten photographs

The master prints used to prepare these
portfolios were approved and initialed by
Paul Strand in 1975 and 1976 and printed
by Richard Benson in 1976 and 1977. Limited
to an edition of 100 numbered copies and
ten artist's proofs, each portfolio is signed
by Hazel Strand on her husband's behalf.
Each print bears the authorized seal of the
Paul Strand Foundation.

Ten silver prints mounted and matted to
16 x 20 inches.
Introduction by Cesare Zavattini.
$9,500.

**Special subscriber price of $8,550 through
January 15, 1995.
After January 15, 1995, the price of any
remaining portfolios will go up to $12,500.**

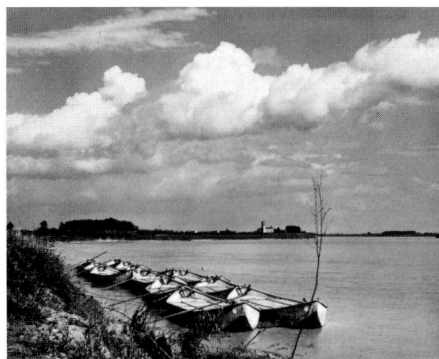 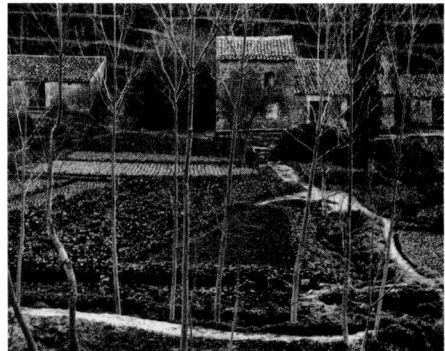

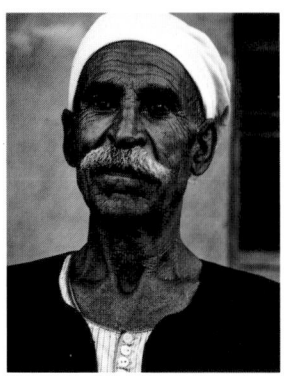 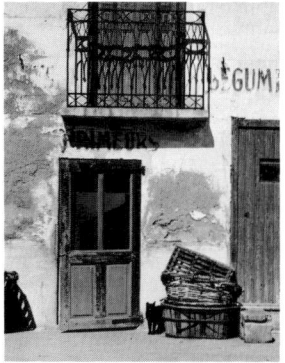 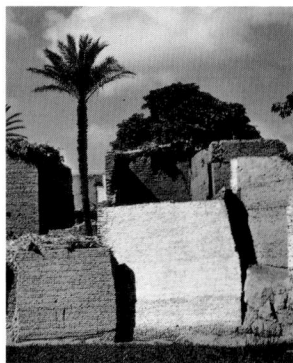

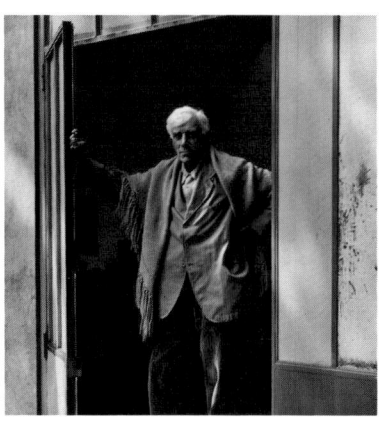 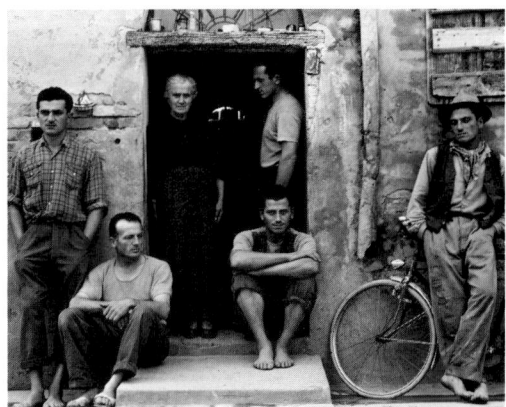

**Selected images from this portfolio:**
*The River Po*, Luzzara, Italy, 1953 (image 6 13/16 x 8 5/8), *Landscape*, Sicily, 1954
(image 6 13/16 x 8 9/16), *Sheik Abdel Hadi Misyd*, Attar Farm, Delta, Egypt, 1959 (image 9 1/4
x 7 1/4), *Shop*, Le Bacarès, Pyrénées-Orientales, France, 1950 (image 7 1/8 x 5 11/16),
*Bani Salah*, Fayyum, Egypt, 1959 (image 12 1/16 x 9 13/16), *Georges Braque*, Varangéville,
France, 1957 (image 9 5/8 x 7 5/16), *The Family*, Luzzara, Italy, 1953 (image 8 9/16 x 10 13/16)

Included but not illustrated: *Fall in Movement*, Orgeval, France, 1973 (image 13 1/8 x 10 5/16),
*Tir A'Mhurain*, South Uist, Hebrides, 1954 (image 9 5/16 x 11 13/16), *Iris and Stump*, Orgeval, France, 1973
(image 10 1/2 x 11 3/4)

# PHOTOGRAVURES

Paul Strand considered photogravure perfectly suited to his work because of the technique's capacity to achieve the "almost infinite tonal values which lie beyond the skill of the human hand."

In the hands of a master printer, hand-pulled photogravures possess a luminous quality often unmatched by any other process of photographic reproduction. The process is accomplished by creating a copper printing plate from a photographic positive; the plate yields exquisite tonality on papers printed under thousands of pounds of pressure. The resulting image possesses the truest and subtlest photographic tones possible, with the texture a nearly continuous tone, as a result of the microscopic three-dimensionality of the intaglio surface. Aperture and Jon Goodman of the Photogravure Workshop, in cooperation with generous institutional and private donors, have revived the photogravure process; lost for over forty years, it was the preferred printing method of many nineteenth- and early-twentieth-century photographers.

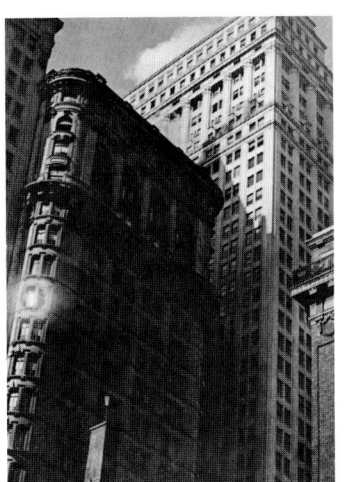
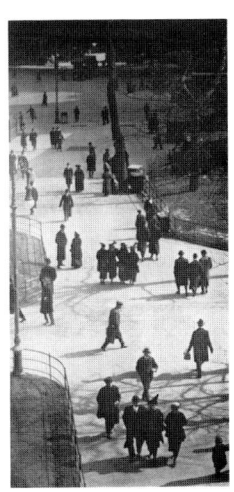
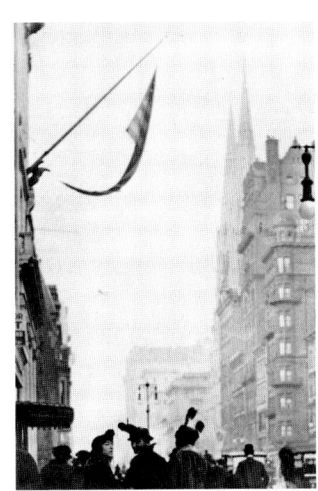

The Formative Years, 1914 – 1917
A portfolio of ten hand-pulled photogravure prints

Produced from Strand's original negatives in 1983, the edition is limited to 300 sets, boxed and numbered, and 30 artist's proofs.
Introduction by Ben Lifson.
ISBN: 0-89381-125-4. $1,800.
**We've extended our recent warehouse relocation offer for this portfolio — Special subscriber price $950.**

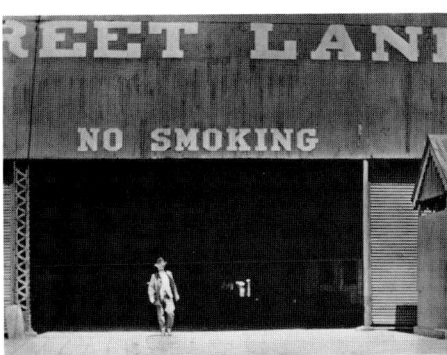
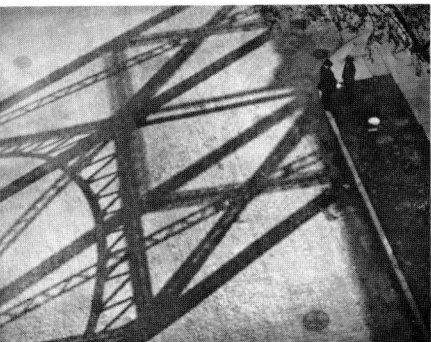

**Selected images from this portfolio:**
*From the El*, New York, 1917 (image 12 13/16 x 9 1/8), *City Hall Park*, New York, 1915 (image 13 1/8 x 6 1/4), *Fifth Avenue*, New York, c. 1915 (image 12 1/4 x 8), *Hudson River Pier*, New York, c. 1914 (image 9 1/4 x 12 1/4), *From the Viaduct, 125th Street*, New York, 1915 (image 10 x 12 7/8), *Yawning Woman*, New York, c. 1916 (image 12 1/2 x 9 1/2), *Man, Five Points Square*, New York, 1916 (image 9 1/2 x 10 1/4), *Railroad Sidings*, New York, 1914 (image 12 7/16 x 9 7/16)

Included but not illustrated:
*Still Life, Pear and Bowls*, Twin Lakes, Connecticut, 1916 (image 10 1/16 x 11 1/4),
*Abstraction, Porch Shadows*, Twin Lakes, Connecticut, 1916 (image 9 1/2 x 13)

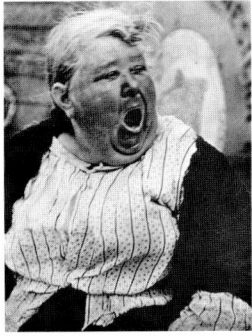
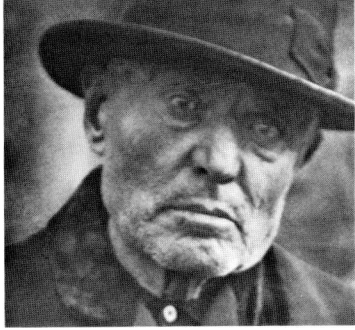
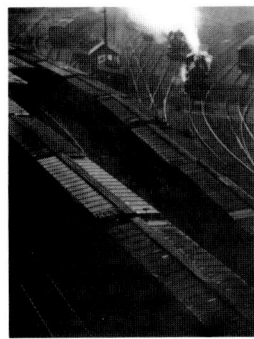

# ORDER FORM

Please send me the following Paul Strand
prints, portfolios, and photogravures:

| | |
|---|---|
| | $ |
| | $ |
| | $ |
| | $ |

Shipping & handling charges    $

      Each print and portfolio:

        Domestic $15.00

        Canada/Mexico $30.00

        Other foreign (air) $50.00

Subtotal    $

NY residents
add 8.25% sales tax    $

Canadian residents add 7% GST
(Reg. No. R125658724)    $

Total    $

Name *(please print)*

Address

City       State

Zip       Phone

○ My check or money order in U. S. funds, payable to Aperture, is enclosed.

○ Please charge my    ○ Visa    ○ Mastercard    ○ American Express

Card No.       Expiration date

Signature

Special shipping instructions

Note: As the supply of these prints, portfolios, and photogravures is limited, this offer is subject
to availability. After January 15, 1995, the prices of any remaining items may change without
notice. Please allow 4 – 6 weeks for delivery.

Printed in U.S.A.       STR

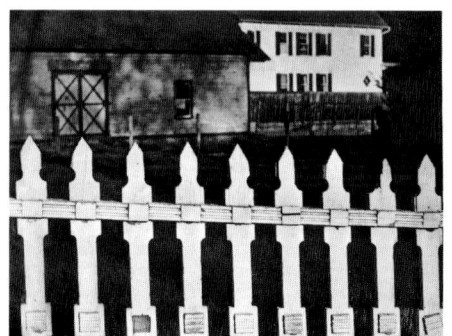

*The White Fence*, Port Kent, New York, 1916

Produced in an edition of 300, each hand-pulled, dust-grain photogravure (image 9 1/2 x 12 3/4)
is numbered and bears the authorizing stamp and signature of the director of the Paul Strand
Archive. ISBN: 0-89381-476-8. $450.
**We've extended our recent warehouse relocation offer for this print —**
**Special subscriber price $175.**

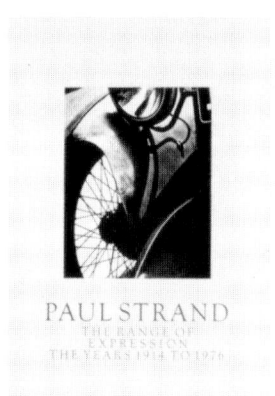

*The Range of Expression, 1914 – 1976*

A hand-pulled photogravure poster. Produced in 1982 by Aperture and Jon Goodman of the
Photogravure Workshop to celebrate a traveling exhibition of Strand's work, this poster features
the image *Wire Wheel*, New York, 1917 (image 13 x 10 1/4).
Edition limited to 75 hand-pulled, dust-grain gravures. Poster 27 x 19 inches. $350.
**Special subscriber price $150.**

APERTURE · 20 EAST 23RD ST · NY, NY 10010 · TEL 212 598 4205 · 800 929 2323 (24 HRS) · FAX 212 598 4015

# PAUL STRAND

"THE WORK OF PAUL STRAND HAS BECOME A LEGEND. . . . TIME AND AGAIN, PHOTOGRAPHERS COMING IN BRIEF CONTACT WITH ITS FORCE AND ITS EXTRAORDINARY BEAUTY HAVE FELT THE SHOCK OF CATALYST. STRAND HAS BEEN A DISCOVERER OF PHOTOGRAPHIC FORMS AND CONCEPTS OF OUR TIME."
— NANCY NEWHALL

Selected works in this catalog will be on view from November 22, 1994, through January 10, 1995, at Aperture's Burden Gallery, 20 East 23rd Street, New York, NY 10010. Hours: Tuesday through Saturday, 10:00 am to 6:00 pm.

They may also be viewed by appointment. Please call the Burden Gallery at 212 505 5555 x 326.

While other Aperture limited-edition prints of comparable quality now sell for $3,500, this print — available for the first time — is being offered at a **special subscriber price of $950 through January 15, 1995.**

This limited-edition platinum print was made from the original 5-by-7 negative under the direction of Richard Benson, who worked closely with Paul Strand at the end of Strand's life. Limited to an edition of 150 numbered copies and 15 unnumbered artist's proofs, each print bears the authorizing stamp & signature of the director of the Paul Strand Archive.
Image 8 1/8 x 6 7/16 inches.
Matted to 20 x 16 inches.
ISBN: 0-89381-588-8.

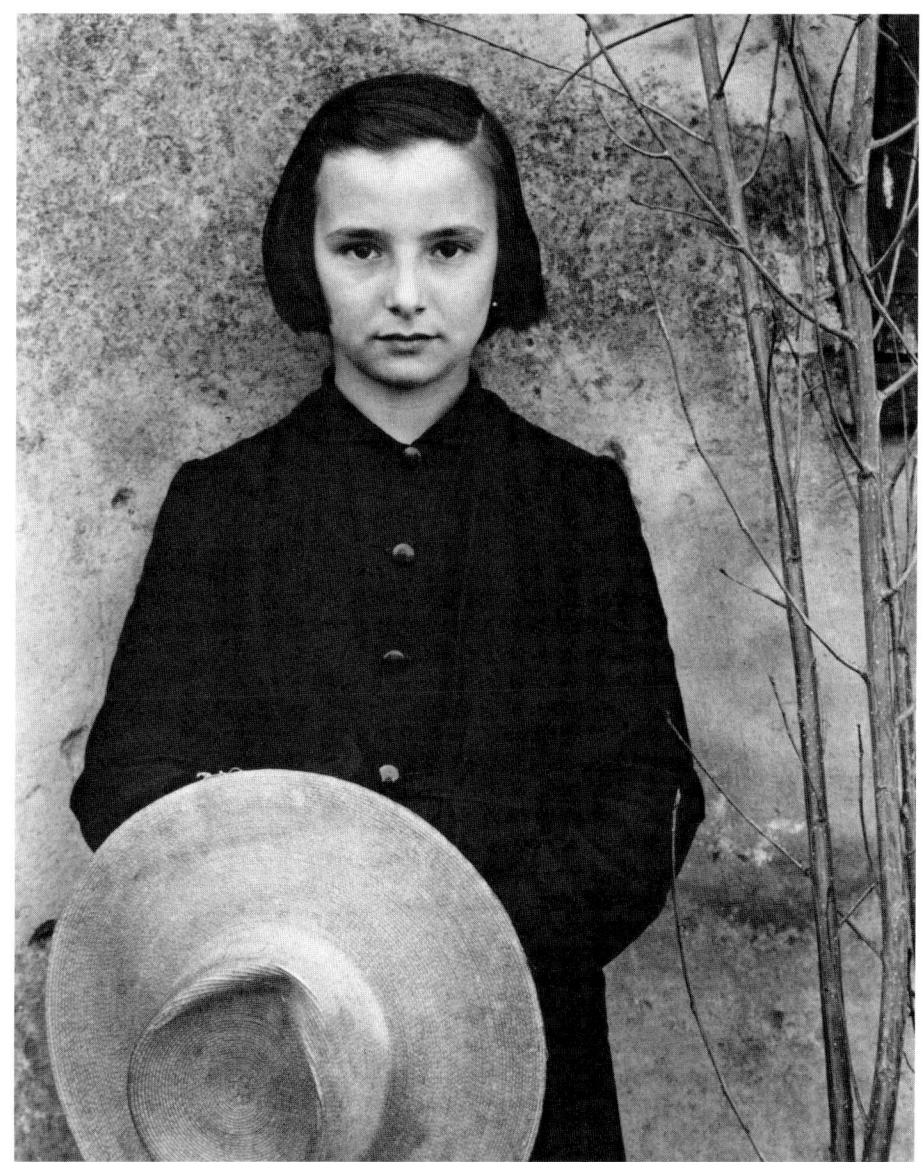

*Tailor's Apprentice*, Luzzara, Italy, 1953

APERTURE · 20 EAST 23RD ST · NY, NY 10010 · TEL 212 598 4205 · 800 929 2323 (24 HRS) · FAX 212 598 4015

# LIMITED-EDITION PRINTS

Paul Strand is recognized as one of photography's greatest printers, yet throughout most of his working life he seldom made more than a few prints of even his most famous images. In his final years, however, at the urging of friends, he dedicated himself to making additional prints of selected images drawn from his entire life's work. Toward this end, he labored for many months in 1975 and 1976 with printer Richard Benson at the Strand home in Orgeval, France.

The results of this inspired collaboration, four portfolios and three individual prints, are being offered for purchase in limited editions by Aperture. Of interest to the connoisseur and the collector, as well as to museums and galleries, these masterworks are handsomely matted and presented in archival cases. All master prints were personally approved by Strand and signed by the photographer or, after his death, by his wife, Hazel Kingsbury Strand.

No further photographic prints will be made from the negatives of these images except for purposes of study, and none of the study prints will be offered for sale. This is a unique opportunity to acquire photographs whose value will only increase over the years.

Each of the limited-edition prints contains a beautifully designed introductory essay by a noted critic, curator, or historian, and is encased in its own cloth portfolio and matted in four-ply museum-quality matte board.

Printed from the original negative, this edition is limited to 100 numbered copies and ten artist's proofs. Each print is numbered and the text folio bears the authorized seal of the Paul Strand Archive.

Palladium, 6 3/4 x 8 9/16 inches.
Matted to 18 1/4 x 14 1/2 inches.
$3,500.
**Special subscriber price $3,150.**

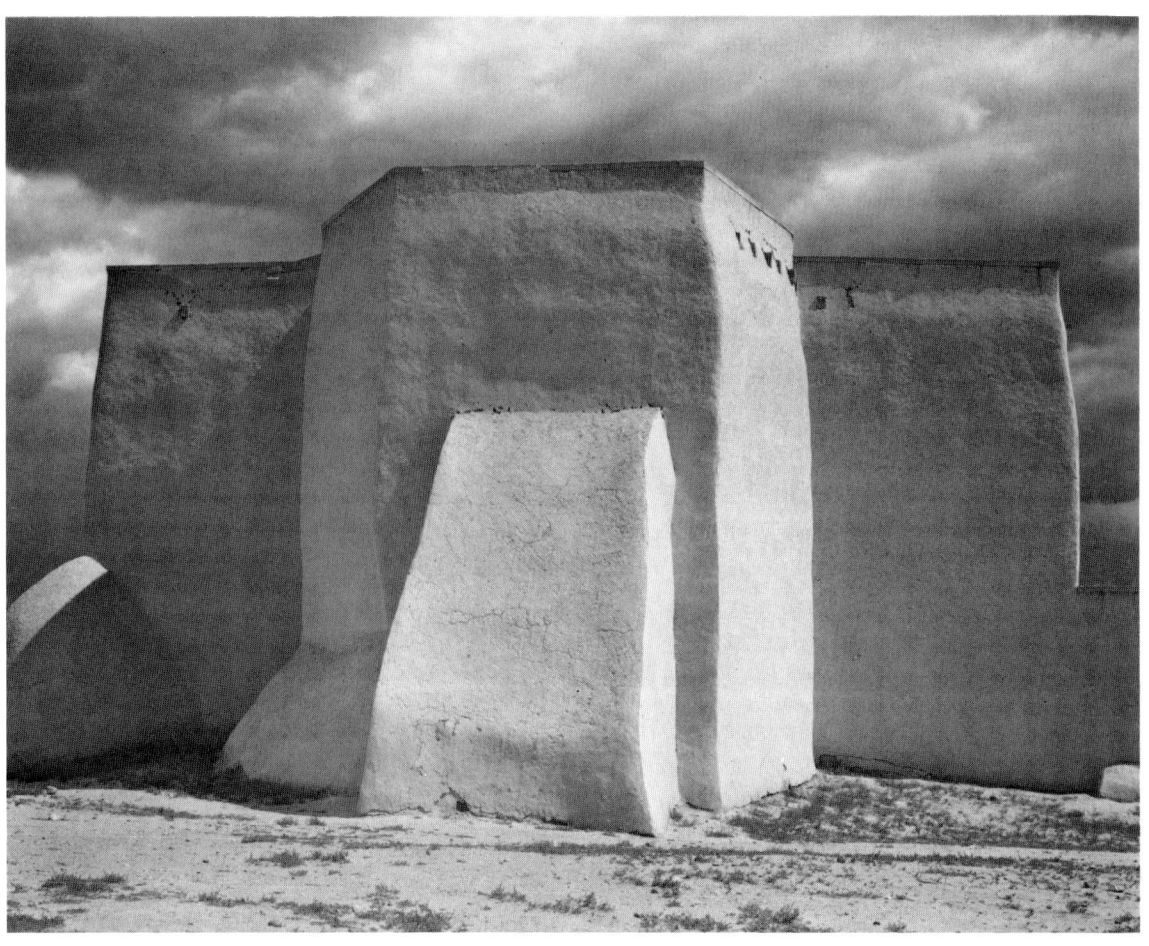

*St. Francis Church*, Ranchos de Taos, New Mexico, 1931